THE **BIG** BOOK OF
QUICK &
HEALTHY
RECIPES

KIRSTEN HARTVIG

THE **BIG** BOOK OF QUICK & HEALTHY RECIPES

365

DELICIOUS & NUTRITIOUS MEALS IN UNDER 30 MINUTES

DUNCAN BAIRD PUBLISHERS

LONDON

Dedication: to Al Hart and Essie Jain

Thank you to Amanda Preston, Bob Ashby, Bob Saxton, Catherine Frances, Charlotte Charmetant, Esther Gillett, Fiona Gilmore, Françoise Nassivet, Geoffrey Cannon, Helouise Sarrat, Jennifer Maughan, Joyce Thomas, Julia Charles, Kathy Mitcherson, Nic Rowley, Paul Charmetant, Peter Firebrace, Sue Mitcherson, Tara Firebrace and Zoë Stone for their help, inspiration and support. Special thanks to chef François Salies for his invaluable contribution to the recipes.

The Big Book of Quick & Healthy Recipes
Kirsten Hartvig

Conceived, created and designed
by Duncan Baird Publishers Ltd
Sixth Floor
Castle House
75–76 Wells Street
London W1T 3QH

Managing Editor: Julia Charles
Editor: Zoë Stone
Managing Designer: Manisha Patel
Designer: Sailesh Patel
Commissioned Photography: William Lingwood
Photography Assistant: Estelle Cuthbert
Stylists: Joss Herd (food) and Helen Trent

Library of Congress Cataloging-in-Publication Data is available

Distributed in the United States by Publishers Group West

ISBN-10: 1-84483-107-8
ISBN-13: 9-781844-831074

10 9 8 7 6 5 4 3 2 1

Typeset in Frutiger and MetaPlus
Color reproduction by Scanhouse, Malaysia
Printed in China by Imago

CONTENTS

INTRODUCTION

The Big Book of Quick and Healthy Recipes is based on the concept that healthy food should be available to all, and that it is possible to create tasty, nutritious meals without spending a lot of money, time or effort.

Whatever your experience as a cook, this book will enable you to create a healthy meal in half an hour, 365 days of the year, using fresh, high-quality, varied seasonal ingredients prepared with minimal processing to ensure maximum taste and nutritional value. It offers all the choice necessary for a varied and interesting diet, and makes it possible for people of all different dietary preferences, habits and needs to eat together. The book draws on ethnic influences from all over the world, and blends modern nutritional science with tried and tested natural healthy-eating principles.

The recipes are divided into four chapters reflecting the changing seasons. All the dishes are rated and explained for health features, including calorie and cholesterol count, nutrient content and medicinal value. Every dish is a nourishing, balanced meal in itself, and most dishes give meat, vegetarian and vegan options – the basic recipe being the same for each. I have also provided serving suggestions for a number of the recipes, which are, of course, optional and may be tailored to suit your needs and preferences.

Special dietary requirements are catered for because an increasing number of people suffer from some form of food allergy, or need to avoid certain foods for health reasons. In each recipe, it is possible to see at a glance whether it contains wheat or gluten, solinaceae (see page 7), or citrus, and suggestions for alternatives to dairy products are also given.

Recipes for each season are divided into seven groups; Soups, Salads and Raw Foods, Pasta Dishes, Ethnic Dishes, Omelets, Pancakes and Pizzas, Broils, Bakes and Casseroles and Sweet Fruit Dishes. These categories are based on the old principle that recommends eating the same type of meal on the same day each week. In natural medicine, it is also thought to be good for health to have a "fruit only" day once a week, so most of the fruit recipes can be used both for main meals and desserts. All main meals can be used as appetizers, too.

If you don't want to choose a different category of food each day of the week, the nutritional information given with each recipe enables you to plan your meals not only by taste and ingredients, but also according to what you feel you need each day in order to maintain (or regain) maximum health.

HOW TO USE THIS BOOK

This book enables you to make a healthy meal in half an hour, 365 days a year. Every dish actively promotes health and provides a nourishing, balanced meal in itself. The recipes are arranged according to season, and make use of fresh seasonal ingredients. They are also organized into seven different categories so you can choose a different type of meal each day of the week.

There is a set of icons by each recipe that shows the health-promoting features of each dish. This makes it easy for those with special dietary requirements to choose suitable meals, and enables you to check at a glance whether the meal you choose contains ingredients you would prefer to avoid – wheat or gluten, solinaceae (tomatoes, bell peppers, eggplants, potatoes, paprika and Tabasco sauce), or citrus. ✪ indicates "boosts immunity"; ♥ "good for the heart or circulation"; ◖ "an aid to detox"; ✕ "low in calories"; ✿ "contains wheat or gluten"; ◔ "contains solinaceae"; and ◗ "contains citrus". The icons are present when this quality applies to the recipe. So, for example, if a dish helps to boost immunity and it contains wheat or gluten, both the star and the wheat or gluten icon will appear beneath the recipe name.

Multi-choice ingredients make it possible to cater for people with different food preferences using the same basic recipe. Every recipe has a vegan option which contains no meat, dairy or other animal products, and there is a nutritional table that gives the calorie counts for average portions of the meat or dairy version (calories) and the vegan version (vegan calories) of each recipe. The cholesterol ratings only apply to dishes containing meat and/or dairy. The vegan versions are all 100 per cent cholesterol free.

Beneath this is a star rating system for the nutrients found in each recipe to help you to choose daily meals that enhance health and help prevent disease. Three stars means the dish contains a large amount of the given nutrient, two stars a medium amount and one star a low level. All the listed nutrients are important for general well-being. For example, polyunsaturates (polyunsats) include *essential fatty acids* vital for normal hormone production and immunity, and are thought to protect against heart disease. Antioxidants such as vitamins A, C, E, zinc and selenium are all important for healthy skin, good eyesight and strong immunity. Calcium is necessary for healthy bones, iron is essential to the blood and circulation, and B vitamins are important for the nervous system. When you are feeling run-down, the book makes it simple to choose recipes high in antioxidants that give your immune system a boost. If you are under a lot of stress, you should choose recipes high in B vitamins. If you are concerned about your blood fat levels, you can choose recipes low in cholesterol and high in polyunsaturates.

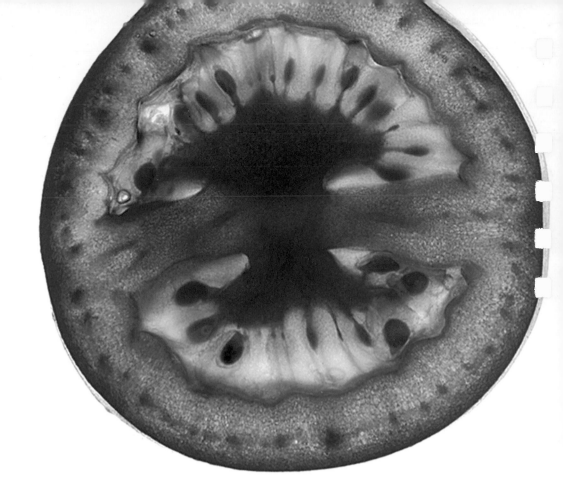

HEALTHY EATING
BASICS

Healthy eating involves using fresh ingredients and gentle cooking methods to enhance natural flavors without the need for artificial additives. However, this doesn't have to mean spending a lot of time and effort in the kitchen, it is more a question of getting organized.

First you need to rethink your attitude toward shopping and cooking: let it be part of your daily routine instead of an inconvenience that has to be "fitted in". Planning a weekly menu and writing shopping lists makes it cheaper, quicker, and easier to shop. Seeking out good local food stores and markets can pay back handsomely in terms of time and money, as well as offering the benefits of connecting you with your local environment and like-minded people.

Cooking doesn't have to be a challenge reserved for special occasions — it can be an enjoyable part of everyday life that enables you to feel better and have more energy for living. What we eat becomes part of us, and connects us to the vitality of life. So make your kitchen a playground where you relax, experiment, and enjoy preparing healthy meals.

CHOOSING INGREDIENTS

Vegetables: are best eaten young before they begin to coarsen and lose their color. Buy vegetables as fresh as possible, preferably from "box schemes" or vegetable markets. Supermarket vegetables have often traveled long distances and have been stored for longer than local market produce.

Fruit: is most tasty when picked ripe, but ripe fruit doesn't travel and keep as well as unripe fruit, so it is often picked early and artificially ripened when en route from producer to consumer. Locally-grown, naturally-ripened, organic fruits have the most flavor and are more nutritious.

Herbs and spices: keep a selection of fresh and dried herbs, and spices in your kitchen. Stand bunches of fresh herbs in glasses of cold water, or buy individual herbs in pots and keep them on the windowsill. Spices have more flavor if you buy them whole and use them freshly ground (in a mortar or a coffee grinder). Fresh herbs have been used in the recipes unless specified otherwise. To substitute dried herbs for fresh, use a third of the amount.

Cheese: taste cheese before you buy it, and buy small quantities at a time. Store in the bottom of the fridge, wrapped in foil or plastic wrap.

Eggs: always use free-range eggs, and buy organic whenever possible.

Fish: really fresh fish is free of odor, but is not so easy to come by these days. If you have a local fishmonger, ask for your fish to be cleaned and boned while you wait. If you don't have access to local fresh fish, buy frozen. Remember that fish from fish farms are often fed a diet supplemented with antibiotics, hormones and other drugs.

Shellfish: fresh shellfish are heavy with seawater and their shells tightly closed. When you buy oysters or mussels, ask your fishmonger to shuck them.

Meat: buy organic, free-range meat to avoid hormones and other drug residues in your diet. Intensive farming has made it more difficult to find natural, unspoilt meats, so make sure you know the source of your butcher's meat. Animals that live on a natural diet and have access to fresh air and sunshine have fewer illnesses than those that spend their time in cramped, indoor conditions.

Game: animals that live in the wild have more meat and less fat in their flesh, and the fat is higher in polyunsaturates. Farmed game is cheaper than wild game, but inferior in terms of quality and taste.

Seitan: is a form of wheat gluten with a high-protein, low-fat content, and no cholesterol. It is usually sold in strips, and can be used as an alternative to meat. It is available from most health food shops.

Soy beans: are a versatile and extremely nutritious food that can be turned into textured meat substitutes, such as **soy chunks, tempeh** and **tofu. Soy milk, soy yogurt, soy cheese** and **soy cream** are good alternatives to dairy products. Soy beans are also used to make **miso** and **soy sauce. Genuine tamari** is a wheat-free type of soy sauce, and is referred to as "tamari" in the recipes.

Tempeh: is a form of bean curd originating in Indonesia but now popular all over the world. A fine source of protein, it contains no saturated fats, and is one of the few vegetable products to contain vitamin B12. Tempeh resembles chicken in taste and texture, and is available from health food and ethnic shops.

Tofu: is also a soy bean curd. Another alternative to meat, it is widely available from health food shops and supermarkets. Tofu originated in China and has been eaten in the Far East for more than 2000 years. It is low in calories, high in protein and calcium, low in fat, and contains no cholesterol.

Grains, flour, pasta, and bread: whole wheat and whole grain products have a higher nutritional value than refined products because many important nutrients are contained in the outer layers of the kernel, which are removed in the refining process. However, some refined foods (for example, pasta) have a finer texture than their whole grain counterparts, and are easier to cook and digest, so you may want to experiment with white/whole grain blends.

Rice: white rice is quicker to cook than whole grain, but less nutritious because, as with other grains, the important nutrients are found just under the skin.

Oils: cold-pressed extra virgin olive oil is best to use for stir-frying because it is not affected as much by heat as polyunsaturated oils such as **grapeseed** or **sunflower oil**. However, in some recipes the thinner polyunsaturated oils give better results. French dressing is easier to whisk into an even texture when made with olive oil, but polyunsaturated oils contain more essential fatty acids and are therefore healthier. I prefer to use a mixture of both.

Margarine/butter: choose unhydrogenated polyunsaturated vegetable margarine. If you use butter, buy organic.

Stock: read the ingredient list on the package of ready-made stocks and stock cubes so you will know what they contain. Avoid flavor enhancers such as monosodium-glutamate. Many also contain tomatoes, which you should avoid if you are allergic to solinaceae. Choose meat, fish, or vegetable stock according to your preference where no particular type is specified.

Vinegar: choose red or white wine vinegar for use in cooked dishes and dressings. Balsamic vinegar gives a rich caramel flavor, but should be used sparingly as it can be overpowering.

Lemon juice: is an excellent addition to salad dressings, providing both flavor and vitamin C. It prevents discoloration (for example, of avocados, artichokes, or apple slices) and gives dressings a lighter color.

Salt: grey unrefined sea salt is not as pretty as white refined table salt, but it contains valuable trace elements and is less concentrated and thus better for health.

Black pepper: freshly ground black pepper gives a much more peppery flavor than pre-ground pepper.

Sugar: raw cane sugar is preferable to white refined sugar because it contains small amounts of minerals and is less concentrated.

Brewer's yeast flakes: are high in protein, calcium, iron, and B vitamins. They have a nut-like flavor and make a useful alternative to Parmesan.

HOT SHOPPING TIPS

You can improve the quality of what you eat without it adding extra to your food budget. For example, buying fresh products is more cost effective than buying "ready meals" because processed foods are usually prepared from poor quality ingredients, plus some additives to give longer shelf life, brighter colors, and a stronger taste. With fresh foods, what you see is what you get, and by cutting out the middle man you can create your own naturally fresh and healthy diet, reaping all the benefits of unadulterated ingredients without having to bear the cost of processing, packing, and storing.

As consumers we have real power to influence the economic, social, and technological processes that affect how food is produced and prepared by making active choices about what we eat and where our food comes from. By choosing ingredients that are produced in ways we agree with, we can help create an agricultural and food distribution system that supports gentle, ecologically sensitive, organic growing methods, both locally and in other parts of the world. By expressing a preference for natural, unadulterated, organically-grown foods, we can contribute to the growth of sustainable agriculture worldwide.

Research has shown that the nutrient content of fruits and vegetables was considerably higher before the widespread adoption of chemicals in food growing. Luckily, the tide is turning as more incentives are offered to farmers to convert to organic production by governments responding to consumer pressure. The cumulative effect is that more local and imported organic foods are becoming available at lower prices, thus creating a sustainable, balanced, happier lifestyle for food producers and consumers alike.

In summary, to ensure that you purchase high-quality, fair trade foods for maximum taste and nutritional value, follow the practical and simple shopping tips outlined below:

• Select ingredients that are organically grown, seasonal, and local.
• When buying products from further afield (such as spices and tropical fruits), choose organic, fair trade foods wherever possible. That way you support local producers in other parts of the world too.
• Avoid genetically modified foods. Organic produce is not genetically engineered, and expressing a preference for natural foods reduces the incentive to develop more GMOs.
• Choose fresh, unprocessed ingredients when available.
• When buying processed foods, read the list of ingredients on the label and make sure you know what you are buying.

HOT COOKING TIPS

• **Read your chosen recipe** through before you start cooking, then collect all the ingredients, and prepare them as described in the ingredients list (for example, "2 carrots, chopped") before you start cooking. The amounts in each recipe are for two people, so you can easily halve them to cook for one, or double them to cook for four.

• **Cooking soup**: the trick is to get as much of the taste as possible out of the ingredients and into the water. Sauté the ingredients before adding the preheated liquid or, alternately, place all the ingredients in a pot with cold water and salt, and let them all heat up together.

• **Cooking fish**: fish are fragile and should be gently cooked to avoid them drying out and disintegrating.

• **Cooking meat**: meat usually needs to be "sealed" at the beginning of the cooking process. Sauté it first, set aside and add to the dish later on.

• **To sauté** means to gently stir-fry over a relatively low heat thus avoiding high-temperature frying, which destroys nutrients and is generally bad for health. Prepare all the ingredients and place them in separate piles. Heat a little oil in a pan, then add ingredients to the pan, one pile at a time, starting with the hardest (which will take the longest to cook), and finishing with the most watery.

• *Al dente* is an Italian expression and means "slightly chewy". Pasta loses its taste and texture if over-cooked and so is best served al dente. Vegetables cooked al dente are slightly crisp with their flavor and bright colors intact.

• **Blanching** means to cook in boiling water for just a few minutes. Use plenty of boiling water and quickly rinse in cold water afterward to stop the cooking process.

• **Purée whole fresh tomatoes** instead of peeling them or using canned ones. This will improve the flavor of your dish and conserve important nutrients found in the skins.

• **Use olive oil** as it is more stable than other fats and oils, and does not form trans fats (found in hydrogenated oils, margarines, and butter) when heated.

• **Fresh herbs**: rosemary, thyme, sage, marjoram, oregano, and bay leaf all have strong flavors and can withstand cooking. More delicate herbs, such as chives, tarragon, mint, and basil, should be added at the last moment to preserve their flavor. Use fresh herbs because, as well as contributing flavor, they add medicinal value to your diet. Garnish salads and cooked dishes with freshly chopped herbs.

• **Salads**: discard the coarsest leaves, cut off the base, and wash lettuce and other green leaves in cold water. Gently dry, then wrap in a cloth (or put in a plastic bag), and store in the fridge until ready to use. Add dressing to salads just before serving.

• **Mushrooms**: cut off the base of the stalks, place in a colander, briefly rinse in cold water, and pat dry before using. Clean wild mushrooms by very gently scraping the stems and cups with a small, sharp knife. Morels should be washed and carefully checked for small insects and worms before cooking.

- **Rice**: whole grain brown rice takes longer to cook than white rice (up to approximately 40 minutes), so put it on before you start preparing the rest of the ingredients.
- **Stock**: vegetable cooking water makes a quick and useful stock. Cool it down and keep it in a clean jar in the fridge for up to three days.
- **Heat stock** before you add it to a dish, thereby keeping the temperature of your dish even and speeding up cooking time.
- **Avoid frying** at very high temperatures to guard against the production of harmful chemicals.
- **Peel or scrub?** The highest concentration of taste and nutrients in fruit and vegetables is found just under the skin, and is lost with peeling. Scrubbing with a hard brush is just as quick, and is all that is needed for most organic foods. However, if you are not able to use organic ingredients, it is advisable to peel your fruit and vegetables because most chemical residues (for example, pesticides, herbicides, and antibiotics) are found in the peel.
- **Purées**: using an electric hand blender is the quickest and easiest way to purée as it avoids removing the dish from the pan, then pouring it back into the pan and reheating. Hand blenders are also easy to clean.
- **Nuts and seeds:** lightly toasting nuts and seeds brings out their flavor. Toast in a dry, heavy-based skillet over a medium–low heat. Remove the pan from the heat as soon as the first seeds start to brown or pop. Add a little salt or soy sauce to enhance the taste.
- **Preheat the oven** to reduce cooking time. Make sure your oven is set at the right temperature before you put anything in it.
- **Baking blind:** to avoid a pastry-based dish turning soggy, place the rolled-out pastry in a tart or pie pan, cover with dried lima beans or lentils, and bake "blind" in a preheated oven for 10–15 minutes while you prepare the remaining ingredients. Remove the beans and let cool.
- **Weights and measures:** imperial weights and measurements are given for the recipes.
- **Cooking temperatures:** oven temperatures are given in degrees Celsius, degrees Fahrenheit and gas mark for each recipe. Remember if you have a fan-assisted oven, that you need to reduce the temperature slightly (usually by approximately 20 degrees) and/or adjust the cooking times. Please refer to manufacturer's guidelines for more specific information on adjusting the temperature and time of your oven, if applicable.

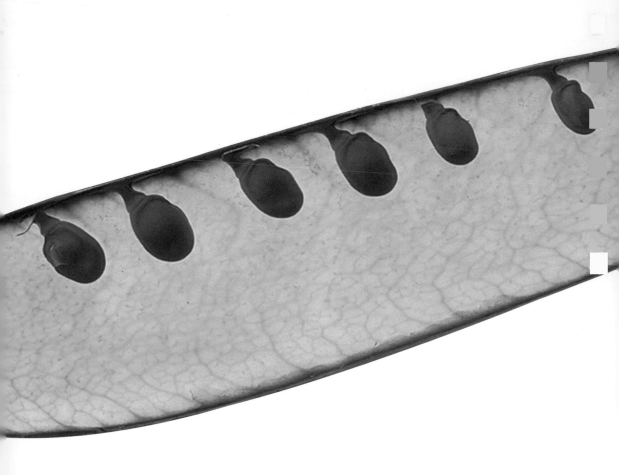

SPRING
RECIPES

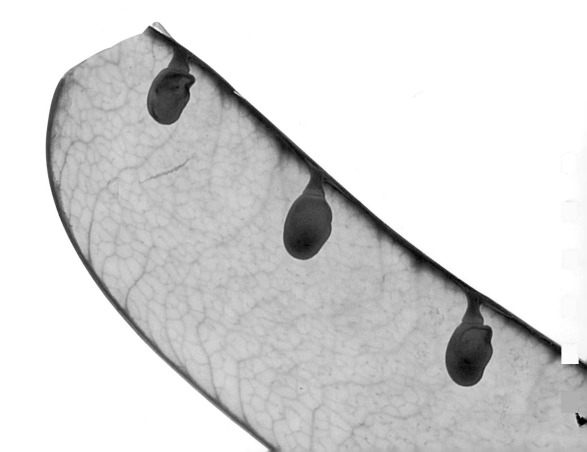

Spring is the time of waking up after the still winter. In nature, energy rises and green shoots appear everywhere and, as the light grows stronger, so does our need to recharge our batteries and have a good clean out. Young nettle shoots, dandelion leaves, sorrel, and cress are bursting with vitamins and minerals to replenish the body, and they are also excellent remedies for detoxifying.

Spring is the best time to go on detox cures and regimes because the various spring greens are full of new nourishment, antioxidants, and phyto-chemicals that help us shed the winter cold. It is a time of new life and new beginnings, and the pastel-colored flowers all around bear witness to the fruits to come.

What a joy to cook with sparkling fresh ingredients after a winter using stored roots! The first asparagus is followed by a myriad of sunny, spring feasts of strawberries, cherries, mushrooms, new carrots, and potatoes, green beans, fresh herbs, and tender zucchini. Colorful meals, high in nutrients and low in calories, replace heavier winter meals. The sun is back, and with it come the plentiful foods and enthusiasm we need to enjoy the delights of the new season.

001 ARTICHOKE HEART SOUP

CALORIES	314
CHOLESTEROL	7
VEGAN CALORIES	285
POLYUNSATS	★★☆
ANTIOXIDANTS	★★★
CALCIUM	★★☆
IRON	★★☆
B VITAMINS	★★☆

4 globe artichokes
2 tbsp lemon juice
2 tbsp olive oil
1 shallot, sliced
1 small potato, diced
1 tomato, puréed

3½ cups vegetable stock
2 tbsp small pasta shapes
salt and black pepper to taste
1 handful parsley, finely
 chopped

Peel the leaves off the artichokes, cut the bases into quarters, and remove the choke and any remaining leaf edges with a sharp knife. Plunge the artichoke hearts into cold water with the lemon juice. Heat the oil in a saucepan and gently soften the shallot. Add the potato and the artichoke hearts, stir-fry for 2 minutes, then add the tomato, heat through and pour in the stock. Bring to a boil, then add the pasta, and simmer for 10–15 minutes. Season with salt and pepper, garnish with the parsley, and serve with bread and cheese, or soy cheese.

002 ASPARAGUS SOUP

CALORIES	305
CHOLESTEROL	7
VEGAN CALORIES	285
POLYUNSATS	★★☆
ANTIOXIDANTS	★★☆
CALCIUM	★★☆
IRON	★★☆
B VITAMINS	★★☆

½ lb asparagus
2 tbsp olive oil
1 small onion, chopped
1 small carrot, chopped
2 medium potatoes, chopped
3¾ cups vegetable stock

1 small bunch fresh parsley,
 chopped
½ cup milk/soy milk
salt and black pepper to taste
parsley to garnish, finely
 chopped

Chop the ends off the asparagus, and peel off any coarse outer skin with a potato peeler. Cut off the tips and steam them separately for 5–6 minutes. Chop the remaining asparagus into chunks. Gently heat the oil in a large saucepan and sweat the onion, carrot, potatoes, and asparagus chunks for a couple of minutes before adding the vegetable stock and the parsley. Bring to a boil and gently simmer for 15 minutes. Remove from the heat, pour in the milk, purée, and season. Add the asparagus tips, gently reheat, and serve garnished with parsley.

003 CATALAN THYME AND GARLIC SOUP

CALORIES	149
CHOLESTEROL	0
VEGAN CALORIES	149
POLYUNSATS	★★☆
ANTIOXIDANTS	★★☆
CALCIUM	★☆☆
IRON	★☆☆
B VITAMINS	★☆☆

2¼ cups water
2 tsp fresh thyme
2 cloves garlic, chopped

salt and black pepper to taste
olive oil for drizzling
1 handful croûtons

Bring the water to a boil in a saucepan with the thyme, garlic, and a little salt and pepper. Simmer for 2–3 minutes, check the seasoning, drizzle with a little oil, and garnish with croûtons before serving.

004 CHINESE GREEN ASPARAGUS SOUP

CALORIES	265
CHOLESTEROL	0
VEGAN CALORIES	265
POLYUNSATS	★★★
ANTIOXIDANTS	★★★
CALCIUM	★★☆
IRON	★★☆
B VITAMINS	★★☆

2 tbsp olive oil
7 green asparagus spears, sliced
1 small stick celery (with leaves), sliced
4 red radishes, sliced
1 clove garlic, finely chopped

1 tsp fresh ginger, finely chopped
2½ cups spinach leaves, chopped
2 tsp tamari (soy sauce)
1 tbsp sesame oil
3 cups vegetable stock
salt and black pepper to taste

Stir-fry the asparagus, celery, radishes, garlic, and ginger in a Dutch oven with the olive oil for 2 minutes. Add the spinach, tamari, and sesame oil and fry for another 30 seconds. Pour in the stock, bring to a boil, and simmer for 15 minutes. Season and serve hot.

005 SAVOY CABBAGE SOUP

CALORIES	369
CHOLESTEROL	0
VEGAN CALORIES	369
POLYUNSATS	★★☆
ANTIOXIDANTS	★★★
CALCIUM	★★☆
IRON	★★☆
B VITAMINS	★★☆

4⅓ cups vegetable stock
2 tbsp olive oil
1 small leek, sliced
2 potatoes, cubed
1 carrot, cubed
1 slice celery root, cubed
¼ Savoy cabbage, shredded

1 bay leaf
1 tsp paprika
a few sprigs each of parsley, sage, rosemary and thyme, chopped
1 handful small pasta shapes
salt and black pepper to taste

Bring the stock to the boil in a Dutch oven with the other ingredients and simmer for 15 minutes. Season and serve with whole wheat bread.

006 HARISSA SOUP

CALORIES	498
CHOLESTEROL	0
VEGAN CALORIES	498
POLYUNSATS	★☆☆
ANTIOXIDANTS	★★★
CALCIUM	★★☆
IRON	★★★
B VITAMINS	★★☆

½ hot chili pepper, chopped
2 cloves garlic, crushed
1 tsp coriander seeds
1 tsp ground cumin
2 tbsp olive oil
2 scallions, sliced
1 carrot, diced
1 stick celery, sliced
1 cup green beans, sliced

1 lb ripe tomatoes, puréed
1¼ cups flageolet beans, cooked or canned
1½ cups garbanzos, cooked or canned
3½ cups vegetable stock
salt and black pepper to taste
1 handful mint, chopped

In a mortar, pound the chili, garlic, coriander, and cumin with a little oil. Then gently heat the remaining oil in a large Dutch oven, and add the onion and the vegetables. Heat through, add the tomatoes, beans, garbanzos, and chili paste. Stir for 1 minute before adding the stock and a little salt. Bring to a boil and simmer for 15 minutes. Season with salt and pepper, garnish with mint, and serve.

007 HOT NETTLE SOUP

CALORIES	258
CHOLESTEROL	0
VEGAN CALORIES	258
POLYUNSATS	★☆☆
ANTIOXIDANTS	★★★
CALCIUM	★★☆
IRON	★★★
B VITAMINS	★★☆

4⅓ cups vegetable stock
7oz fresh nettle tips, washed
2 tbsp olive oil
½ tsp cayenne pepper
1 pinch saffron threads
1 bay leaf
1 clove garlic, crushed

1 red onion, halved and sliced
1 potato, diced
1 carrot, sliced
1 stick celery, finely chopped
3 tbsp navy beans, cooked or
    canned
salt and black pepper to taste

Bring the stock to a boil in a Dutch oven with the nettles and the rest of the ingredients. Heat through and simmer for 15 minutes. Purée, adjust the seasoning, and serve with croutons.

008 PORTUGUESE CABBAGE SOUP

CALORIES	461
CHOLESTEROL	25
VEGAN CALORIES	394
POLYUNSATS	★★☆
ANTIOXIDANTS	★★★
CALCIUM	★★☆
IRON	★★★
B VITAMINS	★★☆

3½ cups vegetable stock
3 small potatoes,
    quartered and thinly sliced
½ Spanish onion, thinly sliced
1½ cups savoy cabbage,
    shredded

1 tsp mustard seeds
1 tsp paprika
2 tbsp olive oil, plus some for frying
salt and black pepper to taste
¼ lb spicy sausage (pork/soy),
    sliced

Bring the stock to a boil in a Dutch oven with the potatoes, onion, spring greens, mustard seeds, paprika, olive oil, and some salt and pepper. Heat through and simmer for 15 minutes. Meanwhile, fry the sausage slices in a frying pan with a little oil. When the soup is ready, check the seasoning, garnish with the fried sausage slices, and serve.

009 FRENCH ONION SOUP

CALORIES	368
CHOLESTEROL	0
VEGAN CALORIES	368
POLYUNSATS	★★☆
ANTIOXIDANTS	★☆☆
CALCIUM	★☆☆
IRON	★☆☆
B VITAMINS	★★☆

2 tbsp olive oil
1¼ cups onions, finely chopped
1 tbsp wheat flour
4⅓ cups vegetable stock

1 tbsp port wine
salt and black pepper to taste
2 thin slices bread, broiled

Heat the oil in a Dutch oven over a low–medium heat and stir-fry the onions until soft. (Don't let them brown too much.) Sprinkle with the flour and stir for 1 minute. Slowly add the stock and the port, bring to a boil, simmer for 20 minutes, and season. Place a thin slice of broiled bread in the bottom of each bowl and pour the soup on top. Serve immediately.

SPICY BEET SOUP

★◐☒◿

CALORIES	296
CHOLESTEROL	28
VEGAN CALORIES	368
POLYUNSATS	★★★
ANTIOXIDANTS	★★★
CALCIUM	★☆☆
IRON	★★☆
B VITAMINS	★★☆

1 tbsp grapeseed oil
1 tsp ground cumin
1 cinnamon stick
½ tsp ground cloves
1 tsp freshly ground black pepper
1 cup raw beet, diced

3 tomatoes, diced
2¼ cups vegetable stock/
   water
salt to taste
¼ cup crème fraîche/coconut
   cream

Heat the oil in a pan, add the spices and stir for 10 seconds. Add the beet, stir for a further 30 seconds, then add the tomatoes. Stir-fry for 1 minute before adding the stock or water. Bring to a boil and simmer for 15 minutes, then season. Take off the heat, remove the cinnamon stick, purée and add the cream. Serve with croûtons or toast.

011 SPRING VEGETABLE SOUP

CALORIES	298
CHOLESTEROL	0
VEGAN CALORIES	298
POLYUNSATS	★☆☆
ANTIOXIDANTS	★★★
CALCIUM	★☆☆
IRON	★★☆
B VITAMINS	★★☆

2 tbsp olive oil
2 scallions, sliced
1 small potato, sliced
1 small carrot, chopped
5 fresh tomatoes, puréed
the tips from ½ lb of
   asparagus
¾ cup peas

3 red radishes, sliced
2¼ cups vegetable stock
1 tsp maple syrup
1 tbsp tarragon, finely chopped
salt and black pepper to taste
a little Parmesan/brewer's yeast
   flakes (optional)

Heat the oil in a Dutch oven. Gently sweat the scallions, potato, and carrot
for 5 minutes. Add the tomatoes. Heat through, then add the asparagus,
peas, and radishes. Add the stock, maple syrup, and a little salt. Bring to
a boil and simmer for 10 minutes. Add the tarragon, season, sprinkle with
Parmesan or brewer's yeast flakes (if using), and serve.

012 HIMALAYAN NETTLE SOUP

CALORIES	93
CHOLESTEROL	0
VEGAN CALORIES	93
POLYUNSATS	★☆☆
ANTIOXIDANTS	★★★
CALCIUM	★★☆
IRON	★★★
B VITAMINS	★★☆

9oz young nettle tips
4⅓ cups vegetable stock
½ tsp black pepper
1 tsp ginger, chopped

1 tbsp wheat flour mixed with a little
   milk/soya milk
salt to taste

Pick and wash the nettles using gloves. Bring the stock to a boil in a pan.
Add the nettle tips, pepper, ginger, and a little salt. Simmer for 15 minutes.
Blend and thicken with the flour while stirring continuously. Check the sea-
soning and serve with rice.

013 TIBETAN BOETUK

CALORIES	502
CHOLESTEROL	55
VEGAN CALORIES	416
POLYUNSATS	★★☆
ANTIOXIDANTS	★★☆
CALCIUM	★★☆
IRON	★★☆
B VITAMINS	★★☆

⅔ cup wheat flour
2 tbsp olive oil
3 scallions, sliced
1 clove garlic, crushed
1 tsp ginger, chopped
1 pinch asafoetida
1 pinch grated nutmeg
1 pinch saffron threads

½ cup lean lamb chunks/
   1oz soy chunks
   (dry weight), rehydrated
1 tbsp tamari (soy sauce)
2 tomatoes, chopped
4 red radishes, sliced
1 cup green peas
4⅓ cups vegetable stock

Mix the flour with a little salt and enough water to make a stiff dough.
Roll the dough into a thin snake and cut into ½in dumplings. Set aside.
Heat the oil in a pan, add 2 scallions, followed by the garlic and ginger,
and fry for 1 minute. Then add the spices and the lamb or soy chunks and
fry for a further 5 minutes. Add the tamari, heat through, then add the
tomatoes. Turn down the heat and simmer for a few minutes before adding
the radishes, peas, and stock. Bring to a boil and add the dumplings.
Simmer for 8–10 minutes. Finely chop the remaining scallion, sprinkle over
the soup, and serve.

014 SPROUTING SPRING SALAD

★♥◐✖◢

CALORIES	316
CHOLESTEROL	0
VEGAN CALORIES	316
POLYUNSATS	★★☆
ANTIOXIDANTS	★★★
CALCIUM	★★☆
IRON	★★★
B VITAMINS	★★☆

1 large handful Iceberg lettuce
1 handful arugula
1 Belgian endive, sliced
   lengthwise
¾ cup fresh peas
1 small zucchini, finely sliced
1 handful alfalfa sprouts

Basic French dressing:
1 tbsp lemon juice
1 clove garlic, crushed
2 tsp Dijon mustard
salt and black pepper to taste
3 tbsp olive oil

To make a basic French dressing, mix the lemon juice, garlic, mustard, salt, and pepper in a large salad bowl. Slowly add the oil and whisk until smooth and creamy. Shred the lettuce and place it in the bowl along with the other ingredients. Add the dressing, toss well, and serve immediately.

015 SALADE PRINTANIÈRE

★✖◢◢

CALORIES	260
CHOLESTEROL	168
VEGAN CALORIES	371
POLYUNSATS	★★☆
ANTIOXIDANTS	★★★
CALCIUM	★★☆
IRON	★★★
B VITAMINS	★★☆

1 cup green beans,
   cooked and halved
½ bunch radishes, sliced
8 mushrooms, sliced
juice of 1 lemon
2 tbsp olive oil

1 tbsp tarragon, chopped
salt and black pepper to taste
10 cherry tomatoes, halved
12 large shrimp, cooked and
   shelled/⅓ cup Brazil nuts, halved

Mix the green beans, radishes, and mushrooms in a salad bowl. Make a vinaigrette by whisking the lemon juice, oil, tarragon, salt, and pepper in a bowl. Pour two-thirds of the vinaigrette over the mixed vegetables and gently toss, then divide between two large plates. Dip the tomatoes in the remaining vinaigrette and arrange them around the edge of each plate. Garnish with the shrimp or Brazil nuts, and serve with French baguette.

016 SMOKY SWEDISH SALAD

★♥◐✖◢

CALORIES	390
CHOLESTEROL	22
VEGAN CALORIES	382
POLYUNSATS	★★★
ANTIOXIDANTS	★★★
CALCIUM	★★☆
IRON	★☆☆
B VITAMINS	★★★

oil for frying (optional)
¾ cup smoked herring fillets/
   4oz smoked tempeh, cubed
1 raw beet, chopped into
   thin sticks
1 carrot, chopped into thin sticks
1 apple, quartered, cored, and
   finely chopped

1 scallion, finely sliced
2 tbsp light almond butter
1 tbsp tarragon vinegar
1 tbsp lemon juice
1 tsp Dijon mustard
½ tsp ground coriander
½ tsp dried thyme
salt and black pepper to taste

If you are using tempeh, stir-fry in a skillet with a little oil until golden. Mix the beet, carrot, apple, and scallion in a salad bowl. Make a dressing by mixing the almond butter with the vinegar, lemon juice, mustard, coriander, thyme, salt, and pepper in a bowl. Add a little water to get a smooth and creamy consistency. Gently mix the dressing with the salad and garnish with the herring or tempeh. Serve with a bowl of green lettuce or curly endive, and slices of whole grain or rye bread.

017 ◄ SALMON WITH MANGO AND ASPARAGUS SALAD

⭐❤️💧🌿

CALORIES	615
CHOLESTEROL	96
VEGAN CALORIES	349
POLYUNSATS	★★☆
ANTIOXIDANTS	★★★
CALCIUM	★★☆
IRON	★★☆
B VITAMINS	★★★

1 tbsp olive oil
10oz salmon fillet, boned and
  flaked/3oz seitan, cubed
½ lb asparagus spears, trimmed
  and chopped
2 handfuls lamb's lettuce
½ Florence fennel bulb, sliced

1 mango, pitted, peeled,
  and cubed
1 scallion, finely chopped
½ cup plain/soy yogurt
1 tsp Dijon mustard
salt and black pepper to taste

Stir-fry the salmon or seitan in a frying pan with the oil for 2–3 minutes, until it begins to brown. Blanch the asparagus in a saucepan of boiling water with a little salt for 2–3 minutes, drain and set aside. Divide the lamb's lettuce between two large plates. Add the fried salmon or seitan, the asparagus, fennel, mango, and scallion. To make the dressing, place the yoghurt in a small bowl, add the mustard, salt, and pepper. Mix well and pour over the 2 salads. Serve with crusty bread.

018 GREEN BEAN SALAD

❤️💧❌🌿

CALORIES	393
CHOLESTEROL	0
VEGAN CALORIES	393
POLYUNSATS	★★★
ANTIOXIDANTS	★★☆
CALCIUM	★★☆
IRON	★★★
B VITAMINS	★★☆

1 red bell pepper, quartered
  and deseeded
½ lb green beans, blanched
2 scallions, sliced
1 handful parsley

2 tbsp walnut oil
2 tsp balsamic vinegar
salt and black pepper to taste
1 handful walnuts, shelled

Broil the red bell pepper quarters until the skin is completely black and charred. Cool, discard the skin, and cut into strips. Make the dressing by whisking the oil, vinegar, salt, and pepper in a salad bowl. Add the red bell pepper, green beans, scallions, and parsley, and gently toss. Garnish with the walnuts and serve.

019 SPRING CRUDITÉS WITH RAVIGÔTE

⭐❤️💧❌

CALORIES	397
CHOLESTEROL	0
VEGAN CALORIES	397
POLYUNSATS	★★☆
ANTIOXIDANTS	★★★
CALCIUM	★★☆
IRON	★★★
B VITAMINS	★★★

2 Belgian endive, sliced lengthwise
2 cups shiitake mushrooms, sliced
  and fried
¼ lb asparagus tips
1 large handful fresh fava beans,
  shelled
¼ cauliflower, cut into small florets
1 beet, cut into thin sticks
1 tbsp red wine vinegar

1 pinch salt
1 tsp mustard
½ tsp each of chopped tarragon and
  fine herbs
1 tsp each of chopped parsley and
  chervil
1 spring onion, finely chopped
2 tsp capers, chopped
3 tbsp olive oil

Divide the crudités between 2 large plates. To make the dressing, purée the vinegar, salt, mustard, herbs, scallion, and capers. Slowly add the oil and mix to an even consistency. Sprinkle the dressing onto the crudités and serve with broiled bread.

020 TARAMASALATA AND GREEK SALAD

CALORIES	199
CHOLESTEROL	382
VEGAN CALORIES	201
POLYUNSATS	★★★
ANTIOXIDANTS	★★★
CALCIUM	★★★
IRON	★★★
B VITAMINS	★★☆

4oz jar red caviar/1 cup smoked
    tofu, crumbled
2 tbsp lemon juice
1 tsp grated lemon zest
3 tbsp water
1 small shallot, finely chopped
1 clove garlic, finely chopped
2 tbsp fresh bread crumbs

1 tbsp tomato catsup (optional)
salt and black pepper to taste
1 small lettuce, shredded
1 carrot, grated or cut into peelings
1 large ripe tomato, sliced into boats
1 tbsp capers
10 Greek olives, pitted
2 tbsp parsley, chopped

Make the taramasalata by puréeing the red caviar or smoked tofu with the lemon juice, lemon zest and water. Add the shallot, garlic, bread crumbs, and tomato catsup (if using). Season and keep in the fridge until needed. Place the lettuce in a salad bowl and top with the carrot, tomato, capers, olives, and parsley. Serve with the taramasalata and warm pitta bread.

021 ASPARAGUS AND TOMATO SALAD

CALORIES	264
CHOLESTEROL	0
VEGAN CALORIES	264
POLYUNSATS	★★☆
ANTIOXIDANTS	★★☆
CALCIUM	★☆☆
IRON	★☆☆
B VITAMINS	★★☆

½lb white asparagus, peeled
    and ends cut off
2 tomatoes, sliced
1 pinch salt and black pepper

1 tbsp lemon juice
3 tbsp olive oil
1 small bunch chives, chopped

Boil the asparagus in a pan with salted water for approximately 10 minutes. Drain, then chop the asparagus into 1¼in pieces, place on a serving plate and cover with the tomato slices. To make the vinaigrette, whisk the salt, pepper, lemon juice, and olive oil in a bowl, and spoon over the tomatoes. Garnish with the chives and serve immediately.

022 FLORENCE FENNEL SALAD

CALORIES	249
CHOLESTEROL	0
VEGAN CALORIES	249
POLYUNSATS	★★★
ANTIOXIDANTS	★★★
CALCIUM	★★☆
IRON	★☆☆
B VITAMINS	★★☆

2 Florence fennel bulbs, halved
    lengthwise and finely sliced
    (reserve the tops to garnish)
6 radishes, sliced
1 carrot, cut into fine sticks
1 apple, quartered, cored, and
    cubed

1 scallion, finely sliced
1 tbsp light almond butter
1 tbsp tarragon vinegar
1 tbsp lemon juice
1 tsp Dijon mustard
salt and black pepper to taste

Mix the fennel, radishes, carrot, apple, and scallion in a salad bowl. Make the dressing by mixing the almond butter with the vinegar, lemon juice, mustard, salt, and pepper in a bowl. Add a little water to get a smooth and creamy consistency. Gently toss the dressing with the salad, garnish with fennel tops, and serve with bread and pâté.

023 ▲ CHINESE CABBAGE SALAD

★♥◆✕⊘

CALORIES	97
CHOLESTEROL	0
VEGAN CALORIES	97
POLYUNSATS	★☆☆
ANTIOXIDANTS	★★★
CALCIUM	★☆☆
IRON	★★☆
B VITAMINS	★★☆

1 small Chinese cabbage, finely chopped
1 small white radish, finely chopped
1 tsp salt
½ tsp cayenne pepper
1 clove garlic, finely chopped
1 tsp ginger, finely chopped
2 scallions, finely chopped
1 carrot, grated
¾ cup peas, fresh or frozen, blanched

Place the Chinese cabbage and the white radish in a salad bowl, sprinkle with salt and cayenne pepper. Mix well, add the garlic, ginger, scallions, carrot, and peas. Mix again and serve with broiled bread and pâté.

024 AVOCADO, SPINACH AND PEA SALAD

CALORIES	411
CHOLESTEROL	0
VEGAN CALORIES	411
POLYUNSATS	★★★
ANTIOXIDANTS	★★★
CALCIUM	★★★
IRON	★★★
B VITAMINS	★★☆

6 cups fresh spinach leaves,
  sliced
1 avocado, diced
1⅓ cup green peas, fresh or
  defrosted
1 tbsp tarragon vinegar

½ tsp maple syrup
1 clove garlic, crushed
salt and black pepper to taste
2 tbsp wheat germ oil
1 small bunch watercress, chopped
1 tbsp pumpkin seeds

Mix the spinach, avocado, and peas in a large salad bowl. To make the
dressing, whisk the vinegar, maple syrup, garlic, salt, and pepper in a
bowl. Slowly add the oil, whisk to a smooth consistency, then toss with the
salad. Garnish with watercress and pumpkin seeds, and serve with bread.

025 SALADE D'ASPÈRGE

CALORIES	430
CHOLESTEROL	120
VEGAN CALORIES	226
POLYUNSATS	★★☆
ANTIOXIDANTS	★★☆
CALCIUM	★★☆
IRON	★★☆
B VITAMINS	★★☆

½ lb white asparagus, peeled and
  ends cut off
2 chicken breasts/1 cup tofu,
  sliced
2 handfuls mixed salad leaves

1 tbsp white wine vinegar
2 tbsp olive oil, plus some for frying
salt and black pepper to taste
1 tbsp chives, chopped

Cook the asparagus in a pan with boiling water and a little salt until tender
(5–10 minutes, depending on size). Fry the chicken or tofu in a skillet with
a little oil and set aside. Make a vinaigrette by whisking the vinegar, oil,
salt, and pepper in a bowl. Divide the salad leaves between two large
plates and garnish them with the fried chicken or tofu slices, and the
cooked asparagus. Drizzle with the vinaigrette and garnish with chives.
Serve with broiled bread.

026 MESCLUN SALAD

CALORIES	315
CHOLESTEROL	19
VEGAN CALORIES	289
POLYUNSATS	★★☆
ANTIOXIDANTS	★★☆
CALCIUM	★★☆
IRON	★★☆
B VITAMINS	★★☆

1 curly endive, sliced
1 handful lamb's lettuce
1 handful young dandelion leaves
1 handful arugula
1 handful oakleaf lettuce
1 tbsp sorrel, chopped
2 tbsp chervil, chopped

3 tbsp olive oil
1 tbsp lemon juice
1 clove garlic, crushed
1 pinch raw cane sugar
salt and black pepper to taste
10 anchovy fillets/20 olives, pitted

Make the vinaigrette in a salad bowl by whisking the olive oil, lemon juice,
garlic, sugar, salt, and pepper. Add the salad ingredients and gently toss.
Garnish with the anchovies or olives and serve.

027 ▲ SPAGHETTI WITH ARTICHOKES, BEANS, AND SPINACH

CALORIES	599
CHOLESTEROL	0
VEGAN CALORIES	599
POLYUNSATS	★★☆
ANTIOXIDANTS	★★★
CALCIUM	★★☆
IRON	★★★
B VITAMINS	★★★

5oz spaghetti
2 tbsp olive oil
1 scallion, sliced
1 clove garlic, chopped
1 red bell pepper, halved and sliced
½ cup fava beans, fresh
   or frozen

2¾ cup fresh spinach, chopped
4 artichoke hearts, sliced
2 tbsp tomato paste
½ tsp raw cane sugar
1 tbsp marjoram
salt and black pepper to taste

Boil the spaghetti in plenty of salted water with a little oil. Meanwhile, gently heat the oil in a large saucepan. Add the onion, garlic, and red bell pepper and gently fry for 2 minutes. Stir in the beans, spinach, and artichoke hearts. Add the tomato paste, sugar, and marjoram, and a little water, if necessary. Cover and very gently simmer for 10 minutes. Season and serve with the cooked spaghetti.

028 PASTA WITH SAUSAGE AND ITALIAN TOMATO SAUCE

⭐ 🤍 💧 🍳 🌾 ☕

CALORIES	705
CHOLESTEROL	13
VEGAN CALORIES	671
POLYUNSATS	★★☆
ANTIOXIDANTS	★★★
CALCIUM	★★☆
IRON	★★★
B VITAMINS	★★★

7oz tricolor fusilli
1¼ cups sausage (meat/soy)
2 tbsp olive oil
1 scallion, chopped
1 generous cup fresh peas
1 small pickled red bell

pepper, sliced
1 cup passata (sieved tomato)
2 handfuls arugula or 2 curly
endive
salt and black pepper to taste
1 handful parsley, chopped

Cook the fusilli in plenty of boiling water with a little salt and oil. Chop the sausage into chunks. Heat the oil in a heavy-based skillet, add the chunks of sausage and the scallion. Stir-fry over a medium heat until the sausage begins to brown. Add the peas, pickled pepper, and passata, bring to a boil and simmer for 10 minutes. Arrange the salad leaves on two large plates. Drain the cooked pasta and place in the middle of each plate. Top with the sauce, season, garnish with the parsley, and serve.

029 LINGUINI WITH BEET SAUCE

⭐ 🤍 🌾

CALORIES	507
CHOLESTEROL	8
VEGAN CALORIES	519
POLYUNSATS	★☆☆
ANTIOXIDANTS	★★☆
CALCIUM	★★☆
IRON	★★★
B VITAMINS	★★☆

7oz linguini
1 tbsp olive oil
1 small red onion, halved
and sliced
1 raw beet, diced
2 tbsp red wine
2 tbsp water or vegetable stock

1 tbsp balsamic vinegar
1 small bunch flat-leaf parsley,
chopped
salt and black pepper to taste
¼ cup Parma ham/smoked
tempeh, diced

Cook the linguini in plenty of boiling water with a little salt and oil. Heat the oil in a Dutch oven. Add the onion and beet and gently stir-fry for 5 minutes. Add the red wine, water or stock, vinegar, and parsley, and bring to a boil. Simmer until the beet is soft, then season. Mix the drained pasta into the sauce. Garnish with the ham or tempeh and serve hot.

030 FETTUCCINE WITH TUSCAN SAUCE

⭐ 🤍 🌾

CALORIES	762
CHOLESTEROL	53
VEGAN CALORIES	707
POLYUNSATS	★★★
ANTIOXIDANTS	★★☆
CALCIUM	★★☆
IRON	★★☆
B VITAMINS	★★☆

2 tbsp olive oil
⅔ cup boned hare (or rabbit)
saddle/seitan, diced
1 small red onion, finely chopped
1 clove garlic, finely chopped
1 tbsp pine kernels
½ Florence fennel bulb, sliced

½ cup vegetable stock
¾ square semisweet chocolate
1 tbsp red wine vinegar
1 tbsp oregano, chopped
salt and black pepper to taste
7oz fettucine

Heat the oil in a Dutch oven, add the hare (or rabbit) or seitan, onion, garlic, pine kernels, and fennel, one by one, and stir-fry over a medium–high heat for 5 minutes. Add the stock and the chocolate, bring to a boil, cover and simmer for 10 minutes. Add the vinegar and oregano, heat through and season. Cook the fettuccine in plenty of boiling water with a little salt and oil. Drain and serve with the sauce and a green salad.

031 CORN PASTA WITH ARUGULA AND SUN-DRIED TOMATOES

CALORIES	659
CHOLESTEROL	5
VEGAN CALORIES	646
POLYUNSATS	★★★
ANTIOXIDANTS	★★★
CALCIUM	★★☆
IRON	★★☆
B VITAMINS	★★☆

7oz corn pasta
1 bunch arugula, chopped
10–12 black olives, pitted
   and chopped
10–12 sun-dried tomatoes, chopped

2 tbsp safflower oil
1 tbsp lime juice
salt and black pepper to taste
1–2 tbsp Parmesan/soy cheese,
   freshly grated

Cook the pasta in plenty of boiling water with a little salt and olive oil. Meanwhile, mix the arugula with the olives, sun-dried tomatoes, safflower oil, lime juice, salt, and pepper in a large serving bowl. Drain the cooked pasta and add to the salad. Check the seasoning, sprinkle with the Parmesan or soy cheese, and serve.

032 TAGLIATELLE WITH FAVA BEANS

CALORIES	599
CHOLESTEROL	0
VEGAN CALORIES	599
POLYUNSATS	★★☆
ANTIOXIDANTS	★★★
CALCIUM	★★☆
IRON	★★★
B VITAMINS	★★★

7oz tagliatelle
1 tbsp olive oil
1 scallion, finely chopped
1 clove garlic, finely chopped
1 handful parsley, finely
   chopped

1 cup small fava beans (shelled
   weight), fresh or frozen
½ cup water
salt and black pepper to taste
a little Parmesan/brewer's yeast
   flakes (optional)

Cook the tagliatelle in plenty of boiling water with a little salt and oil. Meanwhile, heat the oil in a separate pan, add the scallion, garlic, and parsley and very gently stir-fry for 5 minutes until soft. Add the beans and the water. Season, bring to a boil and cook for 5 minutes. Remove from the heat, mash half the bean mixture to a coarse paste and return to the pan with the whole beans. Check the seasoning and heat through. Drain the cooked pasta, then add to the sauce, and stir. Sprinkle with Parmesan or brewer's yeast flakes (if using) and serve immediately.

033 PENNE WITH ASPARAGUS AND MUSHROOM SAUCE

CALORIES	543
CHOLESTEROL	0
VEGAN CALORIES	543
POLYUNSATS	★★☆
ANTIOXIDANTS	★★☆
CALCIUM	★☆☆
IRON	★☆☆
B VITAMINS	★★★

7oz penne pasta
½ lb green asparagus, trimmed
2 tbsp olive oil
1 shallot, finely chopped
1¾ cups mushrooms, sliced

¼ cup vegetable stock
1 tsp cornstarch dissolved in a little
   cold water
1 tbsp tamari (soy sauce)
salt and black pepper to taste

Cook the penne in plenty of boiling water with a little salt and oil. Cut the asparagus into penne-sized lengths, then stir-fry them in the olive oil together with the shallot and the mushrooms for 5 minutes. Add the stock, bring to a boil and simmer for 2–3 minutes, or until the asparagus is tender. Pour in the dissolved cornstarch and the tamari, and cook until the sauce thickens. Season with salt (if necessary) and plenty of black pepper. Drain the cooked pasta and add to the sauce. Serve immediately.

034 ▼ PASTA PRIMAVERA

CALORIES	563
CHOLESTEROL	0
VEGAN CALORIES	563
POLYUNSATS	★★☆
ANTIOXIDANTS	★★★
CALCIUM	★★☆
IRON	★★☆
B VITAMINS	★★☆

7oz tricolor fusilli
2 tbsp olive oil
2 scallions, chopped
1 small carrot, cut into
　　thin sticks
¼ lb celery root, cut into
　　thin sticks
¼ lb snow peas

¼ lb young nettle tips or baby
　　spinach leaves, chopped
½ cup vegetable stock or water
1 tbsp lemon juice
1 tsp Dijon mustard
salt and black pepper to taste
1 handful watercress, chopped

Cook the pasta in plenty of boiling water with a little salt and oil. Meanwhile, heat 1 tablespoon of oil in a Dutch oven and gently stir-fry the scallions for 30 seconds, then add the carrot, celery root, snow peas, and nettle tips or spinach leaves. (Only touch raw nettles with gloves on. Once cooked they lose their sting.) Stir-fry for a further 2 minutes, then add the stock or water. Bring to a boil and simmer for 5 minutes. Add the lemon juice, mustard, and the remaining 1 tablespoon of oil, and season. Drain the cooked pasta and mix with the vegetables. Garnish with watercress and serve immediately.

035 PENNINI WITH
BLACK TRUMPET MUSHROOMS

CALORIES	884
CHOLESTEROL	525
VEGAN CALORIES	647
POLYUNSATS	★★★
ANTIOXIDANTS	★★★
CALCIUM	★★☆
IRON	★★☆
B VITAMINS	★★☆

10oz chicken livers/5oz
   seitan, cut into chunks
1 tbsp wheat flour
grapeseed oil for (stir-)frying
7oz pennini
1 shallot, chopped
¼ lb black trumpet

mushrooms (craterellus)
3 tbsp dry white wine
4 tbsp chicken/vegetable stock
3 tbsp crème fraîche/soy cream
salt and black pepper to taste
1 small bunch chives, finely
   chopped

Coat the chicken livers or seitan in the flour and a little salt and pepper,
then place them in a skillet and fry with some oil over a high heat until
brown. Remove and set aside. Meanwhile, boil the pennini in plenty
of salted water with a little oil. Add a little more oil to the skillet and
stir-fry the shallot and the mushrooms, then remove and set aside. Add
the wine to the pennini pan and reduce to half the volume, then add the
stock and let it reduce, too. Add the cream, followed by the fried shallot
and mushrooms. Let simmer until the sauce thickens. Add the fried livers
or seitan, check the seasoning, and serve with the cooked pennini,
garnished with chopped chives.

036 SALADE DE PÂTES

CALORIES	663
CHOLESTEROL	86
VEGAN CALORIES	634
POLYUNSATS	★★☆
ANTIOXIDANTS	★★★
CALCIUM	★★☆
IRON	★★☆
B VITAMINS	★★★

7oz fresh linguini
10oz fresh tuna fillets/
   6oz package tempeh and 1
   sheet of nori seaweed, toasted
   and crushed
juice of ½ lemon
10 salted anchovy fillets (soaked for
   10 minutes)/10 black olives, pitted

1 dash red wine vinegar
2 tbsp olive oil
black pepper to taste
1 small Florence fennel,
   finely sliced
5 cherry tomatoes
1 tbsp parsley, finely
   chopped

Cook the linguini in plenty of boiling water with a little salt and oil. Cool
the pasta under running water, drain and set aside. Place the tuna or
tempeh on a baking sheet, add the crushed nori (if using), drizzle with oil
and lemon juice, and bake in a preheated oven at 220°C/425°F/gas mark
7 for 5–10 minutes. Meanwhile, purée the anchovies or olives, vinegar, oil,
and pepper to a smooth consistency (and pass through a sieve afterward
if you are worried about the fishbones). Mix the fennel with the cooked
pasta and the sauce. Divide between 2 plates, top with the baked tuna
or tempeh slices and cherry tomatoes, and serve garnished with parsley.

037 VERMICELLI WITH CURRIED OYSTER MUSHROOMS

CALORIES	335
CHOLESTEROL	0
VEGAN CALORIES	335
POLYUNSATS	★★☆
ANTIOXIDANTS	★★☆
CALCIUM	★☆☆
IRON	★★☆
B VITAMINS	★★☆

7oz vermicelli
2 tbsp olive oil
1 tsp curry powder
2 scallions, sliced
1 tsp ginger, finely chopped

4½ cups oyster mushrooms, sliced
1 tbsp cilantro leaves, chopped
salt and black pepper to taste

Cook the vermicelli in plenty of salted water with a little oil. Heat the oil in a skillet or wok, add the curry powder and the scallions, and stir-fry for 30 seconds, then add the ginger and the mushrooms and stir-fry over a medium heat for a further 5 minutes. Add the cilantro, season, and serve with the cooked, drained pasta and a green salad.

038 CHINESE FIVE-SPICE NOODLES

CALORIES	358
CHOLESTEROL	182
VEGAN CALORIES	341
POLYUNSATS	★★☆
ANTIOXIDANTS	★★☆
CALCIUM	★★☆
IRON	★★☆
B VITAMINS	★★☆

2 tbsp safflower oil
1 clove garlic, finely chopped
4 scallions, sliced
⅔ cup shrimp, cooked and shelled/1 cup marinated tofu, cubed
2½ cups fresh spinach, chopped
1 tsp ginger, grated

1 tbsp tamari (soy sauce)
1 tsp Chinese five-spice
1 tbsp Chinese rice wine or dry sherry
1 tsp raw cane sugar
7oz Chinese rice noodles
1 tbsp salted sesame seeds (gomasio), toasted

Heat the oil in a wok or large pan and stir-fry the garlic, scallions, and shrimp or tofu over a medium heat for 3 minutes. Add the spinach, ginger, and tamari, and stir-fry for a further minute, then add the five-spice, wine or sherry, and sugar. Lower the heat and very gently simmer for 3–4 minutes. Check the seasoning. Cook the noodles as indicated on the package. Serve topped with the sauce and garnished with sesame seeds.

039 TAGLIATELLE AUX MORILLES

CALORIES	826
CHOLESTEROL	166
VEGAN CALORIES	623
POLYUNSATS	★★☆
ANTIOXIDANTS	★★☆
CALCIUM	★★☆
IRON	★★☆
B VITAMINS	★★☆

200g (7oz) fresh tagliatelle
10oz turbot fillets/
    1¼ cups tofu
oil for frying
10 small morel mushrooms
juice of ½ lemon

4 tsp old Rivesaltes wine or dry sherry
½ cup fish/vegetable stock
½ cup crème fraîche/soy cream
salt and black pepper to taste

Cook the tagliatelle in boiling water with a little salt and oil. Cut the tofu into strips (if using). Fry the fillets or tofu in a pan with the oil, and set aside (keep warm). Clean and halve the morels, then fry them in the same pan for 3 minutes. Add the lemon juice and reduce until almost evaporated, then add the wine or sherry and the stock, and reduce to half the volume. Add the cream and very gently simmer until the sauce thickens, then season. Divide the cooked pasta between two plates, arrange the fillets or tofu strips next to the pasta, and top with the sauce. Serve immediately.

040 CHENG MAI STIR-FRY
❋♥◊✖

CALORIES	338
CHOLESTEROL	0
VEGAN CALORIES	338
POLYUNSATS	★★★
ANTIOXIDANTS	★★★
CALCIUM	★★☆
IRON	★★☆
B VITAMINS	★★★

1¾ cups cauliflower
1¾ cups purple sprouting broccoli
1½ cups oyster mushrooms
2 tbsp grapeseed oil
1 clove garlic, crushed

1 cup snow peas
1 cup baby corn
2 tbsp tamari (soy sauce)
½ cup bean sprouts

Chop the cauliflower into florets, and cut the broccoli and mushrooms into slices, and set aside. Heat the oil in a wok. Add the garlic and fry for 10 seconds, then add the snow peas, cauliflower florets, and broccoli slices, one by one, stirring continuously. Stir-fry for a further 2 minutes, then add the mushroom slices and the corn. Heat through, add the tamari, and stir. Turn down the heat, cover, and simmer for 5 minutes (adding a little water if necessary). Add the bean sprouts, heat through, and serve hot with rice or noodles.

041 LEBANESE SPINACH
❋♥◊🌿

CALORIES	553
CHOLESTEROL	11
VEGAN CALORIES	547
POLYUNSATS	★★★
ANTIOXIDANTS	★★★
CALCIUM	★★★
IRON	★★★
B VITAMINS	★★★

olive oil for frying
1 onion, halved and sliced
1lb 2oz fresh spinach,
    roughly chopped
2 large slices bread, chopped
    into cubes

1 cup plain/soy yogurt
1 clove garlic, crushed
1 tbsp mint, chopped
2 tbsp pine kernels, toasted
salt and black pepper to taste

Gently sweat the onion in a large Dutch oven with a little oil until soft. Add the spinach, heat through, cover and very gently simmer until soft, approximately 10 minutes, then season. Make the dressing by whisking together the yogurt, garlic and mint. Season and set aside. Fry the bread in a skillet with a little oil until golden to make croûtons, then place half of them in a serving bowl, add the cooked spinach, followed by the yogurt dressing. Top with the remaining croûtons and garnish with the toasted pine kernels. Serve immediately.

042 ASIAN ASPARAGUS
❋♥◊✖◗

CALORIES	263
CHOLESTEROL	0
VEGAN CALORIES	263
POLYUNSATS	★★☆
ANTIOXIDANTS	★★★
CALCIUM	★★☆
IRON	★★☆
B VITAMINS	★★☆

½ lb green aspargus, trimmed
    and peeled
2 tbsp olive oil
½ tsp ground cumin
1 stalk lemon grass, finely sliced
2 tsp ginger, finely chopped
2 carrots, cut into sticks
2 scallions, sliced

1 tbsp tamarind paste dissolved in
    1 cup hot water
1 handful bean sprouts
1 tbsp tamari (soy sauce)
1 tsp maple syrup
1 tbsp lemon juice
salt and black pepper to taste
    (optional)

Cut the asparagus into 2in pieces. Heat the oil in a wok. Add the spices, then the asparagus, carrots, and scallions and stir-fry for 5 minutes. Add the dissolved tamarind paste. Simmer until the asparagus is tender, then add the bean sprouts, tamari, maple syrup, and lemon juice. Heat through, season (if using), and serve with rice or noodles.

043 PROVENÇAL LEMON POTATOES
⭐❤💧✖🌿🥥

CALORIES	300
CHOLESTEROL	0
VEGAN CALORIES	300
POLYUNSATS	★★☆
ANTIOXIDANTS	★★★
CALCIUM	★★☆
IRON	★★☆
B VITAMINS	★★☆

3½ cups small potatoes, kept
   whole and unpeeled
2 tbsp olive oil

½ lemon (unpeeled), chopped
1 tsp herbes de Provence
salt and plenty of black pepper

Boil the potatoes in lightly salted water until tender, approximately 10
minutes. Drain and set aside. Heat the oil in a large pan, add the boiled
potatoes, lemon, and herbs. Stir continuously until the potatoes are well
coated with herbs. Season and serve on a bed of fresh arugula.

044 ◄ INDONESIAN TEMPEH AND VEGETABLES
⭐❤

CALORIES	440
CHOLESTEROL	0
VEGAN CALORIES	440
POLYUNSATS	★★★
ANTIOXIDANTS	★★☆
CALCIUM	★★☆
IRON	★★☆
B VITAMINS	★★★

4 tempeh slices, cut into sticks
2 tbsp tamari (soy sauce)
2 tbsp olive oil
1 clove garlic, sliced
1 tbsp ginger, chopped
1 green chili, deseeded and sliced
¾ cup baby corn, kept whole

1 cup snow peas, kept whole
2 cups oyster mushrooms,
   kept whole
2 scallions, sliced
1 tbsp toasted sesame oil
salt and black pepper to taste

Marinate the tempeh in the tamari while you prepare the other
ingredients. Then stir-fry the marinated tempeh with the olive oil
in a large pan or wok, add the remaining ingredients (except for
the sesame oil), one by one, and stir-fry for a few more minutes.
Add the sesame oil, season, and serve with noodles.

045 GERMAN SALAD
⭐❤🥥

CALORIES	487
CHOLESTEROL	48
VEGAN CALORIES	508
POLYUNSATS	★★★
ANTIOXIDANTS	★★★
CALCIUM	★★☆
IRON	★★☆
B VITAMINS	★★☆

1½ cups small potatoes, boiled
   and coarsely chopped
1 red apple, cored and chopped
1 tbsp mayonnaise/soy
   mayonnaise
1 large cornichon, diagonally sliced
2 small herring fillets/⅓ cup walnut
   halves, shelled

2 tbsp parsley, chopped
1 beet, cooked and sliced
½ small red onion, finely sliced
2 tsp white wine vinegar
½ tsp mustard
1 tbsp walnut oil
salt and black pepper to taste

Place the boiled potatoes and the apple in a salad bowl and mix in the
mayonnaise. Top with the cornichon and herring or walnuts. Garnish with
parsley, cooked beet, and red onion. Make the dressing by whisking the
vinegar, mustard, oil, salt, and pepper, and sprinkle over the salad
just before serving.

046 BAKED ENDIVE AND BEET

CALORIES	659
CHOLESTEROL	34
VEGAN CALORIES	568
POLYUNSATS	★★★
ANTIOXIDANTS	★★☆
CALCIUM	★★★
IRON	★★★
B VITAMINS	★★☆

2 large Belgian endive, quartered lengthwise
1 beet, sliced
6 sun-dried tomatoes, sliced
½ cup chopped walnuts
2 tbsp olive oil

1 tbsp lemon juice
salt and black pepper to taste
1 handful Dutch/soy cheese, grated
2 tbsp fresh bread crumbs

Preheat the oven to 200°C/400°F/gas mark 6. Place the quartered endive and the beet slices in a shallow baking dish. Scatter the sun-dried tomato slices and the chopped walnuts on top, drizzle with oil and lemon juice, and season. Top with the grated cheese and the bread crumbs. Bake in the oven for 20 minutes (adding a little water if necessary), and serve.

047 SENGALESE YASSA

CALORIES	400
CHOLESTEROL	120
VEGAN CALORIES	277
POLYUNSATS	★★★
ANTIOXIDANTS	★★★
CALCIUM	★★★
IRON	★★★
B VITAMINS	★★★

1¼ cups chicken breast/ 9oz seitan, sliced
1 tbsp groundnut oil or grapeseed oil
1 large onion, grated

juice of 2 limes
1 tsp Tabasco sauce
2 tbsp water
salt and black pepper to taste

Make a marinade of the oil, onion, lime juice, and Tabasco sauce. Brush the chicken or seitan with the marinade and broil (or grill) until well browned. Pour the remaining marinade into a skillet, heat through, add the cooked chicken or seitan, and the water, cover and simmer until tender, approximately 15 minutes. Season, and serve with boiled rice and steamed Savoy cabbage, Swiss chard, or curly kale.

048 AFRICAN-STYLE FAVA BEANS

CALORIES	178
CHOLESTEROL	0
VEGAN CALORIES	178
POLYUNSATS	★☆☆
ANTIOXIDANTS	★★★
CALCIUM	★★☆
IRON	★★☆
B VITAMINS	★★★

2 tbsp olive oil
2 tsp ground cumin
2 cloves garlic, chopped
1¾ cups fresh fava beans, shelled

3 tbsp lemon juice
2 tbsp parsley, chopped
salt and cayenne pepper to taste
1 tsp paprika

Gently heat the oil in a Dutch oven, add the cumin and the garlic, and stir-fry for 15 seconds. Add the fresh fava beans and stir for a further 15 seconds, then add enough water to cover the beans, bring to a boil, and simmer for approximately 10 minutes until the beans are soft. Add the lemon juice and the parsley. Mash some of the cooked beans with a spoon. Season and serve garnished with the paprika on a bed of millet or couscous.

049 ▼ SPRING MASALA

★ ▨

CALORIES	421
CHOLESTEROL	210
VEGAN CALORIES	490
POLYUNSATS	★★★
ANTIOXIDANTS	★★★
CALCIUM	★★☆
IRON	★★★
B VITAMINS	★★☆

1 tbsp grapeseed oil
1 small red onion, chopped
1 clove garlic, chopped
1 tsp turmeric
1 small fresh or dried green chili, chopped
1 tsp ginger, chopped
2 carrots, chopped
1 cup shrimp, cooked and

peeled/½ cup cashew nuts
approximately 1 cup coconut milk
1 tsp garam masala
salt to taste
⅔ cup green peas, shelled
1 handful cilantro leaves, chopped

Heat the oil in a heavy-based pan and gently stir-fry the onion and garlic for a few minutes until they begin to soften. Add the turmeric, chili, ginger, and carrots and stir-fry for a further 2 minutes before adding the shrimp or cashews. Stir for a further minute, then add the coconut milk and the garam masala, and simmer for 5–10 minutes until the carrots are cooked (adding more coconut milk if necessary). Season, add the peas and heat through. Garnish with the cilantro leaves and serve with rice.

050 GREEK RAGOÛT

CALORIES	401
CHOLESTEROL	0
VEGAN CALORIES	401
POLYUNSATS	★☆☆
ANTIOXIDANTS	★★☆
CALCIUM	★★☆
IRON	★★☆
B VITAMINS	★★☆

2 tbsp olive oil
1 leek, sliced
5 small potatoes,
  chopped
7oz fresh green beans
1¾ cups vegetable stock,
  heated

1 tbsp tomato paste
1 dash honey
1 tsp fresh or dried oregano, plus
  some to garnish
salt and black pepper to taste
1 tbsp lemon juice

Heat the oil in a medium Dutch oven and sauté the leek for 3 minutes. Add the potatoes and the trimmed beans and sauté for a further 2 minutes, then add the heated stock, tomato paste, honey, and oregano, and season. Bring to a boil and cook until the potatoes are tender, approximately 15 minutes. Add the lemon juice, check the seasoning, garnish with a sprinkle of oregano, and serve.

051 KOREAN SALAD

CALORIES	352
CHOLESTEROL	0
VEGAN CALORIES	352
POLYUNSATS	★★★
ANTIOXIDANTS	★★★
CALCIUM	★★☆
IRON	★★☆
B VITAMINS	★★☆

2 carrots, cut into thin
  diagonal sticks
1¾ cups white radish, cut into
  thin diagonal sticks
½ cucumber, cut into diagonal
  sticks
½ tsp salt

1 tbsp (rice) vinegar
1 dash tamari (soy sauce)
1 pinch raw cane sugar
1 dash Tabasco sauce
1 tbsp toasted sesame oil
2 tbsp almonds, chopped and
  toasted

Place the carrots, radish, and cucumber sticks in a salad bowl. Sprinkle with the salt, and mix well. To make the dressing, whisk together the vinegar, tamari, sugar, and Tabasco sauce. Then add the oil and whisk again. Pour the dressing over the salad, garnish with the toasted almonds, and serve with pan bread.

052 MEXICAN CASSEROLE

CALORIES	820
CHOLESTEROL	165
VEGAN CALORIES	552
POLYUNSATS	★★☆
ANTIOXIDANTS	★★★
CALCIUM	★★☆
IRON	★★★
B VITAMINS	★★☆

oil for frying
1¼ cups loin of lamb, diced/
  2¼oz soy chunks (dry weight),
  rehydrated
1 onion, sliced
½ red bell pepper, sliced
½ green bell pepper, sliced
1 clove garlic, crushed
1 small hot chili, kept whole

1 tomato, chopped
1 cup white wine
1 pinch dried thyme
1 bay leaf
2⅓ cups kidney beans, cooked or
  canned
salt and cayenne pepper
  to taste

Heat a little oil in a Dutch oven and fry the lamb or soy chunks over a high heat. Set aside. Fry the onion, red and green bell peppers, and garlic in the same pan with a little more oil. Add the chili, tomato, white wine, thyme, and bay leaf. Bring to a boil, cover, and simmer for 10 minutes. Add the beans and cook for 5 minutes. Add the cooked lamb or soy chunks, heat through, and season. Serve with corn bread.

053 EGGLESS OMELET PRINTANIÈRE

CALORIES	350
CHOLESTEROL	0
VEGAN CALORIES	350
POLYUNSATS	★★★
ANTIOXIDANTS	★★☆
CALCIUM	★★☆
IRON	★★☆
B VITAMINS	★★☆

basic eggless omelet batter:
⅔ cup wheat flour
½ tsp salt
1 tsp baking powder
1 pinch saffron threads
1 cup water
black pepper to taste

filling:
2 tbsp fresh peas, blanched
1 tbsp mint, finely chopped
oil for frying

To make the basic eggless batter, mix the flour, salt, baking powder, and saffron in a bowl. Add the water, whisk to a smooth batter, and season. Heat a little oil in a skillet. Pour in the batter and spread it evenly to form a thin pancake. Turn down the heat and cook slowly until the top begins to firm. Spread the peas and mint over half of the omelet, fold, and fry on each side for 30 seconds. Remove from the heat and serve.

054 TOFU OMELET AUX FINE HERBES

CALORIES	248
CHOLESTEROL	0
VEGAN CALORIES	248
POLYUNSATS	★★★
ANTIOXIDANTS	★★☆
CALCIUM	★★★
IRON	★★☆
B VITAMINS	★★☆

batter:
1 cup tofu, crumbled
½ cup soy/rice milk
1 tbsp wheat flour
1 tsp baking powder
salt and black pepper to taste

filling:
2 tsp each of finely chopped chives,
    parsley and chervil or tarragon
oil for frying

Blend the tofu with the milk. Transfer to a mixing bowl, add the flour and the baking powder, and season. Add the herbs and mix again. Heat a little oil in a skillet. Pour in the tofu batter and spread it evenly over the skillet. Turn down the heat and gently cook until the top side is firm. Sprinkle with oil, turn, and cook the other side. Remove from the heat and serve.

055 SPICY SPRING OMELET

CALORIES	376
CHOLESTEROL	408
VEGAN CALORIES	399
POLYUNSATS	★★★
ANTIOXIDANTS	★★☆
CALCIUM	★★★
IRON	★★☆
B VITAMINS	★★☆

omelet:
4 eggs
½ tsp salt
1 clove garlic, crushed
or 1 portion basic eggless omelet
    batter (see above)

filling:
oil for frying
⅓ cup ham/tempeh, diced
4 cups fresh spinach, chopped
1 tsp hot chili sauce (optional)
salt and black pepper to taste

Heat a little oil in a skillet and fry the ham or tempeh. Add the spinach, turn down the heat, and simmer until the spinach is wilted, then add the chili sauce (if using), and season. Beat the eggs with the salt, add the garlic, and season. Alternately, prepare the eggless batter. Heat a little oil in a skillet and pour in your chosen batter. Push back the edges of the mixture to let any uncooked egg run underneath the omelet. Repeat until the omelet has set and the underside is brown. Cover with the filling, fold in half, cook for 30 seconds, remove from the heat and serve.

056 OMELET À LA JARDINIÈRE

CALORIES	397
CHOLESTEROL	391
VEGAN CALORIES	406
POLYUNSATS	★★★
ANTIOXIDANTS	★★★
CALCIUM	★★☆
IRON	★★☆
B VITAMINS	★★★

omelet:
4 eggs, beaten
salt and black pepper to taste
or 1 portion basic eggless omelet
    batter (see p.41)

filling:
1 handful green beans, trimmed
1 carrot, cut into thin sticks
1 small cauliflower, cut into florets
²/₃ cup green peas

Cook the trimmed beans, carrot, and cauliflower in a pan with a little salted water until just tender. Drain and set aside. Prepare your chosen batter and set aside. Heat a little oil in a skillet, add the cooked vegetables and the peas, and gently stir-fry for 2–3 minutes. Pour the batter over the vegetables and cook like a thick pancake. Serve hot.

057 CRÊPES WITH MUSHROOM FILLING

CALORIES	614
CHOLESTEROL	238
VEGAN CALORIES	544
POLYUNSATS	★★☆
ANTIOXIDANTS	★★☆
CALCIUM	★★☆
IRON	★★☆
B VITAMINS	★★★

basic egg pancake batter:
1 cup wheat flour
2 eggs, beaten
½ cup milk/soy milk
½ cup water
1 tbsp grapeseed oil/butter
1 pinch salt
or 1 portion basic eggless pancake
    batter (see below)

filling:
a little olive oil, plus some for frying
    crêpes
4½ cups mushrooms, sliced
1 shallot, chopped
1 clove garlic, chopped
1 tbsp all-purpose flour
pinch nutmeg
²/₃ cup milk/soy milk

To make the basic egg batter, mix the batter ingredients and set aside. Stir-fry the mushrooms, shallot, and garlic in a Dutch oven with the oil. Sprinkle with flour and nutmeg, lower the heat and stir for 1 minute. Add the milk to make a thick sauce, and season. Pour the batter into an oiled skillet. Fry the crêpes for 2 minutes on each side. Top with the filling, roll and serve hot.

058 PANCAKES WITH SPINACH FILLING

CALORIES	642
CHOLESTEROL	57
VEGAN CALORIES	642
POLYUNSATS	★★★
ANTIOXIDANTS	★★★
CALCIUM	★★☆
IRON	★★★
B VITAMINS	★★☆

basic eggless pancake batter:
1 cup wheat flour
1 tsp baking powder
1 pinch salt
½ cup soy milk
½ cup water
2 tbsp grapeseed oil
oil for frying

filling:
4 cups fresh spinach
1 tbsp wheat flour
½ cup soy cream/crème
    fraîche
pinch nutmeg and salt to taste
a little soy/Gruyère cheese
    (optional)

To make the basic eggless batter, mix the batter ingredients and set aside. Gently cook the spinach in a saucepan of water until soft. Add the flour and stir for 30 seconds, then add the cream, heat and season. Heat a little oil in a skillet, pour in the batter and fry the pancakes for 2 minutes on each side. Top with 1 tablespoon of filling, roll and place in a baking dish. Sprinkle with soy or Gruyère cheese and broil or bake at 230°C/450°F/gas mark 8 for a few minutes until the cheese melts. Serve hot.

059 ▼ CHEESY POTATO AND ARUGULA PANCAKES

★ 🌢 🌿 🥜

CALORIES	732
CHOLESTEROL	242
VEGAN CALORIES	667
POLYUNSATS	★★☆
ANTIOXIDANTS	★★★
CALCIUM	★★☆
IRON	★★☆
B VITAMINS	★★☆

pancakes:
1 portion basic pancake batter (see opposite page)
olive oil for frying

filling:
3 cups potatoes, chopped

2 cloves garlic, crushed
1 small fresh or dried red chili, chopped or crumbled
7oz fresh arugula, chopped
⅓ cup Gruyère/soy cheese, grated
salt to taste

Boil the potatoes in salted water until soft. Meanwhile, mix all the batter ingredients and set aside. Heat 1 tablespoon of oil in a large Dutch oven and fry the garlic and chili for 30 seconds. Add half the arugula and stir. Remove from the heat. Stir in the cooked potatoes, the Gruyère or soy cheese, and the remaining arugula. Mash, mix, and season. Heat a little more oil in a frying pan and fry the pancakes for 2 minutes on each side. Top with 1–2 tablespoon of filling. Roll the pancakes, and serve.

060 CORN PANCAKES WITH SPICY PEAS

CALORIES	749
CHOLESTEROL	0
VEGAN CALORIES	749
POLYUNSATS	★★★
ANTIOXIDANTS	★★☆
CALCIUM	★★☆
IRON	★★☆
B VITAMINS	★★☆

pancakes:
1 cup cornstarch
1 cup wheat flour
1 tbsp baking powder
½ tsp salt
2 tbsp corn oil, plus some for frying
1¼ cups water

filling:
1 scallion, sliced
1 tsp ground cumin
1 clove garlic, crushed
1½ cups garbanzos, cooked or
    canned
⅔ cup fresh peas
½ cup vegetable stock
1 dash Tabasco sauce
salt and black pepper to taste

Mix the 2 flours with the baking powder, salt, corn oil and water, and whisk to a smooth consistency. Set aside. Stir-fry the scallion in a Dutch oven with 1 tablespoon of oil, then add the cumin and the garlic. Heat through, add the garbanzos, and stir for 1 minute. Add the peas, stock, and Tabasco sauce, and season. Let the peas simmer while you heat a little more oil in a skillet and fry approximately six pancakes. Divide the filling among the pancakes and serve.

061 PIZZA CASSUOLA

CALORIES	524
CHOLESTEROL	57
VEGAN CALORIES	406
POLYUNSATS	★★☆
ANTIOXIDANTS	★★☆
CALCIUM	★★☆
IRON	★★☆
B VITAMINS	★★☆

1 pizza base
2 tomatoes, chopped
salt to taste
6 anchovy fillets/12 black olives,
    pitted and chopped

1 tbsp capers
1 tbsp oregano
1 cup mozzarella/soy cheese,
    grated
black pepper to taste

Preheat the oven to 240°C/475°F/gas mark 9 and warm a baking sheet. Cover the pizza base with the chopped tomatoes. Sprinkle with salt. Top with the anchovies or olives, capers, and oregano. Sprinkle with grated cheese, and bake in a hot oven for approximately 15 minutes. Garnish with black pepper and serve hot with a side salad.

062 ◄ PIZZA PEPPERONI

CALORIES	609
CHOLESTEROL	54
VEGAN CALORIES	489
POLYUNSATS	★★☆
ANTIOXIDANTS	★★☆
CALCIUM	★★☆
IRON	★★☆
B VITAMINS	★★☆

1 pizza base
2–3 tbsp tomato sauce, passata
    or sauce tomate concassé
    (see p.115)
2 cups fresh spinach, sautéed
1 clove garlic, crushed

½ cup spicy sausage (pork/soy),
    sliced and fried
1 tsp each dried thyme & oregano
salt and black pepper to taste
1 cup mozzarella/soy cheese,
    grated

Preheat the oven to 240°C/475°F/gas mark 9 and warm a baking sheet. Spread the tomato sauce over the pizza base and top with the sautéed spinach, garlic, and spicy sausage. Sprinkle with the herbs, season, and sprinkle with the grated cheese. Bake in a hot oven for approximately 15 minutes. Serve hot with a side salad.

063 SPRING SPECIAL

CALORIES	592
CHOLESTEROL	38
VEGAN CALORIES	515
POLYUNSATS	★★☆
ANTIOXIDANTS	★★★
CALCIUM	★★★
IRON	★★★
B VITAMINS	★★★

1 pizza base
2–3 tbsp tomato sauce, passata or
  sauce tomate concassé
  (see p.115)
1 handful arugula leaves, chopped
1 cup mozzarella/soy cheese,
  grated
1 clove garlic, crushed

8 asparagus spears, trimmed
  and blanched
1 tbsp grated Parmesan/brewer's
  yeast flakes
oregano to taste
salt and black pepper to taste
1 tbsp olive oil

Preheat the oven to 240°C/475°F/gas mark 9 and warm a baking sheet.
Spread the tomato sauce over the pizza base. Add the arugula and the
mozzarella or soy cheese, then the garlic and asparagus. Sprinkle with
Parmesan or brewer's yeast flakes, and season. Drizzle with oil and bake
in a hot oven for approximately 15 minutes. Serve hot.

064 SPICY VEGAN PIZZA

CALORIES	467
CHOLESTEROL	0
VEGAN CALORIES	467
POLYUNSATS	★☆☆
ANTIOXIDANTS	★★☆
CALCIUM	★★★
IRON	★★★
B VITAMINS	★★☆

1 pizza base
2–3 tbsp tomato sauce, passata or
  sauce tomate concassé
  (see p.115)
1 tsp hot chili paste
1 clove garlic, crushed
1 cup smoked tofu, crumbled
1 handful arugula, chopped
oil for stir-frying

¾ cup tiny cauliflower florets
⅔ cup fresh peas
1 carrot, grated
2 scallions, sliced
1 tbsp tamari (soy sauce)
salt and black pepper to taste
1 tbsp parsley or dill
oregano to taste

Preheat the oven to 220°C/425°F/gas mark 7 and warm a baking sheet.
Cover the pizza base with the tomato sauce and the chili paste. Sprinkle
with the garlic. Add the crumbled tofu and the arugula. Stir-fry the
vegetables in a wok with a little oil, then stir in the tamari. Add to the
pizza, and season. Bake in a hot oven for approximately 15 minutes.
Garnish with the herbs and serve hot with a side salad.

065 SICILIAN PIZZA

CALORIES	716
CHOLESTEROL	45
VEGAN CALORIES	641
POLYUNSATS	★★★
ANTIOXIDANTS	★★★
CALCIUM	★★★
IRON	★★★
B VITAMINS	★★☆

1 pizza base
10 sun-dried tomato halves
1 tbsp olive oil
1 Florence fennel bulb, chopped
⅔ cup fresh peas, shelled
1 clove garlic, crushed

⅓ cup anchovies/black
  olives, pitted
1 tbsp oregano
salt and black pepper to taste
1 cup mozzarella/soy cheese,
  grated

Preheat the oven to 240°C/475°F/gas mark 9 and warm a baking sheet.
Cover the pizza base with the sun-dried tomato halves. Sprinkle with
the oil and top with the fennel, fresh peas, garlic, anchovies or olives,
and oregano. Season, sprinkle with the grated mozzarella or soy cheese,
and bake in a hot oven for approximately 15 minutes. Serve hot with a
side salad.

066 QUICK CHESTNUT BOURGUIGNONNE

CALORIES	469
CHOLESTEROL	0
VEGAN CALORIES	469
POLYUNSATS	★★☆
ANTIOXIDANTS	★★☆
CALCIUM	★★☆
IRON	★★☆
B VITAMINS	★★☆

2 tbsp olive oil
1 cup bottled chestnuts, drained
1 shallot, quartered
7oz button mushrooms, kept whole
1 clove garlic, chopped
1 tbsp wheat flour

½ cup red wine
1 bay leaf
1 tsp dried thyme
1 tbsp parsley, finely chopped
2 tsp tomato paste
½ cup vegetable stock, heated
salt and pepper to taste

Gently heat the oil in a large pan and stir-fry the chestnuts and shallot for 3 minutes. Add the mushrooms and garlic, turn up the heat and stir-fry for a further 2 minutes. Stir in the flour and add the remaining ingredients. Bring to a boil, cover, and simmer for 20 minutes. Serve with rice.

067 SPRING GREEN RISOTTO

CALORIES	690
CHOLESTEROL	0
VEGAN CALORIES	690
POLYUNSATS	★★☆
ANTIOXIDANTS	★★★
CALCIUM	★★☆
IRON	★★☆
B VITAMINS	★★☆

4 tbsp olive oil
1 small leek, sliced
1 cup risotto rice
¼ lb fresh curly kale leaves

2¼ cups vegetable stock, heated
3 tbsp white wine
salt and black pepper to taste

Heat the oil in a large pan or wok and gently soften the leek for 2–3 minutes. Add the rice and stir-fry for 2 minutes, then add the curly kale leaves and let them wilt for 1 minute. Add the stock and the wine, season, cover, and very gently simmer until the rice is cooked. Check from time to time (and add a little water if necessary). Serve with walnut bread.

068 BELGIAN ENDIVE CASSOLETTES

CALORIES	558
CHOLESTEROL	286
VEGAN CALORIES	359
POLYUNSATS	★★★
ANTIOXIDANTS	★★★
CALCIUM	★★★
IRON	★★★
B VITAMINS	★★★

5 large Belgian endive, quartered lengthwise
2 cups young dandelion leaves, chopped
3 tbsp lemon juice
1 tsp maple syrup
salt and black pepper to taste
2 tbsp grapeseed oil, plus some for cooking

1 lb 2oz small fresh scallops, shucked and trimmed/1¼ cups marinated tofu, diced
1 pinch cayenne pepper
1 tbsp port wine
2 tbsp vegetable margarine or butter
1 tsp lemon zest
1 tbsp parsley

Place the Belgian endive and dandelion leaves in a large Dutch oven, add 2 tablespoons of the lemon juice, the maple syrup, salt, and pepper, and gently soften in a little oil for 8–10 minutes. Meanwhile, heat the oil in a skillet over a low heat and fry the scallops or tofu cubes until they begin to brown. Add the cayenne pepper, with the port wine, the remaining tablespoon of lemon juice, and the margarine or butter. Place the cooked endive in a heated serving dish and arrange the fried scallops or tofu on top. Garnish with lemon zest and parsley, and serve with rice or bread.

069 ▲ SPICY BEAN BURGERS
⭐❤️🌾⬭

CALORIES	541
CHOLESTEROL	0
VEGAN CALORIES	541
POLYUNSATS	★★★
ANTIOXIDANTS	★★☆
CALCIUM	★☆☆
IRON	★★☆
B VITAMINS	★★☆

1 packed cup red kidney beans,
   cooked or canned and drained
1 shallot, finely chopped
½ cup hazelnuts, finely chopped
1 tsp ginger, finely
   chopped

1 pinch cayenne pepper
2 tsp tamari (soy sauce)
2 tbsp bread crumbs
2 tbsp soy flour
salt to taste
oil for grilling or frying

Mash or purée the kidney beans (with a little water, if necessary) to
a coarse paste, add the shallot, hazelnuts, ginger, cayenne pepper,
tamari, bread crumbs, and soy flour, and mix well. Season and shape
into 4 flat burgers. Brush the burgers with oil and grill over hot embers.
Alternately, fry the burgers in hot oil. Serve on a toasted bun with all the
usual burger trimmings.

070 FENNEL, SEAFOOD, AND POTATO BAKE

CALORIES	474
CHOLESTEROL	53
VEGAN CALORIES	402
POLYUNSATS	★★★
ANTIOXIDANTS	★★★
CALCIUM	★★☆
IRON	★★☆
B VITAMINS	★★★

1 tbsp olive oil
3 cups trimmed monkfish,
    cut into chunks and seasoned/
    2oz soy chunks (dry weight),
    soaked with 2 tbsp mixed
    seaweed
1½ potatoes, quartered
    and parboiled
1 Florence fennel bulb, sliced

1 red onion, sliced
4 sun-dried tomato halves,
    chopped
1 lemon, thinly sliced
⅓ cup vegetable/fish stock,
    heated
1 small handful parsley,
    chopped
salt and black pepper to taste

Preheat the oven to 220°C/425°F/gas mark 7. Heat the oil in a large
skillet over a high heat and fry the monkfish or soy chunks for 2 minutes.
Grease a baking dish and arrange the parboiled potatoes on the bottom.
Add the slices of fennel, onion, tomato and lemon, in layers, and finish
with the fried monkfish or soy chunks. Then add the heated stock,
garnish with chopped parsley, and season. Cover and bake in a hot
oven for 20 minutes. Serve with rice or French baguette.

071 CÔTELETTES PRINTANIÈRE

CALORIES	721
CHOLESTEROL	176
VEGAN CALORIES	396
POLYUNSATS	★★☆
ANTIOXIDANTS	★★★
CALCIUM	★★☆
IRON	★★★
B VITAMINS	★★★

6 small carrots, kept whole
2 artichoke bottoms
1 zucchini, chopped into fine sticks
1 cup green beans, chopped
6 long red radishes, kept whole
2 tbsp olive oil
6 lamb chops/5oz seitan,
    sliced

6 mushrooms, finely chopped
juice of 1 lemon
1 tbsp parsley, finely
    chopped
1 clove garlic, chopped
salt and black pepper to taste
3 small new potatoes, steamed

Blanch the carrots, artichokes, zucchini, beans, and radishes in a
saucepan of boiling water until just tender. Drain and set aside. Sauté
the chops or seitan with 1 tablespoon of oil in a skillet until just cooked,
add the mushrooms and sauté until they give off their juices. Add the
lemon juice and half the parsley. In a separate pan, stir-fry the cooked
vegetables in 1 tablespoon of oil with the garlic, and season. Place the
chops or seitan, and the mushrooms on a warmed plate. Arrange the
cooked vegetables and the steamed potatoes in a fan next to them.
Garnish with the remaining parsley and serve.

072 FILLETS WITH MUSTARD AND SAGE SAUCE

CALORIES	544
CHOLESTEROL	110
VEGAN CALORIES	433
POLYUNSATS	★☆☆
ANTIOXIDANTS	★★☆
CALCIUM	★☆☆
IRON	★★★
B VITAMINS	★★★

oil for roasting
1 cup loin of lamb/tempeh,
  sliced
1 shallot, chopped
1 sprig fresh sage, chopped
½ cup white wine

½ cup stock
1 tbsp whole grain mustard
1 tsp cornstarch
  dissolved in a little cold water
  (optional)
salt and black pepper to taste

Heat a little oil in a pan over a high heat and roast the lamb or tempeh for 3 minutes on each side. Add the shallot and the sage and gently fry them without letting them brown. Pour in the wine and let it reduce to half its volume, then add the stock and the mustard and simmer for 5 minutes. Season, and add the dissolved cornstarch if the sauce is too thin. Heat through. Place the roasted fillet or tempeh and the sauce on a warmed plate and serve with steamed potatoes and French beans.

073 BRAISED BRUSSELS SPROUTS

CALORIES	213
CHOLESTEROL	13
VEGAN CALORIES	177
POLYUNSATS	★☆☆
ANTIOXIDANTS	★★★
CALCIUM	★★☆
IRON	★★☆
B VITAMINS	★★☆

1½ cups Brussels sprouts, halved
1 tbsp olive oil
juice and zest of ½ orange
¼ cup bacon/½ cup tofu, diced

1 carrot, diced
1 tsp wholegrain mustard
salt and black pepper to taste

Place the Brussels sprouts in a heavy-based Dutch oven with the rest of the ingredients. Bring to a boil, cover and very gently simmer until the Brussels sprouts are tender, approximately 20 minutes. Stir from time to time (adding a little water if necessary). Season, and serve with rice.

074 SPINACH BOUILLABAISSE

CALORIES	337
CHOLESTEROL	196
VEGAN CALORIES	309
POLYUNSATS	★★☆
ANTIOXIDANTS	★★★
CALCIUM	★★★
IRON	★★★
B VITAMINS	★★★

1 tbsp olive oil
1 leek, sliced
2 potatoes, chopped
2 cloves garlic, chopped
6 cups fresh spinach, chopped
¾ cup vegetable stock,
  heated

½ tsp ground coriander
½ tsp turmeric
salt and cayenne pepper
  to taste
1 handful parsley, chopped
2 eggs/1 cup marinated tofu,
  diced

Gently stir-fry the leek and potatoes in a large pan or Dutch oven with the olive oil for 5 minutes. Add the garlic and the spinach and stir-fry for 5 minutes, then add the stock and the spices, and season. Bring to a boil, add the parsley, and simmer. Crack the eggs on top or add the marinated tofu, and continue to simmer for 10 minutes. Serve immediately with bread and cheese or soy cheese.

075 SHIITAKE STIR-FRY

■■■■

CALORIES	339
CHOLESTEROL	0
VEGAN CALORIES	339
POLYUNSATS	★★★
ANTIOXIDANTS	★★★
CALCIUM	★★☆
IRON	★★★
B VITAMINS	★★☆

oil for stir-frying
4½ cups shiitake mushrooms,
  sliced
1 clove garlic, finely chopped
2 scallions, chopped
1 small Chinese cabbage, chopped
1 carrot, cut into thin sticks
3 cups broccoli, cut into florets
12 ears of corn

¾ in cube ginger,
  finely chopped
2½ cups snow peas
2 tbsp tamari (soy sauce)
1 cup vegetable stock
1 tbsp maple syrup
1 tbsp cornstarch dissolved in a
  little water

Heat a little oil in a wok. Add the mushrooms, garlic, and onions. Stir-fry for 1 minute, then add the Chinese cabbage, carrot, broccoli, corn, and ginger. Heat through and add the snow peas. Stir-fry for a further 2 minutes, then add the tamari, stock, maple syrup, and dissolved cornstarch. Stir until the sauce thickens. Serve with rice or noodles.

076 ASPARAGUS TART

■■■

CALORIES	618
CHOLESTEROL	31
VEGAN CALORIES	559
POLYUNSATS	★★★
ANTIOXIDANTS	★★☆
CALCIUM	★★☆
IRON	★★☆
B VITAMINS	★★☆

8oz ready-made tart dough,
  rolled out thinly
½ lb asparagus, trimmed and
  blanched
1 cup tofu, crumbled

⅓ cup milk/soy milk
salt and black pepper to taste
⅓ cup Cheddar/soy cheese,
  grated

Use the pastry to line an 8in tart pan, scatter with a handful of dried beans and bake blind at 220°C/425°F/gas mark 7 for 10–15 minutes. Let cool and remove the beans. Place the cooked asparagus in the pastry shell. Blend the tofu with the milk, season, and pour over the asparagus. Top with Cheddar or soy cheese and return to the oven. Bake for 10–15 minutes until it begins to brown. Serve with a salad.

077 CELERY ROOT SCHNITZEL

■■■■■■

CALORIES	316
CHOLESTEROL	98
VEGAN CALORIES	323
POLYUNSATS	★★★
ANTIOXIDANTS	★★★
CALCIUM	★★☆
IRON	★★☆
B VITAMINS	★★☆

1 large celery root, cut into thick
  slices and peeled
2 tbsp grapeseed oil
1 egg, beaten/1 tbsp soya flour
  dissolved in a little cold water

2 tbsp seasoned fresh bread crumbs
1 lemon, sliced
2 tbsp grated horseradish
1 handful parsley, chopped
1 tbsp capers

Blanch the celery root in a pan of boiling salted water for 3 minutes. Heat the oil in a large skillet. Dip the celery root slices first into the egg or dissolved soy flour, then into the breadcrumbs before frying them until golden. Place a slice of lemon, a little grated horseradish, and a few capers on each schnitzel to garnish. Serve with boiled potatoes, melted butter or vegetable margarine, and chopped parsley.

078 ▲ CHOPS WITH HONEY AND THYME

★🌿🟥

CALORIES	693
CHOLESTEROL	176
VEGAN CALORIES	368
POLYUNSATS	★★☆
ANTIOXIDANTS	★★☆
CALCIUM	★★☆
IRON	★★★
B VITAMINS	★★☆

4 lamb chops/7oz seitan
1 tbsp olive oil
salt and black pepper to taste
2 tsp honey

1 tsp dried thyme
juice of ½ lemon
½ cup dry white wine
1 tbsp tamari (soy sauce)

Preheat the oven to 250°C/500°F/gas mark 10. Sauté the lamb or seitan in the oil in a large Dutch oven, then remove from the dish, season, paint with 1 teaspoon of honey, and sprinkle with thyme. Replace the lamb or seitan in the dish and bake in a hot oven for 10 minutes. Remove the lamb or seitan from the dish (discard the lamb cooking fat) and set aside. Make a sauce by browning 1 teaspoon of honey in the dish and adding the lemon juice, white wine, and tamari. Bring to a boil and reduce to half the volume. Place the lamb or seitan on 2 plates and cover with the sauce. Serve with boiled potatoes and braised Belgian endive.

FRUIT JELLY

⭐❌

CALORIES	195
CHOLESTEROL	0
VEGAN CALORIES	195
POLYUNSATS	★☆☆
ANTIOXIDANTS	★★☆
CALCIUM	★☆☆
IRON	★☆☆
B VITAMINS	★☆☆

1 banana, peeled and chopped
1 sweet apple, cored and chopped
2 dates, pitted

½ cup apple juice
1 tsp agar-agar

Purée the banana, apple, dates, and apple juice, and pour into a pan. Whisk in the agar-agar until it is dissolved. Bring to the boil, then pour the mixture into two small serving bowls and refrigerate until set. Serve with crème fraîche or soy cream.

080 RUBY-RED SALAD

⭐💧❌🌰

CALORIES	152
CHOLESTEROL	0
VEGAN CALORIES	152
POLYUNSATS	★☆☆
ANTIOXIDANTS	★★★
CALCIUM	★★☆
IRON	★★☆
B VITAMINS	★★☆

1 ruby-red grapefruit, peeled
  and chopped
1 papaya, peeled, deseeded,
  and cubed

1 small bunch mint, chopped
1 tsp ground cinnamon
1 tsp maple syrup (optional)

Divide the grapefruit and papaya between two plates, garnish with mint, sprinkle with cinnamon and maple syrup (if using), and serve.

081 APPLE, CHERRY, AND WALNUT CRÊPES

⭐🌿

CALORIES	676
CHOLESTEROL	227
VEGAN CALORIES	592
POLYUNSATS	★★★
ANTIOXIDANTS	★★☆
CALCIUM	★★☆
IRON	★★☆
B VITAMINS	★★☆

crêpes:
1 portion basic pancake batter
  (see p.42)

filling:
1 apple, quartered, cored,
  and thinly sliced
1¾ cups fresh cherries,
  pitted and halved
2 tbsp chopped walnuts
maple syrup
grapeseed oil for frying

Mix all the batter ingredients and set aside. Combine the apple, cherries, and walnuts in a bowl with a little maple syrup. Heat a little oil in a frying pan, pour in the batter, and fry the pancakes for 2 minutes on each side. Top with a couple of tablespoons of filling, roll the crêpes, and serve hot.

082 EXOTIC FRUIT SALAD

⭐♥❌🍃

CALORIES	279
CHOLESTEROL	0
VEGAN CALORIES	279
POLYUNSATS	★☆☆
ANTIOXIDANTS	★★★
CALCIUM	★★☆
IRON	★☆☆
B VITAMINS	★☆☆

1 orange, peeled and sliced
1 banana, peeled and sliced
1 pear, cored and sliced
1 apple, cored and sliced
1 kiwi, peeled and sliced
½ pink grapefruit, peeled
  and chopped

6 lichees, peeled, halved, and pitted
4 slices dried mango, cut into strips
1 tsp honey
juice of ½ lime
2 tsp ginger, finely chopped
1 carambola, sliced

Mix the fresh fruit (except for the carambola) in a glass bowl. Add the dried mango strips. Melt the honey in a pan with the lime juice and ginger, and pour over the fruit. Gently toss, decorate with carambola and serve.

083 APPLE TART

CALORIES	356
CHOLESTEROL	0
VEGAN CALORIES	356
POLYUNSATS	★★★
ANTIOXIDANTS	★★☆
CALCIUM	★☆☆
IRON	★☆☆
B VITAMINS	★☆☆

7oz ready-made tart dough, rolled out thinly
3½ cups tart apples, cored and finely sliced
a little lemon juice
a little grapeseed oil
1 pinch raw cane sugar
1 pinch ground cinnamon

Preheat the oven to 220°C/425°F/gas mark 7. Use the pastry to line an 8in tart pan. Sprinkle the apple slices with a little lemon juice to prevent discoloration and add them in concentric circles to cover the whole pastry base. Sprinkle with a little oil, sugar, and cinnamon. Bake in a hot oven for 15–20 minutes until the apples begin to brown. Serve with crème fraîche or soy cream.

084 BAKED PEARS WITH HONEY AND BRAZIL NUTS

CALORIES	336
CHOLESTEROL	0
VEGAN CALORIES	336
POLYUNSATS	★★★
ANTIOXIDANTS	★★★
CALCIUM	★☆☆
IRON	★☆☆
B VITAMINS	★☆☆

1 tbsp grapeseed oil
2 large, ripe pears, halved, cored, and sliced
1 tbsp liquid honey
1 tbsp lemon juice
½ cup Brazil nuts, sliced

Preheat the oven to 200°C/400°F/gas mark 6. Grease a small pie pan with the oil, and cover the bottom with the pear slices. Mix the honey with the lemon juice and pour over the pears. Sprinkle with sliced Brazil nuts and a dash of oil. Bake in a hot oven for approximately 15 minutes until the nuts begin to brown. Serve with plain or soy yogurt.

085 APRIL FOOL

CALORIES	255
CHOLESTEROL	6
VEGAN CALORIES	252
POLYUNSATS	★★☆
ANTIOXIDANTS	★★☆
CALCIUM	★★☆
IRON	★☆☆
B VITAMINS	★★☆

2 cups rhubarb, sliced
1 pinch ground cinnamon
1 tsp honey
2 tsp almond butter
1 frozen banana, peeled and chopped
3 large dates, pitted and chopped
¼ cup plain/soy yogurt

Cook the rhubarb with the cinnamon and a little water in a Dutch oven until soft. Add the honey and continue to cook for 2 minutes. Then place the cooked rhubarb in a glass bowl and cool in a water bath. Meanwhile, purée the almond butter with the frozen banana, dates, and yogurt. Gently fold the cooked and cooled rhubarb into the yogurt mixture. Spoon into two glass bowls, and chill before serving.

086 SWEET CHERRY SOUP

CALORIES	202
CHOLESTEROL	0
VEGAN CALORIES	202
POLYUNSATS	★★☆
ANTIOXIDANTS	★★★
CALCIUM	★★☆
IRON	★★☆
B VITAMINS	★★☆

2¼ cups fresh ripe cherries, pitted
juice of 2 oranges
1 tbsp maple syrup

1 cup hot water
4 Brazil nuts, chopped
2 slices lime
2 tbsp mint, chopped

Purée the cherries with the orange juice, maple syrup, and water. Cool, and garnish with Brazil nuts, slices of lime, and mint just before serving.

087 PINEAPPLE COCKTAIL

CALORIES	163
CHOLESTEROL	0
VEGAN CALORIES	163
POLYUNSATS	★☆☆
ANTIOXIDANTS	★★★
CALCIUM	★★☆
IRON	★★☆
B VITAMINS	★★☆

½ pineapple, peeled, cored, and cut into chunks
juice of 1 orange
juice of 1 pomelo

1 pear, cored and cut into chunks
1 tsp ginger, finely chopped
2 slices lemon
2 tsp mint, finely chopped

Purée the pineapple chunks with the orange juice, pomelo juice, pear chunks, and chopped ginger. Pour the mixture into tall glasses, garnish with slices of lemon and chopped mint, and serve.

088 SPRING BERRY SALAD

CALORIES	226
CHOLESTEROL	6
VEGAN CALORIES	226
POLYUNSATS	★★☆
ANTIOXIDANTS	★★★
CALCIUM	★★☆
IRON	★☆☆
B VITAMINS	★★☆

1¼ cups cherries, pitted and halved
1 cup strawberries, hulled and halved
1 cup raspberries

plain/soy yogurt to taste
grated (or unsweetened shredded) coconut to taste
grated semisweet chocolate to taste (optional)

Divide the berries between two glass bowls. Top with yogurt, grated coconut, and grated chocolate (if using), and serve.

089 DRIED FRUIT WITH FRESH STRAWBERRIES

CALORIES	486
CHOLESTEROL	0
VEGAN CALORIES	486
POLYUNSATS	★☆☆
ANTIOXIDANTS	★★☆
CALCIUM	★★☆
IRON	★★☆
B VITAMINS	★★☆

2 dried bananas, chopped
4 dates, pitted and chopped
4 dried figs, chopped
1 handful raisins

1 pear, cored and chopped
1 apple, cored and chopped
20 strawberries, halved

Place all the fruit (except for the strawberries) in a bowl and gently mix. Spoon the mixed fruit onto two plates, garnish with strawberries, and serve with plain yogurt or soy yogurt.

090 SPICY APPLE SALAD

CALORIES	214
CHOLESTEROL	6
VEGAN CALORIES	211
POLYUNSATS	★☆☆
ANTIOXIDANTS	★★★
CALCIUM	★★☆
IRON	★★☆
B VITAMINS	★★☆

2 red apples, cored and sliced
6 red radishes, sliced
1 small mango, peeled and diced

½ cup plain/soy yogurt
1 tsp horseradish, freshly grated

Arrange the apples, radishes, and mango on two plates. Mix the yogurt with the horseradish, then place a spoonful on each plate and serve.

091 ▼ MINTY STRAWBERRIES

CALORIES	176
CHOLESTEROL	0
VEGAN CALORIES	176
POLYUNSATS	★☆☆
ANTIOXIDANTS	★★★
CALCIUM	★☆☆
IRON	★☆☆
B VITAMINS	★☆☆

1¾ cups strawberries, halved
1 pear, cored and diced
1 tsp lemon juice

1 tbsp mint, finely chopped
1 tbsp maple syrup
semisweet chocolate (optional)

Place the strawberries and the pear in a glass bowl. Sprinkle with the lemon juice, mint, maple syrup, and a little grated chocolate (if using). Serve with crème fraîche or soy cream.

SUMMER
RECIPES

Summer is the season of warmth, strong colors, and ripening, sunkissed abundance. In Chinese tradition, summer is yang – the outgoing life force – and offers us the chance to absorb energy into our hearts to use with love and warmth. There is a feeling of plenty, and an almost overwhelming choice of fresh ingredients filled with light and rich flavors.

In the healing traditions, summer is a time for eating foods rich in essential nutrients to boost immunity and strength. The season of fire and heat also inspires us to eat easily-digestible meals, full of vitality, that enable us to use the plenty that surrounds us for creativity and activity.

Trees and bushes are heavy with red fruits and berries. Gardens overflow with green vegetables and fields are filled with golden grains. They all gather energy as they ripen in the sun, and with this energy they make all the nutrients that they – and we – need to be healthy. Create your own high-energy, fresh, summer diet, full of antioxidants, vitamins, minerals, and essential polyunsaturates. Bon appetit!

092 MINTY MELON SOUP

★ ♡ ◐ ✕ ▢

CALORIES	160
CHOLESTEROL	0
VEGAN CALORIES	160
POLYUNSATS	★☆☆
ANTIOXIDANTS	★★★
CALCIUM	★★☆
IRON	★★☆
B VITAMINS	★★☆

1 cantaloupe melon, deseeded, peeled, and chopped
½ cucumber, chopped
1 tbsp maple syrup
2 tsp lemon zest, grated

½ cup water
1 small bunch mint, finely chopped
salt and black pepper to taste
2 tsp lemon juice

Heat the melon and the cucumber in a saucepan with the maple syrup, lemon zest, and water. Simmer for 10 minutes, stirring from time to time. Add the mint. Remove from the heat, purée, season, and add the lemon juice. Allow to cool, then refrigerate before serving.

093 TROPICAL AVOCADO SOUP

★ ♡ ◐ ⊘ ▢

CALORIES	492
CHOLESTEROL	6
VEGAN CALORIES	489
POLYUNSATS	★★★
ANTIOXIDANTS	★★★
CALCIUM	★★☆
IRON	★★☆
B VITAMINS	★★☆

1 avocado, peeled and pitted
1 clove garlic
1 small fresh green chili
1 small bunch chives, chopped, plus some to garnish

1¼ cups coconut milk
½ cup plain/soy yogurt
½ cup vegetable stock
2 tbsp lemon juice
salt and black pepper to taste

Purée the avocado with the rest of the ingredients, and season. Chill well before serving, garnished with chives.

094 MINESTRONE

★ ♡ ❧ ⊘ ▢

CALORIES	456
CHOLESTEROL	0
VEGAN CALORIES	456
POLYUNSATS	★★☆
ANTIOXIDANTS	★★★
CALCIUM	★★★
IRON	★★★
B VITAMINS	★★★

2 tbsp olive oil
1 small onion, chopped
1 carrot, chopped
¼ Florence fennel bulb or 1 stick celery, chopped
1 zucchini, chopped
1 handful white cabbage, finely shredded
3 ripe tomatoes, puréed
2¼ cups vegetable stock

1 glass dry white wine (optional)
salt and black pepper to taste
2 tbsp small pasta shapes
⅓ cup white beans, cooked or canned
1 small bunch parsley and basil, finely chopped
1 clove garlic, crushed
a little Parmesan/brewer's yeast flakes (optional)

Heat the oil in a large Dutch oven and gently stir-fry the onion, carrot, fennel, zucchini, and cabbage (don't let them brown). Add the tomatoes, stock, and white wine (if using), and season. Bring to a boil, add the pasta, cover, and simmer for 10 minutes. Add the beans, parsley, basil, and garlic. Heat through, check the seasoning, sprinkle with Parmesan or brewer's yeast flakes (if using), and serve.

095 SUMMER TOMATO SOUP
⭐♥❌🌰

CALORIES	60
CHOLESTEROL	0
VEGAN CALORIES	60
POLYUNSATS	★☆☆
ANTIOXIDANTS	★★★
CALCIUM	★☆☆
IRON	★★☆
B VITAMINS	★★☆

6 ripe tomatoes,
    quartered
1 scallion, finely chopped

1 small bunch basil, finely
    chopped
salt and black pepper to taste

Purée the tomatoes, then gently heat them in a pan. Add the scallion and the basil, and season. Serve hot or cold.

096 RUBY-RED SOUP
⭐♥💧✖🌰🫒

CALORIES	203
CHOLESTEROL	0
VEGAN CALORIES	203
POLYUNSATS	★★☆
ANTIOXIDANTS	★★★
CALCIUM	★★☆
IRON	★★☆
B VITAMINS	★★☆

1 tbsp olive oil
500g (1lb 2oz) red bell peppers,
    deseeded and sliced
salt to taste

zest and juice of 3 organic blood
    oranges
1 tbsp chopped dill

Heat the oil in a pan and gently fry the bell pepper slices together with a little salt, and the orange zest. Cover and simmer for 15 minutes, stirring from time to time and allowing the bell peppers to cook in their own juices. Remove from the heat and purée the peppers with the orange juice. Reheat, garnish with dill, and serve.

097 MONGOLIAN SOUP WITH DUMPLINGS
⭐♥🌾🌰

CALORIES	680
CHOLESTEROL	0
VEGAN CALORIES	680
POLYUNSATS	★★☆
ANTIOXIDANTS	★★★
CALCIUM	★★☆
IRON	★★★
B VITAMINS	★★★

2 cups wheat flour
½ tsp salt
2 tbsp olive oil
½ tsp fenugreek seeds
1 clove garlic, crushed
1 small red onion
2 tomatoes, chopped
1 tbsp ginger, finely chopped

1 pinch saffron
2 tbsp tamari (soy sauce)
1 small bunch red radishes, sliced
⅓ cup green peas
3 cups vegetable stock
2 scallions, sliced
salt and black pepper to taste

Mix the flour and salt in a bowl. Add enough water to make a stiff dough. Roll the dough on a floured counter into a finger-thick snake. Cut the dough into ½in dumplings and sprinkle with flour. Gently heat the oil in a pan. Add the fenugreek seeds, garlic, and onion. Stir for 2 minutes, then add the tomatoes, spices, and tamari. Stir, cover, and simmer for 5 minutes. Add the radishes and peas. Heat through, pour in the stock, and bring to a boil. Add the dumplings. Boil for 5–6 minutes until the dumplings are cooked. Add the scallions, season, and serve.

098 SOUP WITH PASTA AND SUN-DRIED TOMATOES

CALORIES	401
CHOLESTEROL	0
VEGAN CALORIES	401
POLYUNSATS	★★★
ANTIOXIDANTS	★★★
CALCIUM	★★☆
IRON	★★☆
B VITAMINS	★★☆

4⅓ cups vegetable stock
1 handful pasta shapes
1 handful sun-dried tomatoes, finely chopped
1 scallion, finely chopped
1 small zucchini, finely chopped

4–5 mushrooms, sliced
1 tbsp parsley, finely chopped
1 tbsp basil, finely chopped
salt and black pepper to taste
½ lemon, sliced

Bring the stock to a boil in a pan with the pasta and the rest of the ingredients (except for the lemon). Simmer until the pasta is cooked. Garnish with slices of lemon and serve with thick slices of bread.

099 ZUCCHINI SOUP

CALORIES	181
CHOLESTEROL	0
VEGAN CALORIES	181
POLYUNSATS	★★☆
ANTIOXIDANTS	★★☆
CALCIUM	★☆☆
IRON	★☆☆
B VITAMINS	★☆☆

2 tbsp olive oil
1 small onion, chopped
1 potato, thinly sliced
4 zucchini, sliced
2½ cups vegetable stock

juice of ½ lemon
1 tsp dried thyme
1 tsp dried marjoram
salt and black pepper to taste

Heat the oil in a Dutch oven and gently soften the onion (don't let it brown). Add the potato and the zucchini, and stir-fry for 1 minute, then add the stock. Bring to a boil and simmer for 10 minutes. Add the lemon juice and the herbs. Remove from the heat, purée, and season. Serve with whole wheat bread and cheese or soy cheese.

100 SPANISH AVOCADO SOUP

CALORIES	307
CHOLESTEROL	21
VEGAN CALORIES	280
POLYUNSATS	★★☆
ANTIOXIDANTS	★★★
CALCIUM	★★☆
IRON	★★☆
B VITAMINS	★★☆

1 cup plain/soy yogurt
½ cup milk/soy milk
⅔ cup tomato juice
1 clove garlic, finely chopped
1 ripe tomato, finely chopped
2in cucumber, finely chopped

1 large avocado, pitted and peeled
1 tbsp lemon juice
salt and black pepper to taste
1 sprig tarragon, finely chopped

Mix the yogurt in a bowl with the milk and the tomato juice. Add the garlic, tomato, and cucumber. Mash the avocado in a separate bowl, mixing in the lemon juice as you mash. Then add the avocado to the soup, and season. Garnish with tarragon and serve cool with a couple of ice cubes in each bowl.

101 ORIENTAL SHIITAKE SOUP

CALORIES	220
CHOLESTEROL	0
VEGAN CALORIES	220
POLYUNSATS	★★☆
ANTIOXIDANTS	★★★
CALCIUM	★★☆
IRON	★★☆
B VITAMINS	★★☆

2 tbsp olive oil
1¾ cups fresh shiitake
    mushrooms, sliced
1 scallion, sliced
1 clove garlic, crushed
1 small carrot, finely chopped
1 tbsp ginger, finely chopped

1 small bunch watercress, chopped
1 tbsp tamari (soy sauce)
1 tsp maple syrup
4⅓ cups vegetable stock or water
    with miso to taste
salt and black pepper to taste
1 handful cilantro, chopped

Gently heat the oil in a pan and stir-fry the shiitake mushrooms
with the onion, garlic, and carrot for 3 minutes. Add the ginger,
watercress, tamari, maple syrup, and stock or water with miso. Bring
to a boil, cover, and gently simmer for 5 minutes. Season, garnish with
the cilantro, and serve.

102 SPICY RED LENTIL AND TOMATO SOUP

CALORIES	290
CHOLESTEROL	0
VEGAN CALORIES	290
POLYUNSATS	★★☆
ANTIOXIDANTS	★★★
CALCIUM	★☆☆
IRON	★★☆
B VITAMINS	★★☆

2 tbsp olive oil
2 shallots, chopped
2 cloves garlic, crushed
⅓ cup red lentils, rinsed and
    drained
5 fresh tomatoes, puréed

2¼ cups vegetable stock
1 tsp maple syrup
1 pinch asafoetida
1 pinch cayenne pepper
1 tbsp basil, chopped
salt and black pepper to taste

Gently heat the oil in a large Dutch oven. Add the shallots and fry over
a low heat until soft. Then add the garlic and the lentils and stir-fry for
1 minute before adding the tomatoes. Stir and heat through. Add the stock,
maple syrup, spices, and half the basil. Bring to a boil, cover and simmer
for 15 minutes, or until the lentils are soft. Season, garnish with the
remaining basil, and serve with crusty bread and cheese or soy cheese.

103 MINT AND CUCUMBER SOUP

CALORIES	158
CHOLESTEROL	17
VEGAN CALORIES	149
POLYUNSATS	★☆☆
ANTIOXIDANTS	★★★
CALCIUM	★★☆
IRON	★★☆
B VITAMINS	★★☆

1 handful mint, finely chopped, plus
    some to garnish
1 cucumber, coarsely grated

1¼ cups plain/soy yogurt
1 tbsp lemon juice
salt and black pepper to taste

Mix the mint and the cucumber in a bowl. Stir in the yogurt and the
lemon juice, and season. Chill well. Garnish with mint, and serve with
a few ice cubes in each bowl.

104 ▼ GAZPACHO DEL CAMPO

★♥◊✕⊘⬤

CALORIES	267
CHOLESTEROL	0
VEGAN CALORIES	267
POLYUNSATS	★★☆
ANTIOXIDANTS	★★★
CALCIUM	★★☆
IRON	★★☆
B VITAMINS	★★☆

½ cucumber
3 tomatoes
1 small red onion
½ green bell pepper
1 clove garlic

3 tbsp olive oil
1 tbsp lemon juice
2 tbsp red wine vinegar
salt and black pepper to taste
1 handful dill, finely chopped

Finely chop a quarter of each of the vegetables, and set aside. Purée the remaining vegetables with the garlic, oil, lemon juice, and vinegar to a thick, smooth consistency. Season and chill well. Garnish with the finely chopped vegetables and dill. Serve with a few ice cubes in each bowl, and croûtons.

105 ▲ AVOCADO AND SEAFOOD SALAD
⭐❤️∅◐

CALORIES	286
CHOLESTEROL	6
VEGAN CALORIES	578
POLYUNSATS	★★☆
ANTIOXIDANTS	★★★
CALCIUM	★★☆
IRON	★★★
B VITAMINS	★★☆

1 avocado, halved, pitted, peeled
   and sliced
2 beef tomatoes, sliced
¼ cucumber, sliced
2 tbsp mixed seaweed, soaked
   for 10 minutes and boiled
½ cup shrimp, cooked and peeled/
   ¾ cup walnut halves

juice of ½ lemon
¼ cup plain/soy yogurt
1 small bunch chives, finely
   chopped
1 tsp tomato catsup
a few drops Tabasco sauce
salt and black pepper to taste

Arrange the avocado slices on two plates. Pile the tomato and cucumber
on top. Sprinkle with the boiled seaweed, and garnish with shrimp or
walnuts. Make the dressing by mixing the lemon juice, yogurt, chives,
tomato catsup, and Tabasco sauce in a bowl. Season, and spoon over the
salad. Serve with French baguette.

106   COOL BULGUR TABOULEH

CALORIES	495
CHOLESTEROL	18
VEGAN CALORIES	485
POLYUNSATS	★★★
ANTIOXIDANTS	★★★
CALCIUM	★★☆
IRON	★★★
B VITAMINS	★★☆

⅔ cup bulgur
½ cup smoked salmon, diced/
   garbanzos, cooked or sprouted
2 scallions, chopped
1 small lemon, peeled and diced
1 tbsp each of fresh parsley, mint
   and dill, chopped
2 tomatoes, diced

⅔ cup green peas, fresh or
   defrosted
1 Little Gem lettuce
2 tsp red wine vinegar
1 pinch raw cane sugar
1 pinch salt and black pepper
1 tsp Dijon mustard
2 tbsp wheat germ oil

Put the bulgur in a small pan with twice its volume of water, and a little salt. Bring to a boil and simmer for 8–10 minutes, or until soft. Drain in a sieve. Add the smoked salmon or garbanzos, scallions, lemon, herbs, tomatoes, and peas. Mix well. Divide the lettuce leaves between 2 plates and cover with the bulgur mixture. To make the dressing, mix the vinegar, sugar, salt, pepper, and mustard in a bowl, and slowly whisk in the oil. Sprinkle the dressing over the salads, and serve.

107   SUMMER SALAD

CALORIES	241
CHOLESTEROL	0
VEGAN CALORIES	241
POLYUNSATS	★★★
ANTIOXIDANTS	★★★
CALCIUM	★★☆
IRON	★★☆
B VITAMINS	★★☆

1 Little Gem lettuce, shredded
½ small cauliflower, cut into
   small florets
1 green bell pepper, sliced
½ Florence fennel bulb, finely
   chopped
1 carrot, cut into peelings
5 red radishes, sliced

⅓ cup fava beans, chopped
¼ cucumber, finely sliced
1 small bunch watercress, chopped
1 tbsp walnut oil
1 tsp balsamic vinegar
1 tsp Dijon mustard
salt and white pepper to taste

To make the dressing, whisk the oil, vinegar, mustard, salt, and pepper in a salad bowl. Add the salad ingredients and gently toss. Serve with bread.

108   STUFFED TOMATO SALAD

CALORIES	480
CHOLESTEROL	51
VEGAN CALORIES	284
POLYUNSATS	★★☆
ANTIOXIDANTS	★★★
CALCIUM	★★☆
IRON	★★☆
B VITAMINS	★★☆

1 cup fresh tuna, diced/1 cup dried
   lima beans, cooked or canned
   and drained
juice of 1 lemon
1 tbsp olive oil
6 tomatoes, hollowed out
½ cucumber, finely diced

½ red bell pepper, finely diced
1 small red onion, chopped
12 black olives, halved and pitted
juice of ½ lemon
1 tbsp basil, finely chopped
3 tbsp olive oil
salt and black pepper to taste

Cook the tuna or lima beans with the juice of 1 lemon and 1 tablespoon of oil in a small baking dish in a preheated oven at 220°C/425°F/gas mark 7 for 5–8 minutes. To make the dressing, purée the scooped-out tomato flesh with the lemon juice, basil, oil, salt, and pepper to a thick consistency, and set aside. Place the cooked tuna or lima beans in a bowl with the cucumber, red bell pepper, red onion, and olives. Mix in the dressing. Spoon the salad mixture into the hollowed tomatoes. Serve on a bed of green lettuce.

109 A PLATE OF SUMMER CRUDITÉS

CALORIES	406
CHOLESTEROL	0
VEGAN CALORIES	406
POLYUNSATS	★★★
ANTIOXIDANTS	★★★
CALCIUM	★★☆
IRON	★★☆
B VITAMINS	★★☆

1 red bell pepper, halved
2 carrots
1 small raw beet
2 sticks celery
¼ cucumber
1½ cups chanterelle
  mushrooms, stir-fried in a little oil
4 artichoke hearts, sliced
10 red radishes, kept whole
1 tbsp red wine vinegar
1 pinch salt and black pepper
3 tbsp walnut oil
2 tsp tarragon, chopped
1 tbsp pumpkin seeds, toasted

Broil the bell pepper until the skin becomes black and charred. Cover with a damp dish towel and let cool. Cut the carrots, beet, celery, and cucumber into thin 4in long sticks. Skin the cooled bell pepper and cut the flesh into long sticks. Arrange all the vegetables on 2 large plates. To make the dressing, dissolve the salt and pepper in the vinegar, add the walnut oil and the tarragon, and whisk. Drizzle the dressing over the crudités, and garnish with toasted pumpkin seeds. Serve with toast.

110 BABA GANOUSH

CALORIES	718
CHOLESTEROL	0
VEGAN CALORIES	718
POLYUNSATS	★★★
ANTIOXIDANTS	★★★
CALCIUM	★★★
IRON	★★☆
B VITAMINS	★★☆

1 eggplant
2 tbsp lemon juice
1 tbsp tahini
1 avocado, quartered and pitted
1 carrot, cut into peelings
1 large tomato, chopped
1 small Florence fennel bulb, finely
  chopped
1 bunch watercress, chopped
1 tbsp balsamic vinegar
2 tbsp walnut oil
salt and black pepper to taste

Prick the skin of the eggplant with a fork and broil on all sides until it is soft and the skin charred. Cool under running water, halve and scoop out the flesh with a spoon. Purée the flesh with the lemon juice, tahini, and a pinch of salt. Peel and slice the avocado and mix with the carrot, tomato, fennel, and watercress in a salad bowl. Make the dressing by whisking the vinegar and oil with salt and pepper, pour over the salad, and gently toss. Serve immediately with the baba ganoush and warm pitta bread.

111 CHANTERELLE SALAD

CALORIES	208
CHOLESTEROL	0
VEGAN CALORIES	208
POLYUNSATS	★★★
ANTIOXIDANTS	★★★
CALCIUM	★★☆
IRON	★★☆
B VITAMINS	★★☆

7oz chanterelle mushrooms
1 shallot, finely chopped
2 tbsp flat-leaf parsley, chopped
1 handful radicchio, shredded
1 handful curly endive
¼lb green beans, blanched
1 small yellow zucchini, sliced
1 tbsp white wine vinegar
1 tbsp walnut oil
3 tbsp olive oil, plus some for frying
salt and black pepper to taste
1 small bunch chives, chopped

Make the vinaigrette by mixing the vinegar, oils, salt, and pepper and set aside. Heat a little oil in a pan and gently stir-fry the seasoned chanterelles with the shallot and the parsley for 2 minutes. Remove from the heat and drizzle with half the vinaigrette. Divide the radicchio and the curly endive between 2 large plates, add the green beans and the zucchini. Drizzle with the remaining vinaigrette. Spoon the warm chanterelles on top of the salad and serve garnished with chives.

112 ▲ EGGPLANT AND OLIVE PÂTÉ

⭐❌⌀

CALORIES	146
CHOLESTEROL	0
VEGAN CALORIES	146
POLYUNSATS	★★☆
ANTIOXIDANTS	★★★
CALCIUM	★★☆
IRON	★★☆
B VITAMINS	★★☆

1 tbsp olive oil
1 small red onion, finely chopped
1 eggplant, diced
2 cloves garlic, crushed
2 tsp tamari (soy sauce)

12 cherry tomatoes, blended
1 handful basil
1 tsp Dijon mustard
10 black olives, pitted and chopped
salt and black pepper to taste

Sweat the onion in a skillet with the oil. Turn up the heat, add
the eggplant and stir-fry until soft, approximately 10 minutes. Lower
the heat, add the garlic, tamari, and tomatoes, followed by the basil,
mustard, and olives. Very gently stir-fry for a further 5 minutes. Season
and serve on toasted French bread with plenty of crisp green lettuce and
French dressing (see p.23).

113 CATALAN ROAST BELL PEPPER SALAD WITH WALNUT PÂTÉ

CALORIES	625
CHOLESTEROL	0
VEGAN CALORIES	625
POLYUNSATS	★★★
ANTIOXIDANTS	★★★
CALCIUM	★★☆
IRON	★★☆
B VITAMINS	★★☆

1 yellow bell pepper, quartered
and deseeded
1 red bell pepper, quartered
and deseeded
1 tbsp red wine vinegar
1 tbsp lemon juice
salt and black pepper to taste
1 tsp maple syrup
3 tbsp olive oil, plus some

for puréeing
1 small hot green chili, deseeded
and finely chopped
2 scallions, finely sliced
¾ cup walnuts, shelled
1 clove garlic, crushed
¼ tsp salt
1 green lettuce

Broil the bell peppers until the skins become black and charred. Cover with a damp dish towel and let cool. To make the dressing, whisk the vinegar, lemon juice, salt, pepper, maple syrup, and oil in a bowl, then add the chili and the scallions. Peel the bell peppers and cut the flesh into long strips. Mix the bell peppers with the dressing. To make the pâté, purée the walnuts with the garlic, salt, and enough oil to easily purée to a slightly crunchy consistency. Serve the bell pepper salad with the walnut pâté on a bed of green lettuce, and with fresh country bread.

114 SCANDINAVIAN POTATO AND SAUSAGE SALAD

CALORIES	613
CHOLESTEROL	50
VEGAN CALORIES	478
POLYUNSATS	★★☆
ANTIOXIDANTS	★★☆
CALCIUM	★★☆
IRON	★★☆
B VITAMINS	★★★

olive oil for stir-frying
1 red onion, halved and sliced
1¾ cups spicy sausages
(pork/soy), sliced
1 small zucchini, finely sliced
1 tsp thyme
1 tsp Dijon mustard
2 tsp wheat flour

3 tbsp red wine vinegar
1 tsp maple syrup
salt and black pepper to taste
1 large handful lettuce leaves
3 small potatoes, halved and
boiled
8 cherry tomatoes, halved
10 cornichons

Gently heat 2 tablespoons of oil in a skillet. Add the onion and the sausages and stir-fry for 3 minutes, then add the zucchini and stir-fry for a further 2 minutes. Mix in the thyme, mustard, and flour and cook over a low heat for 1 minute. Add the vinegar, maple syrup, and a little more oil, and continue to stir while the mixture thickens. Season and turn off the heat. Arrange the lettuce leaves on 2 large plates and top with the halved potatoes and the sausage mixture. Garnish with cherry tomatoes and cornichons, and serve immediately.

115 SEAFOOD TABOULEH

CALORIES	425
CHOLESTEROL	140
VEGAN CALORIES	662
POLYUNSATS	★★☆
ANTIOXIDANTS	★★★
CALCIUM	★★☆
IRON	★★★
B VITAMINS	★★★

1 cup couscous
½ tsp Tabasco sauce mixed with
    1 tbsp olive oil
½ cup green peas, fresh or
    defrosted
1 zucchini, finely sliced
2 tbsp mixed seaweed, soaked for
    10 minutes and boiled

½ cup cooked shrimp/
    cashew nuts
1 small scallion, finely chopped
1 clove garlic, crushed
2 tbsp mint, finely chopped
½ lemon, peeled and diced
salt and black pepper to taste

Put the couscous in a small pan with twice its volume of boiling water, and a little salt. Cover and let stand for 10 minutes. Then mix in the Tabasco sauce, followed by the peas, zucchini, seaweed, shrimp or cashews, scallion, garlic, mint, and lemon. Season and serve.

116 ARTICHOKE SALAD

CALORIES	209
CHOLESTEROL	37
VEGAN CALORIES	142
POLYUNSATS	★☆☆
ANTIOXIDANTS	★★★
CALCIUM	★★☆
IRON	★★☆
B VITAMINS	★★☆

4⅓ cups water
1 lemon, quartered
1 onion, quartered
1 pinch raw cane sugar, salt and
    white peppercorns
2 globe artichokes
1 small Butterhead lettuce,

    shredded
1 carrot, finely sliced
2 tomatoes, cut into boats
¼ cucumber, finely sliced
½ cup goat's/soy cheese
cornichons and pickled chilies
    to garnish

Boil the water in a pan. Add the lemon, onion, sugar, and seasoning. Meanwhile, peel the leaves from the artichokes, cut the hearts into quarters, and cut off the choke and any remaining leaf edges. Place the artichoke quarters in the boiling water and simmer for 15 minutes. Cut the cheese into chunks, and arrange the salad ingredients and the cheese on two large plates. Add the cooked artichokes, garnish with cornichons and chilies, and serve with French dressing (see p.23) and baguette.

117 COLLIOURE SALAD

CALORIES	405
CHOLESTEROL	210
VEGAN CALORIES	367
POLYUNSATS	★★☆
ANTIOXIDANTS	★★★
CALCIUM	★★☆
IRON	★★☆
B VITAMINS	★★☆

3 red bell peppers
15 anchovies, desalted and bones
    removed/8 halved pieces of
    salsify and 8 black olives
3 tbsp olive oil
1 tbsp red wine vinegar

1 garlic clove, chopped
1 tbsp parsley, finely chopped
black pepper to taste
2 hard-cooked eggs, quartered/
    ½ cup dried lima beans, cooked,
    or canned and drained

Brush the bell peppers with oil, place them in a baking sheet, and bake in a preheated oven at 250°C/500°F/gas mark 10, turning from time to time until the skins are black and charred. Then peel off the skins while they are still warm, deseed, and cut into thick slices. Arrange the anchovies or salsify, and the olives like sun rays around the edge of a large plate and place the bell pepper slices in the middle of the plate. Drizzle with oil and vinegar, sprinkle with garlic, parsley, and black pepper, and top with hard-cooked egg quarters or lima beans. Serve with bread.

118 ▲ GREEN TAGLIATELLE WITH RED HOT PEPPER SAUCE

CALORIES	829
CHOLESTEROL	150
VEGAN CALORIES	594
POLYUNSATS	★★☆
ANTIOXIDANTS	★★★
CALCIUM	★★☆
IRON	★★★
B VITAMINS	★★★

½ cup chicken/vegetable stock, heated
1 red bell pepper, chopped and deseeded
1 large chicken breast/ 5oz seitan, sliced

2 tbsp olive oil, plus some for frying and tossing
1 pinch cayenne pepper
7oz green tagliatelle
1 tbsp basil, chopped
salt and black pepper to taste

Pour the stock into a small Dutch oven, add the red bell pepper, bring to a boil and simmer for 5 minutes. Meanwhile, fry the chicken or seitan slices in a skillet with a little oil until golden. Set aside. Purée the red bell pepper with the stock, while slowly adding the oil, and season with salt and cayenne pepper. Add the fried chicken or seitan to the sauce and mix Cook the tagliatelle in plenty of boiling water with a little salt and oil. Drain the pasta and return it to the pan. Toss with oil and basil, and season with salt and black pepper. Serve as nests on two large plates with the sauce in the middle.

SPINACH FETTUCCINE
WITH FRESH TOMATO SAUCE

CALORIES	538
CHOLESTEROL	29
VEGAN CALORIES	485
POLYUNSATS	★★☆
ANTIOXIDANTS	★★★
CALCIUM	★★☆
IRON	★★★
B VITAMINS	★★★

7oz spinach fettuccine pasta
2 ripe beef tomatoes,
    puréed
1 tbsp basil, chopped

1 cup mozzarella/soy cheese, cubed
1 tbsp safflower oil
salt and black pepper to taste

Cook the spinach pasta in plenty of boiling water with a little salt and oil. Mix the puréed tomatoes, chopped basil, cheese cubes, and oil in a bowl, and season. Drain the cooked pasta and toss with the sauce. Serve immediately with a green side salad.

BUCKWHEAT NOODLES WITH
SPICY ZUCCHINI SAUCE

CALORIES	777
CHOLESTEROL	57
VEGAN CALORIES	656
POLYUNSATS	★★★
ANTIOXIDANTS	★★★
CALCIUM	★★☆
IRON	★★☆
B VITAMINS	★★☆

1 tbsp olive oil
1 small white onion, finely chopped
1 clove garlic, crushed
1 zucchini, thinly sliced
½ cup sun-dried tomatoes,
    chopped
1 small red chili, deseeded and
    finely sliced

½ cup crème fraîche/soy cream
1 tbsp oregano, finely
    chopped
salt and black pepper to taste
7oz Japanese buckwheat
    noodles
a little grated cheese/soy cheese
    (optional)

Heat the oil in a Dutch oven and sweat the onion and garlic for 5 minutes until soft (don't let them brown). Add the zucchini and cook for 2–3 minutes. Then add the sun-dried tomatoes and the chili, cover and simmer for 5 minutes, stirring from time to time. Add the cream and oregano, and season. Heat through and very gently simmer for 2–3 minutes. Cook the noodles as instructed on the package. Drain and toss with the sauce. Sprinkle with cheese (if using) and serve immediately.

FETTUCCINE WITH SHIITAKE

CALORIES	406
CHOLESTEROL	0
VEGAN CALORIES	406
POLYUNSATS	★☆☆
ANTIOXIDANTS	★★★
CALCIUM	★☆☆
IRON	★★☆
B VITAMINS	★☆☆

7oz fettuccine pasta
1 tbsp olive oil
3½ cups fresh shiitake
    mushrooms, sliced
1 tsp ginger, finely chopped
1 tbsp tamari (soy sauce)
1 cup vegetable stock

1 tsp mirin (Japanese rice wine), or
    dry sherry
2 tbsp flat-leaf parsley, finely
    chopped
1 tsp cornstarch dissolved in a little
    cold water
salt and black pepper to taste

Cook the pasta in plenty of boiling water with a little salt and oil. Heat the oil in a pan and stir-fry the mushrooms until they begin to brown. Add the ginger and the tamari, heat through, then add the stock. Bring to a boil and simmer for 5 minutes. Add the mirin or dry sherry, parsley and dissolved cornstarch. Continue to cook until the sauce thickens, and season. Drain the pasta and stir into the sauce. Serve hot.

LUMACHE WITH SEAFOOD
★♥🌿∅

CALORIES	617
CHOLESTEROL	55
VEGAN CALORIES	636
POLYUNSATS	★★☆
ANTIOXIDANTS	★★★
CALCIUM	★★☆
IRON	★★★
B VITAMINS	★★☆

7oz lumache (pasta snails) or use
  pasta shapes of choice
2 tbsp olive oil
1 cup fresh tuna/7oz marinated
  seitan, diced
1 clove garlic, finely chopped
1 small red bell pepper, quartered,

deseeded and sliced
4 tbsp dried mixed seaweed, soaked
2 ripe tomatoes, chopped
2 anchovy fillets, chopped/8 black
  olives, pitted and chopped
1 tbsp basil, chopped
salt and black pepper to taste

Cook the pasta in plenty of boiling water with a little salt and oil. Heat the oil in a Dutch oven, add the tuna or seitan and fry until lightly browned. Turn down the heat, add the garlic and red bell pepper, and cook until soft. Add the seaweed (with its soaking water), tomatoes, anchovies or olives, and basil, reduce for 5 minutes, then season. Drain the cooked pasta and divide onto two heated plates. Top with the sauce and serve immediately.

PASTA WITH CHUNKY TARRAGON SAUCE
★🌿

CALORIES	1,027
CHOLESTEROL	182
VEGAN CALORIES	734
POLYUNSATS	★★★
ANTIOXIDANTS	★★★
CALCIUM	★★☆
IRON	★★★
B VITAMINS	★★☆

5 oz pasta shapes
1 chicken breast, cut into chunks/
  2oz soy chunks (dry weight),
  rehydrated
all-purpose flour for coating
vegetable oil for frying
1 onion, chopped
⅔ cup white wine

1 cup chicken/vegetable stock
salt and black pepper to taste
1 small bunch tarragon,
  chopped
½ cup crème fraîche/soy cream
1 tsp cornstarch dissolved
  in a little cold water

Cook the pasta shapes in plenty of boiling water with a little salt and oil. Flour the chicken or soy chunks and fry them in a Dutch oven with a little oil. Set aside. Fry the onion in the dish with a little more oil, add the white wine, and let reduce to half the volume. Then add the stock, season, and add half the tarragon. Add the fried chicken or soy chunks and simmer for 20 minutes. Spoon in the cream, bring to a boil, and add the remaining tarragon. Thicken the sauce with the cornstarch. Check the seasoning, and serve hot with the cooked and drained pasta.

PENNE WITH PESTO AND PEAS
★♥🌿

CALORIES	881
CHOLESTEROL	0
VEGAN CALORIES	881
POLYUNSATS	★★★
ANTIOXIDANTS	★★★
CALCIUM	★★☆
IRON	★★★
B VITAMINS	★★☆

7oz penne pasta
3 tbsp pine kernels
½ tsp salt
2 tbsp basil, finely chopped

4 tbsp olive oil
1 clove garlic, crushed (or more
  to taste)
1 generous cup peas

Cook the pasta in plenty of boiling water with a little salt and oil. Grind the pine kernels and salt in a mortar. Add the basil, oil, and garlic. Mix well. Steam the peas in a vegetable steamer for 3–4 minutes. Drain the cooked pasta and place in a large, heated serving bowl. Mix in the pesto, top with the peas, and serve immediately.

125 PASTA WITH GOUJONS IN PIQUANTE SAUCE

CALORIES	958
CHOLESTEROL	125
VEGAN CALORIES	770
POLYUNSATS	★★☆
ANTIOXIDANTS	★★☆
CALCIUM	★★☆
IRON	★★★
B VITAMINS	★★☆

3 cloves garlic, crushed
2 tbsp Dijon mustard
2 tbsp red wine vinegar
3 tbsp vegetable stock
1 tbsp tomato paste
1 tbsp tamari (soy sauce)
5oz pasta of choice
2 tbsp olive oil
1 chicken breast, cut into strips/

2oz soy chunks (dry weight),
  rehydrated
½ Spanish onion, finely sliced
½ cup coconut milk
1 tsp cornstarch diluted in a little
  coconut milk
salt and black pepper to taste
tarragon to garnish

Mix the garlic, mustard, vinegar, stock, tomato paste, and tamari into a sauce in a bowl, and set aside. Boil the pasta in plenty of water with a little salt and oil. Meanwhile, stir-fry the chicken or soy chunks in a Dutch oven with the oil for 3–5 minutes. Add the onion, then the sauce, and bring to a boil. Cover and gently simmer for 5 minutes. Add the coconut milk and the diluted cornstarch, stir, and heat through until the sauce thickens. Season and serve garnished with tarragon and black pepper.

126 LINGUINI WITH PANGRATTATO AND SPICY SAUCE

CALORIES	648
CHOLESTEROL	8
VEGAN CALORIES	724
POLYUNSATS	★★★
ANTIOXIDANTS	★★★
CALCIUM	★★☆
IRON	★★★
B VITAMINS	★★☆

½ cup olive oil, plus 1 tbsp
  for frying
4 cloves garlic, chopped
2 thick slices bread, made into
  coarse crumbs
1 small red chili, chopped
8 anchovy fillets, chopped/

14 sun-dried tomato halves,
  chopped
juice and zest of ½ lemon
salt and black pepper to taste
1 handful flat-leaf parsley, finely
  chopped
7oz linguini pasta

To make the pangrattato, heat the oil over a medium heat in a small pan, add the garlic and cook for 15 seconds, then add the bread crumbs and cook until crisp and golden. Drain, season, and set aside. To make the sauce, heat 1 tablespoon of oil in a pan and gently fry the chili and the anchovies or sun-dried tomatoes for 2–3 minutes. Remove from the heat, add the lemon juice, and season. Cook the pasta in plenty of boiling water with a little salt and oil. Drain and mix with the spicy sauce. Place in a serving dish, sprinkle with the pangrattato, lemon zest, and parsley, and serve immediately.

ROTINI WITH CHEESY ZUCCHINI

127 ▼

CALORIES	714
CHOLESTEROL	44
VEGAN CALORIES	635
POLYUNSATS	★★☆
ANTIOXIDANTS	★★★
CALCIUM	★★★
IRON	★★★
B VITAMINS	★★☆

7oz rotini pasta
1 tbsp olive oil
2 cloves garlic, chopped
4½ cups small zucchini,
   sliced

salt and black pepper to taste
⅔ cup ricotta/soy cheese,
   crumbled
1 handful basil, chopped

Cook the pasta in plenty of boiling water with a little salt and oil. Meanwhile, heat the oil in a heavy-based pan and very gently fry the garlic until soft (don't let it brown). Add the zucchini and gently stir-fry for 4–5 minutes. Season and set aside. Drain the pasta and mix with the zucchini. Add the cheese, check the seasoning, garnish with basil, and serve immediately.

128 SPAGHETTINI WITH
COOL HERBS AND HOT TOMATOES

■♥�◗✦⬮

CALORIES	554
CHOLESTEROL	0
VEGAN CALORIES	554
POLYUNSATS	★★★
ANTIOXIDANTS	★★★
CALCIUM	★★☆
IRON	★★★
B VITAMINS	★★★

7oz spaghettini pasta
2 cloves garlic
1 handful mint
1 handful basil
1 handful oregano
2 large ripe beef tomatoes,
    quartered

1 tbsp capers
1 tsp Tabasco sauce
1 tsp maple syrup
2 tbsp olive oil
salt and black pepper to taste
2 tbsp chopped walnuts

Cook the pasta in plenty of boiling water with a little salt and oil. Coarsely chop the garlic and the herbs, then purée them with the tomatoes, capers, Tabasco sauce, maple syrup, and oil. Season and set aside. Drain the cooked pasta and divide between two large plates. Top with the puréed tomato sauce and garnish with walnuts. Serve immediately.

129 PENNE WITH BRAZIL NUT SAUCE

■♥◗✦⬮

CALORIES	780
CHOLESTEROL	0
VEGAN CALORIES	780
POLYUNSATS	★★★
ANTIOXIDANTS	★★★
CALCIUM	★★☆
IRON	★★☆
B VITAMINS	★★☆

5oz penne pasta
2 tbsp olive oil
1 shallot, chopped
⅓ cup Brazil nuts
2 tbsp fresh bread crumbs

1 red bell pepper, quartered
1 tbsp tamari (soy sauce)
2 tomatoes, chopped
1 clove garlic, crushed
1 tbsp oregano, chopped

Cook the pasta in plenty of boiling water with a little salt and oil. Heat the oil in a skillet or wok and gently stir-fry the shallot for 30 seconds. Add the Brazil nuts and the bread crumbs and stir-fry until they begin to turn brown. Deseed and finely slice the bell pepper quarters and add them to the pan or wok with the tamari. Stir for a further few seconds, then add the tomatoes and the garlic. Heat through. Drain the cooked pasta and mix with the Brazil nut sauce. Garnish with oregano and serve immediately.

130 RICE NOODLES WITH
ORIENTAL SNOW PEA SAUCE

■♥◗

CALORIES	502
CHOLESTEROL	0
VEGAN CALORIES	502
POLYUNSATS	★★★
ANTIOXIDANTS	★★☆
CALCIUM	★☆☆
IRON	★★☆
B VITAMINS	★★☆

1 tbsp grapeseed oil
2 scallions, finely sliced
1 tsp ginger, finely chopped
1 clove garlic, finely chopped
3½ cups snow peas, sliced
½ cup water

1 tbsp tamari (soy sauce)
1 tsp cornflour dissolved in a little
    cold water
1 tbsp toasted sesame oil
salt and black pepper to taste
7oz rice noodles

Gently heat the grapeseed oil in a large skillet or wok. Add the scallions, ginger, garlic, and snow peas and stir-fry for 2 minutes. Stir in the water and the tamari. Bring to a boil and cook for 2 minutes. Add the cornstarch and the sesame oil, stir, and cook until the sauce thickens. Season and set aside (keep warm). Cook the rice noodles as instructed on the package. Drain and toss with the snow pea sauce. Serve hot.

131 SPANISH PAELLA
⭐♥🌿🍳

CALORIES	606
CHOLESTEROL	50
VEGAN CALORIES	581
POLYUNSATS	★★☆
ANTIOXIDANTS	★★★
CALCIUM	★★☆
IRON	★★☆
B VITAMINS	★★★

2 tbsp olive oil
½ Spanish onion
1 clove garlic, crushed
½ cup chicken/tempeh, cut
    into chunks
1½ cups cremini mushrooms,
    sliced
150g (5½oz) long-grain
    semi-whole grain rice

1 pinch saffron threads
1 bay leaf
1 small red bell pepper, quartered,
    deseeded and sliced
1 stick celery (with leaves), sliced
4 ripe tomatoes, puréed
1 cup vegetable stock
1 tbsp oregano, chopped
1 lemon (unpeeled), cut into wedges

Gently heat the oil in a paella pan or a deep skillet. Add the onion and
garlic and stir-fry for 1 minute. Then add the chicken or tempeh and the
mushrooms, and continue to stir-fry until they brown. Add the rice, herbs,
bell pepper, and celery. Stir-fry for 2 minutes, then add the tomatoes
and stock. Bring to a boil and very gently simmer until all the liquid is
absorbed and the rice is cooked (adding more stock or a little water if
necessary). Garnish with oregano and lemon wedges, and serve hot.

132 ORIENTAL STIR-FRY
⭐

CALORIES	556
CHOLESTEROL	138
VEGAN CALORIES	343
POLYUNSATS	★★☆
ANTIOXIDANTS	★★★
CALCIUM	★★☆
IRON	★★★
B VITAMINS	★★☆

2 tbsp tamari (soy sauce)
2 tbsp dry sherry or rice wine
1 tsp cornstarch dissolved in a little
    cold water
1 tsp ginger, finely chopped
1 packed cup lamb fillet/tofu, diced
2 tbsp olive oil

2 scallions, chopped into strips
1 cup broccoli florets, cut into small
    pieces
¾ cup sweetcorn kernels
1 small bunch watercress, chopped
salt and black pepper to taste
stock to taste (optional)

Mix the tamari, sherry or rice wine, dissolved cornstarch, and ginger in a
bowl. Add the lamb or tofu cubes to the mixture. Let marinate while you
chop and prepare the rest of the ingredients. Then heat the oil in a wok
and stir-fry the lamb or tofu with the marinade until all the liquid is
absorbed. Remove from the pan and set aside. Add a little more oil to the
pan and stir-fry the vegetables for 3 minutes. Add the fried lamb or tofu,
mix, and season, adding a little stock (if using). Serve with rice or noodles.

133 PROVENÇALE KIDNEY BEANS
♥🔥❌🌿

CALORIES	266
CHOLESTEROL	0
VEGAN CALORIES	266
POLYUNSATS	★☆☆
ANTIOXIDANTS	★★☆
CALCIUM	★★☆
IRON	★★☆
B VITAMINS	★★☆

1 small red onion, halved and
    sliced
1 clove garlic, sliced
1½ cups kidney beans, cooked
    or canned
2 large ripe tomatoes, chopped

1 small yellow zucchini, sliced
1 tbsp olive oil
¼ cup vegetable stock, heated
2 tbsp basil
⅓ cup small Niçoise olives, pitted
salt and black pepper to taste

Preheat the oven to 220°C/425°F/gas mark 7. Place the first five
ingredients in layers in a baking dish. Drizzle with the oil and the stock,
and scatter over the basil and Niçoise olives. Season and bake in a hot
oven for 15 minutes. Serve with wild rice.

134 ◄ BROCHETTES WITH PILI-PILI SAUCE

CALORIES	592
CHOLESTEROL	168
VEGAN CALORIES	576
POLYUNSATS	★★★
ANTIOXIDANTS	★★★
CALCIUM	★★☆
IRON	★★☆
B VITAMINS	★★★

2 red hot chilies, chopped
2 cloves garlic, chopped
juice of 1 lemon
1 tsp paprika
1 pinch salt
4 tbsp olive oil
10 large shrimp, peeled/1 cup
    smoked tofu, diced

1 sweet potato, cut into chunks
10 button mushrooms, kept
    whole
1 red onion, quartered
10 okra (lady's fingers), halved
1 red bell pepper, cut into chunks
10 cherry tomatoes
2 ears of corn, sliced into chunks

Purée the chilies, garlic, lemon juice, paprika, salt, and oil to a coarse paste and set aside. Alternately spear the shrimp or tofu, sweet potato, mushrooms, onion, okra, red bell pepper, and tomatoes onto two long metal skewers, then place on a baking sheet with the corn chunks and brush with the pili-pili paste. Place the kebabs under a hot broiler and cook until golden, brushing with more pili-pili paste as you turn them. Serve hot with rice or millet.

135 SICILIAN PAPILLOTES

CALORIES	384
CHOLESTEROL	88
VEGAN CALORIES	366
POLYUNSATS	★★★
ANTIOXIDANTS	★★★
CALCIUM	★★☆
IRON	★★☆
B VITAMINS	★★☆

2 tbsp olive oil
1 small eggplant, sliced
1 small zucchini, sliced
4 sun-dried tomatoes, sliced
10 black olives, pitted and sliced
2 fish fillets (sea bream or sea
    bass)/1¼ cups marinated

    tofu, sliced
1 dash of dry white wine
1 tbsp Florence fennel tops or ½ tsp
    fennel seeds
1 pinch dried oregano
salt and black pepper to taste
2 slices lemon

Preheat the oven to 220°C/425°F/gas mark 7. Quickly fry the eggplant and zucchini in a pan with the oil, then mix them with the tomatoes and olives. Divide the mixture into two piles on a large piece of foil. Top with the fish or tofu. Sprinkle with the wine, fennel, and oregano. Season and top with the lemon slices. Make a "tent" with the foil, tightly folded so that the fish or tofu is completely enclosed (but leaving plenty of free space over the fish). Bake in a hot oven for 10 minutes, and serve hot.

136 SOCCA NIÇOISE

CALORIES	553
CHOLESTEROL	0
VEGAN CALORIES	553
POLYUNSATS	★★★
ANTIOXIDANTS	★★★
CALCIUM	★☆☆
IRON	★★☆
B VITAMINS	★★☆

2 cups garbanzo flour
1¼ cups cold water
1¼–2¼ cups hot water

salt and black pepper to taste
olive oil for sprinkling and frying

Preheat the oven to 250°C/500°F/gas mark 10. Place the garbanzo flour in a heavy-based pan and slowly stir in the cold water until smooth. Place the pan over a moderate heat and gradually add the hot water and salt, stirring continuously. Lower the heat and continue to stir until the mixture starts to form a ball. Then spread out the dough evenly in an oiled, shallow baking pan. Sprinkle with the oil and black pepper. Bake in a hot oven for 10 minutes until slightly crisp. Cool and slice, and gently fry the pieces in oil. Drain on paper towels, and serve hot with a tomato salad.

137 CATALAN 10-MINUTE TART

CALORIES	533
CHOLESTEROL	8
VEGAN CALORIES	529
POLYUNSATS	★★★
ANTIOXIDANTS	★★☆
CALCIUM	★★☆
IRON	★★☆
B VITAMINS	★★☆

2 tbsp olive oil
2 shallots, sliced
8 mushrooms, sliced
½ tsp ground cumin
½ tsp ground coriander
1 pinch saffron threads

7oz ready-made tart dough,
 rolled out very thinly
2 large tomatoes, sliced
8 anchovy fillets/12 black olives,
 pitted and sliced
celery salt and black pepper to taste

Preheat the oven to 200°C/400°F/gas mark 6. Heat the oil in a small wok or pan and gently stir-fry the shallots and mushrooms. Add the spices and heat through. Line an 8in tart pan with the tart dough and add the mushroom mixture. Cover with tomato slices and anchovies or olives. Season, bake for 10 minutes or until golden, and serve.

138 BASQUE CHICKEN FRICASSÉE

CALORIES	561
CHOLESTEROL	90
VEGAN CALORIES	466
POLYUNSATS	★★☆
ANTIOXIDANTS	★★★
CALCIUM	★★☆
IRON	★★☆
B VITAMINS	★★☆

2 chicken legs, cut into pieces/
 6oz seitan, cut into chunks
2 tbsp all-purpose flour
olive oil for sautéing and stir-frying
1 large onion, halved
½ red bell pepper, deseeded
½ green bell pepper, deseeded

1 cup white wine
2 tomatoes, peeled and chopped
1 clove garlic, chopped
1 pinch dried thyme
1 bay leaf
½ tsp sugar
salt and black pepper to taste

Preheat the oven to 230°C/450°F/gas mark 8. Flour the chicken or seitan and sauté in a Dutch oven with oil. Set aside. Slice the onion and the red and green bell peppers and stir-fry them in the dish with a little more oil. Add the white wine, tomatoes, garlic, herbs and sugar, and season. Return the chicken or seitan to the dish and bring to a boil. Cover and place in a hot oven for 20 minutes. Check the seasoning and serve with rice.

139 NEPALESE PANCH KOL

CALORIES	289
CHOLESTEROL	0
VEGAN CALORIES	289
POLYUNSATS	★★★
ANTIOXIDANTS	★★★
CALCIUM	★★☆
IRON	★★★
B VITAMINS	★★☆

2 tbsp grapeseed oil
1¼ cups cauliflower, cut into
 small florets
2 small carrots, chopped
½ tsp turmeric
½ cup vegetable stock or
 water
1 small green chili, roughly
 chopped

1–2 cloves garlic, roughly chopped
2 large tomatoes, roughly
 chopped
3 cups fresh spinach, chopped
½ cup peas
12 red radishes, sliced
1 tsp honey
salt and cayenne pepper to taste
cilantro to garnish (optional)

Heat the oil in a heavy-based pan and gently stir-fry the cauliflower and the carrots for 2–3 minutes. Add the turmeric, stir for a further minute, then add the stock or water. Gently simmer while you purée the chili, garlic, and tomatoes. Add the puréed mixture and the fresh spinach to the pan. Bring to a boil and simmer for 10 minutes. Add the peas, radishes, and honey. Stir, heat through, and simmer for a further 3 minutes. Season, garnish with cilantro (if using), and serve with rice or chapati.

MIDDLE EASTERN PUFFS

CALORIES	722
CHOLESTEROL	0
VEGAN CALORIES	722
POLYUNSATS	★★★
ANTIOXIDANTS	★★☆
CALCIUM	★★☆
IRON	★★☆
B VITAMINS	★★☆

1 cup walnuts, shelled
2 tbsp bread crumbs
2 cloves garlic, crushed

½ tsp (pomegranate) molasses
2 tbsp olive oil
8 phyllo pastry sheets

Preheat the oven to 220°C/425°F/gas mark 7. Roughly crush the walnuts in a mortar or a blender. Add the bread crumbs, garlic, molasses, and oil, mix well and season. Cut the phyllo pastry into 4in squares and use two layers of pastry for each square. Place a spoonful of filling along one edge of each square and fold in the sides. Roll each square into a finger shape and firmly press together the edges. Place on a greased baking sheet and bake in the middle of a hot oven until golden, approximately 10 minutes. Serve with a green salad.

141 INDONESIAN SATAY

CALORIES	578
CHOLESTEROL	75
VEGAN CALORIES	540
POLYUNSATS	★★★
ANTIOXIDANTS	★★★
CALCIUM	★★☆
IRON	★★☆
B VITAMINS	★★★

²⁄₃ cup chicken breast/tempeh
8 cherry tomatoes
8 oyster mushrooms
8 pearl onions
1 small yellow zucchini, cut
   into chunks
1 red bell pepper, deseeded and cut
   into triangles

juice of 1 lime
2 cloves garlic, chopped
2 fresh hot chilies, chopped
1 tsp tamarind paste dissolved
   in 1 tbsp water
tamari (soy sauce) to taste
grapeseed oil for blending
3 tbsp peanut butter

Cut the chicken or tempeh into cubes. Spear the tomatoes, mushrooms, onions, zucchini chunks, chicken or tempeh cubes, and bell pepper triangles onto two barbecue skewers and place on a baking sheet. Purée the lime, garlic, chilies, tamarind paste, and tamari with enough oil to make a thick marinade. Brush the kebabs with half the marinade and cook them on a medium–hot barbecue (or under a broiler). Mix the remaining marinade with the peanut butter to make a dip for the kebabs, and serve.

142 EGGPLANT CATALANE

CALORIES	737
CHOLESTEROL	126
VEGAN CALORIES	610
POLYUNSATS	★★☆
ANTIOXIDANTS	★★☆
CALCIUM	★★☆
IRON	★★☆
B VITAMINS	★★★

½ cup olive oil
2 pieces Cornish game hen breast
   (approximately 6oz each)
   /6oz tempeh, sliced
2–3 eggplants, peeled and cut
   lengthwise into ¼in slices

1 portion sauce tomate concassé
   (see p.115)
1 tbsp basil, chopped
1 cup fresh bread crumbs
12 olives, pitted and sliced
salt and black pepper to taste

Brown the game hens or tempeh in a little oil in a skillet over a high heat. Set aside. Add some more oil to the pan and brown the eggplant slices on both sides. Remove and let dry on a kitchen towel. Then place layers of the eggplant slices in a baking dish, alternating with the sauce tomate concassé. Sprinkle with the basil and top with the fried Cornish game hen or tempeh. Sprinkle with bread crumbs and olives, season, and bake at 220°C/425°F/gas mark 7 for 15 minutes. Serve with rice.

143 SUMMER SAMBAL

CALORIES	409
CHOLESTEROL	0
VEGAN CALORIES	409
POLYUNSATS	★★☆
ANTIOXIDANTS	★★★
CALCIUM	★☆☆
IRON	★★☆
B VITAMINS	★★☆

2 fresh red chilies, chopped
2 cloves garlic, chopped
juice from 1 lime
¼ cup roasted peanuts
1 tbsp tamarind paste
1 tbsp raw cane sugar
1–2 tsp tamari (soy sauce)
   (to taste)

2 carrots, chopped into thin sticks
½ Chinese cabbage, finely shredded
¼ lb baby corn ears, halved
   lengthwise
1 mango, peeled and diced
1 cup snow peas,
   diagonally sliced
1 large handful bean sprouts

Purée the red chilies, garlic, lime juice, peanuts, tamarind paste, sugar, and tamari in a bowl with enough water to make a thick, coarse sauce. Place the remaining ingredients in a salad bowl, top with the sauce (sambal), gently toss, and serve.

144 YELLOW ZUCCHINI OMELET

CALORIES	363
CHOLESTEROL	11
VEGAN CALORIES	333
POLYUNSATS	★★☆
ANTIOXIDANTS	★★☆
CALCIUM	★★☆
IRON	★★☆
B VITAMINS	★★☆

batter:
¾ cup wheat flour
1 tsp baking powder
1 pinch saffron threads
⅔ cup soy milk/milk
1 tbsp olive oil
salt and black pepper to taste

filling:
1 yellow zucchini, grated
1 tbsp parsley, finely chopped
oil for frying

Beat the flour and baking powder in a bowl, add the saffron, milk, and olive oil, and season. Then add the grated zucchini and the parsley, and mix well. Heat 1 tablespoon of oil in a skillet. When the oil is quite hot, pour in the omelet batter and spread it evenly to form a thick layer. Turn down the heat and very slowly cook for 10 minutes. Turn and gently cook the other side over a medium heat for 5–7 minutes. Serve with a dressed tomato salad.

145 BASQUE OMELET

CALORIES	235
CHOLESTEROL	417
VEGAN CALORIES	254
POLYUNSATS	★☆☆
ANTIOXIDANTS	★★★
CALCIUM	★★☆
IRON	★★☆
B VITAMINS	★★☆

omelet:
4 eggs
a little milk/water
salt and black pepper to taste
or 1 portion basic eggless omelet
   batter (see p.41)

filling:
oil for frying
½ cup tuna/4 oz seitan, chopped
1 shallot, finely chopped
1 green bell pepper, deseeded and
   finely chopped
1 large ripe tomato, finely chopped
salt and black pepper to taste

Heat a little oil in a skillet and sauté the tuna or seitan with the shallot until they begin to brown. Add the green bell pepper and the tomato, heat through, season, and set aside (keep warm). Beat the eggs in a bowl, add the milk or water, and season. Alternately, prepare the eggless omelet batter. Add a little more oil to the pan, pour in your chosen batter and spread it evenly over the pan. Turn down the heat and gently cook until the omelet is set. Add the filling, fold, remove from the heat, and serve.

146 OMELET FORESTIÈRE

CALORIES	390
CHOLESTEROL	1
VEGAN CALORIES	387
POLYUNSATS	★★★
ANTIOXIDANTS	★★☆
CALCIUM	★☆☆
IRON	★☆☆
B VITAMINS	★★☆

batter:
3 cups potatoes, grated
1 leek, finely chopped
1 tbsp soy milk/milk
salt and black pepper to taste

2 tbsp grapeseed oil

filling:
7oz chanterelle mushrooms, sliced
   and braised

Mix the potatoes and the leek in a bowl to form a coarse, flaky paste, add the milk, and season. Heat the oil in a skillet, add the potato and leek mixture and spread it over the pan to form a ¾in thick layer. Cook until the underside is firm and golden. Spread the cooked chanterelles over one half of the mixture, fold like an omelet, remove from the heat, and serve with pickled cucumber or cucumber salad.

147 ▼ SPANISH OMELET
★ ✿ ◎

CALORIES	360
CHOLESTEROL	391
VEGAN CALORIES	369
POLYUNSATS	★★☆
ANTIOXIDANTS	★★★
CALCIUM	★★☆
IRON	★★☆
B VITAMINS	★★★

omelet:
4 eggs
or 1 portion basic eggless omelet batter (see p.41)
1 small yellow zucchini, grated

filling:
olive oil for frying
1 red bell pepper, deseeded and diced
1 tomato, chopped
1 clove garlic, crushed
1 handful parsley, finely chopped
salt and black pepper to taste

Beat the eggs in a bowl, or alternately, prepare the eggless batter. Add the zucchini. Stir-fry the filling ingredients in a skillet with a little oil for 3 minutes, then add to the batter, and season. Add a little more oil to the pan and pour in the mixture. Turn down the heat and let the mixture cook very slowly for 10 minutes. Turn and cook over a medium heat for a further 5–7 minutes. Then fold in half and serve with spicy tomato sauce.

148 ▼ INSTANT TORTILLAS WITH PEPPER FILLING

CALORIES	774
CHOLESTEROL	75
VEGAN CALORIES	678
POLYUNSATS	★★★
ANTIOXIDANTS	★★★
CALCIUM	★★☆
IRON	★★☆
B VITAMINS	★★★

tortillas:
6 ready-made corn tortillas

filling:
oil for frying
1 small red onion, halved and sliced
¾ cup chicken breast/3oz tempeh, diced

1 small green chili, deseeded and finely chopped
1 tsp ground coriander
½ each of a red, yellow and green bell pepper, deseeded and sliced
1 tbsp tamari (soy sauce)
2 tbsp bean sprouts
1 tbsp cilantro leaves, chopped

Heat a little oil in a wok or skillet and stir-fry the onion. Add the chicken breast or tempeh and fry until golden. Then add the chili and coriander, together with the bell pepper slices, and stir-fry for 3 minutes. Add the tamari (and a little water, if necessary). Turn down the heat and let simmer while you prepare the ready-made tortillas as indicated on the package. Add the bean sprouts and cilantro leaves to the wok or pan. Heat through. Divide the filling among the tortillas, roll, and serve.

149 OYSTER MUSHROOM PANCAKES

⭐🌿🥚

CALORIES	643
CHOLESTEROL	227
VEGAN CALORIES	604
POLYUNSATS	★★★
ANTIOXIDANTS	★★☆
CALCIUM	★★☆
IRON	★★☆
B VITAMINS	★★☆

pancakes:
1 portion basic pancake batter
   (see p.42)
2 tbsp mixed parsley, thyme and
   chives, finely chopped
2 tbsp cheese/soy cheese, grated
grapeseed oil for frying

filling:
1 tbsp olive oil
3½ cups oyster mushrooms,
   sliced
½ cup walnut halves
salt and black pepper to taste
juice of ½ lemon

Mix the batter ingredients in a bowl with the herbs and the cheese. Heat the olive oil in a skillet and stir-fry the mushrooms until their moisture has evaporated. Add the walnuts, season, and set aside. Heat the grapeseed oil in a separate skillet and fry each pancake on one side, then turn and top with a spoonful of mushrooms and walnuts. Fold the pancakes, sprinkle with lemon juice and serve.

150 ASPARAGUS AND CHEESE CRÊPES

⭐💧🌿🥚

CALORIES	750
CHOLESTEROL	242
VEGAN CALORIES	684
POLYUNSATS	★★★
ANTIOXIDANTS	★★☆
CALCIUM	★★★
IRON	★★★
B VITAMINS	★★★

crêpes:
1 portion basic pancake batter
   (see p.42)
grapeseed oil for frying

filling:
1 large ripe avocado, halved

2 tsp white tahini
1 tbsp lemon juice
½ lb fresh asparagus, steamed
½ cup Gruyère/soy cheese/
   brewer's yeast flakes
salt and black pepper to taste

Mix the batter ingredients in a bowl and set aside. Scoop out the avocado flesh and mash it in a bowl with the tahini and the lemon juice. Heat a little oil in a skillet and fry the pancakes. Spread 1 tablespoon of the avocado cream on each pancake, add 3 cooked asparagus spears to each one, and season. Roll and place in a greased baking dish. Sprinkle with cheese or brewer's yeast flakes and broil, or bake in a preheated oven at 220°C/425°F/gas mark 7 until the top is golden. Serve with a salad.

151 PROVENÇAL PANCAKES

⭐💗🌿🥚

CALORIES	742
CHOLESTEROL	21
VEGAN CALORIES	682
POLYUNSATS	★★★
ANTIOXIDANTS	★★★
CALCIUM	★★☆
IRON	★★☆
B VITAMINS	★★★

pancakes:
¾ cup wheat flour (spelt
   if possible)
4 tbsp soy flour
approximately 1¼ cups
   milk/soy milk
2 tbsp olive oil
grapeseed oil for frying

filling:
1 leek, chopped
1 green bell pepper, deseeded and
   sliced
2 large ripe tomatoes, chopped
12 black olives, pitted and chopped
1 tbsp basil, chopped
salt and black pepper to taste

Whisk the two flours with the milk, olive oil, and a pinch of salt. Set aside. Sweat the leek in a pan with a little olive oil for 2 minutes. Add the green bell pepper, tomatoes, olives and basil. Cover and simmer for 5 minutes. Season, and fry the pancakes in a frying pan with grapeseed oil. Place 2 tablespoons of filling on each pancake, fold, and serve.

152 PIZZA MARGHERITA

CALORIES	454
CHOLESTEROL	29
VEGAN CALORIES	401
POLYUNSATS	★☆☆
ANTIOXIDANTS	★★☆
CALCIUM	★★☆
IRON	★★☆
B VITAMINS	★★☆

1 pizza base
2 tbsp tomato sauce, passata or
    sauce tomate concassé (see p.115)

2 ripe plum tomatoes, sliced
oregano to taste
1 cup mozzarella/soy cheese

Preheat the oven to 240°C/475°F/gas mark 9 and warm a baking
sheet. Spread the tomato sauce over the pizza base. Add the tomatoes
and plenty of oregano. Season to taste. Grate the cheese and sprinkle
it over the pizza. Bake in a hot oven for 10–15 minutes. Serve hot.

153 ▼ PESTO PIZZA

CALORIES	862
CHOLESTEROL	67
VEGAN CALORIES	720
POLYUNSATS	★★★
ANTIOXIDANTS	★★★
CALCIUM	★★★
IRON	★★★
B VITAMINS	★★☆

1 pizza base
2 tbsp pesto
10 cherry tomatoes, halved
½ cup spinach, sautéed
1 cup feta cheese/marinated tofu,
    cubed

10 sun-dried tomatoes, chopped
oregano, salt, and black pepper
    to taste
1 cup mozzarella/soya cheese,
    grated

Preheat the oven to 240°C/475°F/gas mark 9 and warm a baking sheet.
Cover the pizza base with the pesto. Top with the cherry tomatoes,
spinach, feta or tofu, and sun-dried tomatoes. Sprinkle with oregano,
season, and sprinkle with mozzarella or soy cheese. Bake in a hot oven
for approximately 20 minutes. Serve hot with a side salad.

154 PIZZA ATHENA

CALORIES	611
CHOLESTEROL	64
VEGAN CALORIES	469
POLYUNSATS	★☆☆
ANTIOXIDANTS	★★★
CALCIUM	★★★
IRON	★★★
B VITAMINS	★★☆

1 large handful fresh spinach
1 pizza base
2 tbsp tomato sauce, passata or
   sauce tomate concassé
   (see p.115)
1 small red onion, chopped
1 cup feta cheese/tofu, cut into
   small chunks

10 Kalamata olives, pitted
1 tomato, sliced
1 tsp thyme
1 tbsp marjoram, chopped
salt and black pepper to taste
1 cup mozzarella/soy cheese,
   grated

Preheat the oven to 240°C/475°F/gas mark 9 and warm a baking sheet. Meanwhile, chop the spinach and blanch it in a pan of boiling water. Drain and set aside. Cover the pizza base with the tomato sauce. Top with the red onion, followed by the cooked spinach, feta or tofu chunks, olives, and tomato slices. Sprinkle with the herbs, and season. Then sprinkle with the grated mozzarella or soy cheese, and bake in a hot oven for approximately 15 minutes. Serve hot with a cucumber and yogurt dip (tzatziki).

155 PIZZA ALLA ROMANA

CALORIES	527
CHOLESTEROL	45
VEGAN CALORIES	452
POLYUNSATS	★★☆
ANTIOXIDANTS	★★★
CALCIUM	★★☆
IRON	★★☆
B VITAMINS	★★☆

1 pizza base
2–3 tbsp tomato sauce, passata or
   sauce tomate concassé
   (see p.115)
1 tsp hot chili paste
1 cup mozzarella/soy cheese,
   grated

1 large ripe tomato, sliced
2 tbsp basil, chopped
1 green bell pepper, halved,
   deseeded and sliced
⅓ cup anchovies/black olives,
   pitted
salt and black pepper to taste

Preheat the oven to 240°C/475°F/gas mark 9 and warm up a baking sheet. Spread the tomato sauce over the pizza base and sprinkle with the hot chili paste, followed by the grated cheese. Top with the tomato slices, basil, green bell pepper slices, and anchovies or olives. Season and bake in a hot oven for approximately 15 minutes. Serve hot with a side salad.

156 SUMMER SPECIAL

CALORIES	595
CHOLESTEROL	97
VEGAN CALORIES	428
POLYUNSATS	★★☆
ANTIOXIDANTS	★★☆
CALCIUM	★★★
IRON	★★☆
B VITAMINS	★★☆

1 pizza base
2 cloves garlic, crushed and
   mixed with 1 tbsp olive oil
1 small zuccini, sliced and
   sautéed
½ cup smoked chicken

breast/smoked tofu, diced
1 cup Camembert/smoked soy
   cheese, thinly sliced
salt and black pepper to taste
2 tbsp herbs (chervil, tarragon,
   basil, and parsley), chopped

Preheat the oven to 240°C/475°F/gas mark 9 and warm a baking sheet. Cover the pizza base with the garlic paste. Top with the zucchini, smoked chicken or tofu, and cheese. Season and bake in a hot oven for approximately 15 minutes. Garnish with more black pepper and the chopped herbs. Serve hot with a side salad.

157 BASQUE PIPERADE

CALORIES	501
CHOLESTEROL	403
VEGAN CALORIES	498
POLYUNSATS	★★★
ANTIOXIDANTS	★★★
CALCIUM	★★☆
IRON	★★★
B VITAMINS	★★★

2 tbsp olive oil
4 tomatoes, chopped
1 red and 1 green bell pepper, sliced
⅓ cup Bayonne ham, diced/
 ½ cup kidney beans, cooked
 or canned

1 packed cup peas
4 eggs, beaten/1 cup crumbled
 tofu and 2 tbsp vegetable
 margarine
salt and black pepper to taste

Heat the oil in a large, heavy-based skillet and gently fry the tomatoes and the bell peppers for 15 minutes. Add the ham or kidney beans and the peas, cover, and cook for a further 5 minutes. Add the beaten eggs to the vegetables and cook until they are scrambled but still quite soft, and season. Alternately, scramble the tofu with the margarine in a separate pan, season, and then add to the vegetables. Serve hot with toast.

158 SESAME AND HONEY GOUJONS

CALORIES	510
CHOLESTEROL	130
VEGAN CALORIES	347
POLYUNSATS	★★★
ANTIOXIDANTS	★★☆
CALCIUM	★☆☆
IRON	★★☆
B VITAMINS	★★☆

2 chicken breasts, sliced/7oz
 seitan, sliced
3 tbsp tamari (soy sauce)
1 tbsp honey
2 tbsp sesame seeds

olive oil for frying
1 clove garlic, chopped
½ tbsp red wine vinegar
black pepper to taste

Marinate the chicken or seitan slices in 1 tablespoon of tamari and half of the honey. Then dip the slices in the sesame seeds until they are completely coated, and fry them with oil in a Dutch oven over a medium heat until brown. Set aside. Fry the garlic for 1 minute, then add the remaining honey, and simmer for 2 minutes until the honey changes color. Add the vinegar and the remaining tamari, heat through and season. Spoon the sauce over the goujons, and serve with rice.

159 POLENTA GRATIN

CALORIES	586
CHOLESTEROL	80
VEGAN CALORIES	505
POLYUNSATS	★★☆
ANTIOXIDANTS	★★☆
CALCIUM	★★☆
IRON	★★☆
B VITAMINS	★★★

olive oil for stir-frying
1 red onion, chopped
⅔ cup chicken breast/ 5 oz seitan,
 diced
12 black olives, pitted and chopped
1 tbsp cilantro
salt and black pepper to taste

2 plum tomatoes, chopped
scant 1 cup polenta
1 stick celery, sliced
1 cup green beans, topped and
 tailed and chopped
1 tbsp Parmesan/brewer's yeast
 flakes

Preheat the oven to 240°C/475°F/gas mark 9. Gently stir-fry the red onion and the chicken or seitan in a wok or a skillet with oil until brown. Add the olives and cilantro, stir for 30 seconds, season, and set aside. Heat 2 tablespoons of oil in a skillet, add the tomatoes and polenta and stir-fry for 2 minutes, then add the celery and beans. Simmer for 5 minutes. Place half the chicken or seitan in a roasting pan, add half the tomato and polenta mixture, then add another layer of chicken or seitan, finishing with a layer of tomato and polenta. Sprinkle with Parmesan or brewer's yeast flakes. Bake for 5 minutes and serve.

160 ▲ BARBECUE WITH RATATOUILLE KEBABS

⭐ ❤️ ⊘

CALORIES	403
CHOLESTEROL	56
VEGAN CALORIES	431
POLYUNSATS	★★☆
ANTIOXIDANTS	★★★
CALCIUM	★☆☆
IRON	★★☆
B VITAMINS	★★☆

1 small red onion, quartered
1 small eggplant, cut into chunks
1 small zucchini, cut into thick slices
1 red bell pepper, cut into triangles
1 green bell pepper, cut into triangles
2 cloves garlic, halved
10 cherry tomatoes
3 tbsp olive oil
2 tsp herbes de Provence
salt and black pepper to taste
2 turkey/ready-made vegetable steaks

Spear the vegetable pieces, garlic halves, and tomatoes alternately onto two metal skewers, brush with oil, sprinkle with herbs, and season. Broil the vegetable kebabs over hot embers, turning frequently. Meanwhile, brush the steaks with oil, and broil until they are brown and cooked through. Serve with the kebabs, chunky cherry tomato sauce and pesto.

161 STEAK PROVENÇALE

CALORIES	718
CHOLESTEROL	176
VEGAN CALORIES	477
POLYUNSATS	★★☆
ANTIOXIDANTS	★★☆
CALCIUM	★★☆
IRON	★★☆
B VITAMINS	★★☆

1 clove garlic, chopped
1 tbsp parsley, finely chopped
3 tbsp fresh bread crumbs
2 medium tomatoes, halved and deseeded
5 large mushrooms, stalks removed and set aside

olive oil for frying
1 shallot, finely chopped
½ clove garlic, finely chopped
4 lamb chops/2 ready-made soy steaks
1 tsp thyme
salt and black pepper to taste

Preheat the oven to 220°C/425°F/gas mark 7. Mix one clove of garlic with the parsley and bread crumbs to make a stuffing. Season the tomatoes and fill them with some of the stuffing. Set aside. Finely chop the mushroom stalks and one of the mushrooms. Heat 1 tablespoon of oil in a Dutch oven and gently fry the shallot, chopped mushroom, and garlic. Mix the mushroom with the remaining stuffing and check the seasoning. Then stuff the four mushrooms and place on a greased baking sheet with the stuffed tomatoes. Bake for 15 minutes. Meanwhile, sprinkle the chops or soy steaks with thyme and season, then broil on both sides. Serve on large plates garnished with the stuffed tomatoes and stuffed mushrooms.

162 SUMMER TAPAS TARTS

CALORIES	607
CHOLESTEROL	23
VEGAN CALORIES	564
POLYUNSATS	★★★
ANTIOXIDANTS	★★★
CALCIUM	★★☆
IRON	★★★
B VITAMINS	★★★

1 cup spelt flour
1 tbsp instant dried yeast
¼ tsp salt
2 tbsp sunflower oil
½ cup tepid water
3 tomatoes, chopped
½ shallot, chopped
1 small red bell pepper, chopped
1 tbsp parsley, chopped
1 tsp paprika
¼ tsp each of sugar and salt

1 dash Tabasco sauce
2 cloves garlic, chopped
½ eggplant, thinly sliced
8–10 cremini mushrooms, thinly sliced
oregano to taste
salt and black pepper to taste
grated mozzarella/soy cheese to taste
2 tbsp brewer's yeast flakes

Preheat the oven to 200°C/400°F/gas mark 6. Combine the flour and yeast with the salt. Add the oil and water and knead to a soft dough. Set aside. Purée the tomatoes, shallot, red bell pepper, parsley, paprika, sugar, salt, Tabasco sauce, and garlic. Set aside. Stir-fry the eggplant in a skillet with a little oil until golden, and set aside. Cut the dough into two and roll it out. Then place each of the rolled out halves in two 4in pie dishes. Add the puréed tomato mixture to each one, followed by a layer of eggplant and mushroom slices. Sprinkle with oregano, season, and sprinkle with grated cheese and brewer's yeast flakes. Bake in the middle of a hot oven for 10–15 minutes or until they begin to brown, and serve.

163 STUFFED MUSHROOMS

CALORIES	686
CHOLESTEROL	48
VEGAN CALORIES	542
POLYUNSATS	★★★
ANTIOXIDANTS	★★★
CALCIUM	★★☆
IRON	★★☆
B VITAMINS	★★☆

2 tbsp olive oil
6 large flat mushrooms, stalks
    removed and chopped
2 tbsp almonds, chopped
2 tbsp fresh bread crumbs

¼ cup soft cheese/
    soy cheese
1 tbsp lemon juice
2 tbsp parsley, chopped
1 tbsp paprika

Preheat the oven to 200°C/400°F/gas mark 6. Fry the mushroom stalks and the almonds in a skillet with a little oil, then mix them with the bread crumbs and the cheese. Season and set aside. Place the mushroom caps upside down on a baking sheet and brush with the lemon juice and the oil. Add the filling and bake in a hot oven for 20 minutes. Garnish with parsley and paprika, and serve with toast and salad.

164 LAMB OR TEMPEH SLICES WITH FLAGEOLET BEANS

CALORIES	565
CHOLESTEROL	99
VEGAN CALORIES	457
POLYUNSATS	★☆☆
ANTIOXIDANTS	★★☆
CALCIUM	★★☆
IRON	★★★
B VITAMINS	★★☆

1 tbsp olive oil
2 leg-of-lamb slices/6oz
    smoked tempeh, sliced
2 shallots, chopped
½ glass dry white wine
½ cup chicken/vegetable
    stock

2 cups flageolet beans,
    cooked or canned
1 clove garlic, chopped
1 pinch dried thyme
salt and black pepper to taste
1 tbsp parsley, finely chopped

Cook the lamb or tempeh in a Dutch oven with the oil for 2 minutes on each side. Set aside. Add the shallots to the pan and gently fry them until soft. Pour in the white wine and let reduce to one-third of its volume. Add the stock, beans, garlic, and thyme, and season. Gently simmer for 10 minutes. Meanwhile, reheat the lamb or tempeh under the broiler. Add the parsley to the beans before serving hot with the lamb or tempeh slices.

165 EGGPLANTS FARCIE

CALORIES	544
CHOLESTEROL	38
VEGAN CALORIES	443
POLYUNSATS	★★☆
ANTIOXIDANTS	★★★
CALCIUM	★★☆
IRON	★★☆
B VITAMINS	★★☆

olive oil for frying
1 eggplant, sliced lengthwise
1 small zucchini, halved and sliced
    lengthwise
2 small potatoes, finely sliced
1 red bell pepper, finely sliced
⅔ cup spicy sausage

(pork/soy), grated
1 thick slice bread, soaked in
    milk/soy milk and grated
1 clove garlic, grated
salt and black pepper to taste
3 tomatoes, puréed
1–2 tsp paprika

Preheat the oven to 220°C/425°F/gas mark 7. Fry the eggplants in a pan with oil until golden and place in the bottom of an oiled baking dish. Add the zucchini, potatoes, and bell pepper in layers. Mix the sausage, bread, and garlic in a bowl, then season and spoon onto the vegetables. Pour the tomatoes over the mixture and make some holes with your finger so that the liquid can run through each layer. Sprinkle with paprika and a little oil. Bake until it begins to brown. Serve hot or cold.

166 BAKED TOMATOES WITH WALNUTS

CALORIES	519
CHOLESTEROL	5
VEGAN CALORIES	507
POLYUNSATS	★★★
ANTIOXIDANTS	★★★
CALCIUM	★★☆
IRON	★★☆
B VITAMINS	★★☆

4 large beef tomatoes
¾ cup chopped walnuts
½ cup peas, blanched
1 clove garlic, crushed
1 tbsp olive oil

1 tsp balsamic vinegar
1 tbsp basil, chopped
salt and black pepper to taste
1 tbsp Parmesan/brewer's yeast
    flakes

Preheat the oven to 220°C/425°F/gas mark 7. Slice off the tops of the tomatoes and set the tops aside. Scoop out the tomato seeds with a teaspoon. Lightly toast the walnuts in a pan and mix in the peas. Add the garlic, oil, balsamic vinegar, and basil. Gently mix and season. Fill the scooped-out tomatoes with the walnut mix and sprinkle with Parmesan or brewer's yeast flakes. Put the tops back on the tomatoes and bake on the top shelf of the oven for 10–15 minutes. Serve with rice or bread, and salad.

167 PISSALADIÈRE

CALORIES	584
CHOLESTEROL	11
VEGAN CALORIES	568
POLYUNSATS	★★★
ANTIOXIDANTS	★★☆
CALCIUM	★★☆
IRON	★★☆
B VITAMINS	★★☆

7 oz ready-made tart dough
2 tbsp olive oil
2½ cups onions, halved
    and sliced
1 clove garlic, chopped
1 tsp dried thyme

1 bay leaf
salt and black pepper to taste
1 tbsp capers
12 anchovy fillets/12 black olives,
    pitted

Preheat the oven to 240°C/475°F/gas mark 9. Roll the dough to an 8in circle and lay on a baking sheet. Gently sauté the onions in a pan with the oil until soft. Add the garlic, thyme, and bay leaf, heat through and season. Pour the onion mixture onto the dough and garnish with capers and anchovies or olives. Bake for 15 minutes. Serve with a green salad.

168 SUMMER KEBABS

CALORIES	676
CHOLESTEROL	138
VEGAN CALORIES	467
POLYUNSATS	★★☆
ANTIOXIDANTS	★★★
CALCIUM	★★★
IRON	★★★
B VITAMINS	★★★

10 cherry tomatoes
1 red bell pepper, cut into chunks
1 yellow zucchini, cut into chunks
1 packed cup lamb fillet/1 cup tofu,
    cut into cubes
1 eggplant, cut into chunks
2 shallots, halved
16 button mushrooms, kept whole
4 bay leaves, halved

marinade:
¾ cup tomato catsup
Juice of 1 lemon
1 tbsp raw cane sugar
6 cloves garlic, crushed
2 tsp thyme
2 tbsp olive oil
1 tbsp mustard

Mix all the marinade ingredients in a bowl. Add the prepared kebab ingredients, and gently mix. Cover and let marinate (for 2 hours, if possible, but a much shorter time will suffice). Then thread the marinated vegetables onto two metal skewers and brush with the marinade. Place the kebabs on a hot barbecue (or under a hot broiler) for 10 minutes, turning from time to time. Serve hot on a bed of boiled rice cooked with saffron, salt, and canned garbanzos, accompanied by a green salad.

169 ▼ LEMON RISOTTO WITH BASIL

CALORIES	533
CHOLESTEROL	9
VEGAN CALORIES	504
POLYUNSATS	★★☆
ANTIOXIDANTS	★★★
CALCIUM	★☆☆
IRON	★★☆
B VITAMINS	★★☆

2 tbsp olive oil
1 leek (with half the top), sliced
2 sticks celery (with leaves), sliced
1 clove garlic, crushed
¾ cup risotto rice
⅓ cup dry vermouth

2¼ cups vegetable stock, heated
1 lemon, quartered and sliced
3 tbsp basil, chopped
2 tbsp Parmesan/1 tbsp brewer's yeast flakes

Heat the oil in a large, heavy-based Dutch oven and gently stir-fry the leek and the celery until soft. Add the garlic and the rice, stir for 1 minute, then add the vermouth. Stir for a further minute, then add the stock. Bring to a boil, cover, and very gently simmer until the rice is cooked. Add the lemon pieces and most of the basil, gently stir, and heat through. Sprinkle with Parmesan or brewer's yeast flakes and the remaining basil, and serve immediately.

170 ▲ POACHED FIGS, APRICOTS, AND CHERRIES

CALORIES	145
CHOLESTEROL	0
VEGAN CALORIES	145
POLYUNSATS	★☆☆
ANTIOXIDANTS	★★☆
CALCIUM	★☆☆
IRON	★☆☆
B VITAMINS	★☆☆

⅔ cup apple juice
1 tbsp brandy (optional)
1 tsp maple syrup
4 fresh figs, quartered

4 apricots, quartered and pitted
8 cherries, halved and pitted
2 tbsp orange juice

Heat the apple juice in a Dutch oven with the brandy (if using) and the maple syrup. Add the figs, apricots, and cherries. Bring to a boil, cover and gently simmer for 5 minutes. Lift out the fruit with a slotted spoon and place them in a salad bowl. Bring the juice back to a boil and reduce to a thick syrup. Pour the syrup over the fruit, add the fresh orange juice, and serve with vanilla ice cream, custard, crème fraîche, or soy cream.

171 APRICOT TART

CALORIES	657
CHOLESTEROL	0
VEGAN CALORIES	657
POLYUNSATS	★★★
ANTIOXIDANTS	★★★
CALCIUM	★★☆
IRON	★★☆
B VITAMINS	★★☆

7oz ready-made tart dough, rolled out
1 lb ripe apricots, pitted and halved, plus 3 for puréeing

2 tbsp liquid honey
1 tbsp almond butter
2 dates, pitted
½ cup apple juice

Preheat the oven to 220°C/425°F/gas mark 7. Cut the dough into a 4in circle, lay it on a baking sheet and prick it in a few places. Arrange the apricot halves on top, cut-side down, and sprinkle with the honey. Bake in the oven for approximately 20 minutes. Purée the almond butter with the three apricots, the dates, and the apple juice, and serve with the tart.

172 SPICY PEACHES

CALORIES	108
CHOLESTEROL	0
VEGAN CALORIES	108
POLYUNSATS	★☆☆
ANTIOXIDANTS	★★☆
CALCIUM	★☆☆
IRON	★☆☆
B VITAMINS	★☆☆

2 large ripe peaches, peeled, pitted and sliced
1 tsp ground cumin
2 tbsp maple syrup

1 tbsp lemon juice
1 pinch cayenne pepper
1 tsp ginger, finely chopped

Place the peaches in a small serving bowl. Roast the cumin in a dry skillet for 15 seconds, then mix with the remaining ingredients. Pour the dressing over the peaches. Serve with pancakes and plain or soy yogurt.

173 WATERMELON SALAD

CALORIES	346
CHOLESTEROL	0
VEGAN CALORIES	346
POLYUNSATS	★★☆
ANTIOXIDANTS	★★★
CALCIUM	★★☆
IRON	★★☆
B VITAMINS	★★☆

½ watermelon, peeled, deseeded, and diced
⅔ cup raspberries
1 nectarine, quartered and diced

4 greengages, quartered
½ honeydew melon
⅔ cup apple juice
½ cup hazelnuts, chopped

Place the watermelon, raspberries, nectarine, and greengages in a glass bowl. Peel, deseed, and dice the honeydew melon and purée it with the apple juice, then pour over the fruit. Garnish with hazelnuts and serve.

174 RHUBARB AND STRAWBERRY COMPÔTE

CALORIES	53
CHOLESTEROL	0
VEGAN CALORIES	53
POLYUNSATS	★☆☆
ANTIOXIDANTS	★★☆
CALCIUM	★★☆
IRON	★☆☆
B VITAMINS	★☆☆

2½ cups rhubarb, sliced
1 tsp vanilla sugar
1½ cups strawberries, hulled

and halved
1 tsp ginger, finely chopped
maple syrup to taste

Place the rhubarb slices in a medium Dutch oven, sprinkle with the vanilla sugar, and cover with water. Bring to a boil and simmer for 10 minutes. Add the strawberries and the ginger. Heat through and simmer for a further 4–5 minutes. Season with maple syrup and serve.

175 SUMMER FRUIT SALAD

CALORIES	268
CHOLESTEROL	0
VEGAN CALORIES	268
POLYUNSATS	★☆☆
ANTIOXIDANTS	★★★
CALCIUM	★★☆
IRON	★★☆
B VITAMINS	★★☆

¼ watermelon
4 apricots, halved and sliced
1 peach, quartered and sliced
10 strawberries, hulled and halved
10 cherries, halved and pitted

20 raspberries
1 peeled banana
1 nectarine
½ cup pure orange juice
1 pinch nutmeg

Peel, deseed, and dice the watermelon and mix with the apricots, peach, strawberries, cherries, and raspberries in a glass bowl. Purée the banana and the nectarine with the orange juice. Divide the fruit between two large glasses, top with the sauce, and garnish with nutmeg. Serve immediately.

176 BERRY SALAD

CALORIES	200
CHOLESTEROL	0
VEGAN CALORIES	200
POLYUNSATS	★★☆
ANTIOXIDANTS	★★★
CALCIUM	★★☆
IRON	★☆☆
B VITAMINS	★☆☆

⅔ cup strawberries, hulled
  and sliced
½ cup each of raspberries,
  blackberries, and blackcurrants

⅔ cup cherries, halved
  and pitted
1 tbsp almond butter
2 apricots, pitted and chopped

Mix the berries in a glass bowl. Purée the almond butter and the apricots with enough water to make a thick cream. Add the cream to the berries and gently coat. Serve immediately.

177 MELON NESTS

CALORIES	153
CHOLESTEROL	0
VEGAN CALORIES	153
POLYUNSATS	★☆☆
ANTIOXIDANTS	★★★
CALCIUM	★☆☆
IRON	★☆☆
B VITAMINS	★☆☆

1 Cantaloupe melon, halved and
  deseeded
4 Little Gem lettuce leaves
10 strawberries, quartered

12 cherries, halved and pitted
2 tbsp lemon juice
2 tsp maple syrup
1 tsp ginger, finely chopped

Scoop out the melon flesh with a melon baller, leaving a ⅛in thick edge of flesh. Shred the lettuce leaves, and arrange them in the hollowed melons. Mix the melon balls with the remaining ingredients. Divide the mixture between the two melon "bowls", and serve immediately.

178 STRAWBERRY SALAD

CALORIES	189
CHOLESTEROL	0
VEGAN CALORIES	189
POLYUNSATS	★☆☆
ANTIOXIDANTS	★★★
CALCIUM	★☆☆
IRON	★★☆
B VITAMINS	★★☆

2 large Iceberg lettuce leaves
½ lb strawberries, halved
1 peach, halved and sliced
1 pear, quartered, cored, and sliced

1 banana, peeled
1 tbsp maple syrup
1 tbsp mint, finely chopped

Divide the lettuce leaves between two plates, and top with three-quarters of the strawberries, and the peach and pear slices. Purée the remaining strawberries with the banana, maple syrup, and enough water to make a thick sauce. Pour over the fruit, garnish with mint, and serve.

179 FRUITY PANCAKES

⭐ 🌾

CALORIES	665
CHOLESTEROL	227
VEGAN CALORIES	581
POLYUNSATS	★★★
ANTIOXIDANTS	★★★
CALCIUM	★★☆
IRON	★★☆
B VITAMINS	★★☆

pancakes:
1 portion basic pancake batter
   (see p.42)

filling:
1 banana, peeled and thinly sliced
1 nectarine, quartered and sliced
8 gooseberries, halved
3 plums, quartered
1 pinch ground cinnamon
2 tbsp hazelnuts, chopped
oil for frying

Mix the batter ingredients and set aside. Combine the fruit in a bowl.
Heat a little oil in a skillet and fry the pancakes for 2 minutes on each side.
Fill each pancake with 2 tablespoons of fruit, sprinkle with cinnamon and
hazelnuts, and serve immediately with lemon wedges and maple syrup.

180 FRUIT BROCHETTES

⭐ ♥ 💧 🌿

CALORIES	447
CHOLESTEROL	0
VEGAN CALORIES	447
POLYUNSATS	★★★
ANTIOXIDANTS	★★★
CALCIUM	★★☆
IRON	★★☆
B VITAMINS	★☆☆

4 small figs
1 pear, cored and quartered
1 banana, peeled and cut
   into chunks
1 thick slice pineapple, peeled and
   cut into chunks

4 small apricots, halved and pitted
4 strawberries
2 tbsp maple syrup
2 tbsp lemon juice
2 tbsp toasted sesame oil

Thread the fruit onto two metal barbecue skewers. Make a marinade of
the maple syrup, lemon juice, and sesame oil in a bowl. Generously brush
the fruit brochettes with the marinade and place on a barbecue (or under a
medium–hot broiler) for 2–3 minutes. Turn, brush again, and cook the
other side for a further 1–2 minutes. Repeat until the fruit begins to turn
golden (don't let it turn soft). Serve hot with plain or soy yogurt.

181 FRUIT PARFAIT

⭐ ♥ 💧 🌿

CALORIES	531
CHOLESTEROL	0
VEGAN CALORIES	531
POLYUNSATS	★★★
ANTIOXIDANTS	★★★
CALCIUM	★★☆
IRON	★★☆
B VITAMINS	★★☆

½ cantaloupe melon, deseeded
⅔ cups raspberries
8 cherries, pitted
1 peach, quartered and diced
½ cup blackberries
2 passion fruit, halved and flesh
   scooped out
1 tbsp lemon juice

2 cloves, crushed in a mortar
¼ tsp each of ground cinnamon and
   ground coriander
1 tbsp almond butter
1 banana, peeled
1 square semisweet chocolate,
   grated (optional)
2 tbsp pistachio nuts, chopped

Scoop out the melon flesh with a melon baller. Layer the berries and the
other fruit (except for the banana) in two tall parfait glasses. Purée the
lemon juice and spices with the almond butter, banana, and enough water
to make a thick cream. Spoon the cream over the fruit mixture and allow it
to run down through the layers. Garnish with chocolate (if using) and nuts,
and serve immediately with a scoop of ice cream or soy ice cream.

182 ▼ HONEY FRUIT SALAD

⭐ ♥ 🔥 ▢

CALORIES	482
CHOLESTEROL	0
VEGAN CALORIES	482
POLYUNSATS	★☆☆
ANTIOXIDANTS	★★★
CALCIUM	★★☆
IRON	★★☆
B VITAMINS	★★☆

²⁄₃ cup dried apricots, raisins, and peaches
1 cup orange juice
1 tsp honey
1 honeydew melon, peeled, deseeded, and cubed
1 banana, peeled and sliced
2 ripe peaches, halved and thinly sliced
8 strawberries, thinly sliced
1 apple, cored and diced
2 tbsp coconut, freshly grated or shredded, unsweetened

Place the dried fruit in a small bowl, cover with the orange juice and honey and let marinate for 10 minutes. Mix the fresh fruit in a large bowl, add the marinated fruit, and sprinkle with coconut. Serve with a sauce made from one banana and eight strawberries, puréed with a little water (optional).

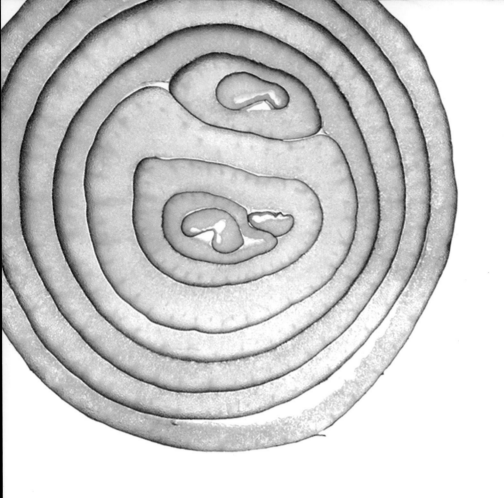

FALL
RECIPES

Fall is the time when the explosive abundance of summer starts to withdraw down into the roots and the earth. As the colors of the fruits, vegetables, and fields change from bright red to golden, it is time to collect some of the plenty, to share the summer's harvest.

In the forest, nuts ripen and game abounds, wild mushrooms appear and deep amber colors herald the parting of the sun. Cooking should reflect the season, with gently simmering stews taking over from hot summer broils. Root vegetables and potatoes, celery and salsify, pumpkin and corn become common ingredients, while sweet chestnuts and mushrooms, pears and apples, blueberries and grapes add color and rich flavors to the fall feast.

This is a good time to clear out the system. Cleansing fall grape cures and fasts can help maximize our immunity in preparation for the colder months ahead. In naturopathic terms, fall is connected with the stomach and the lungs – a chance to digest and store up reserves for the winter, and to take deep breaths of crisp, fresh air to nourish and cleanse the body and mind.

183 FALL VEGETABLE SOUP

CALORIES	318
CHOLESTEROL	0
VEGAN CALORIES	318
POLYUNSATS	★☆☆
ANTIOXIDANTS	★★★
CALCIUM	★★☆
IRON	★★☆
B VITAMINS	★★☆

4⅓ cups vegetable stock
1 leek, sliced
1 slice celery root, diced
1 carrot, sliced
1 potato, diced
1 slice pumpkin, diced

3 tomatoes, blended
1 cup green beans, chopped
1 clove garlic, crushed
2 tbsp olive oil
salt and black pepper to taste
2 tbsp parsley, chopped

Bring the stock to a boil in a large Dutch oven with the leek, celery root, carrot, potato, and pumpkin and simmer for 5 minutes. Then add the tomatoes, together with the green beans, garlic and oil, and season. Cook for a further 5–10 minutes. Add the parsley, check the seasoning, and serve with whole wheat bread.

184 MUSHROOM SOUP

CALORIES	292
CHOLESTEROL	0
VEGAN CALORIES	292
POLYUNSATS	★★☆
ANTIOXIDANTS	★★☆
CALCIUM	★☆☆
IRON	★★☆
B VITAMINS	★★☆

2 tbsp olive oil
1 shallot or small red onion, halved
   and sliced
1 clove garlic, crushed
4½ cups mushrooms, halved
   and sliced

1 tsp ground coriander
3 slices country bread, grated
1 tbsp tamari (soy sauce)
4⅓ cups vegetable stock
salt and plenty of black pepper to
   taste

Gently stir-fry the shallot or onion in a Dutch oven with the oil for 2 minutes. Add the garlic, mushrooms, and coriander and stir-fry for a further 5 minutes before adding the grated bread and the tamari. Continue to stir for 2 minutes, then add the stock. Bring to a boil and simmer for 10 minutes. Season and serve.

185 BEET AND ORANGE SOUP

CALORIES	87
CHOLESTEROL	0
VEGAN CALORIES	87
POLYUNSATS	★☆☆
ANTIOXIDANTS	★★★
CALCIUM	★☆☆
IRON	★★☆
B VITAMINS	★☆☆

1 packed cup raw beet, chopped
1¼ cups water
1 pinch salt

1 cup unsweetened
   orange juice
1 tbsp mint, finely chopped

Place the beets and water in a pan, bring to the boil, and simmer for 20 minutes. Remove from the heat and add the salt and orange juice. Purée to a smooth consistency. Serve hot or cold, garnished with mint.

CHESTNUT SOUP

★♥

CALORIES	481
CHOLESTEROL	23
VEGAN CALORIES	471
POLYUNSATS	★★☆
ANTIOXIDANTS	★★☆
CALCIUM	★★☆
IRON	★★☆
B VITAMINS	★★☆

1⅓ cups peeled chestnuts
4⅓ cups water or stock
2 tbsp olive oil
1 shallot, finely chopped
1 slice celery root, diced
2 tbsp vegetable margarine or butter, chopped
salt and black pepper to taste

Boil the chestnuts in a pan with the water or stock for 5–10 minutes until they begin to disintegrate. Meanwhile, gently sauté the shallot and the celery root with the oil in a skillet over a medium heat until they begin to brown. Add the shallots and the celery root to the pan with the chestnuts and cook for a further 10 minutes. Purée and season (adding a little more water or stock if necessary). Stir in the margarine or butter, check the seasoning, and serve hot with garlic croûtons.

187 SWEET POTATO AND PUMPKIN SOUP ★

CALORIES	444
CHOLESTEROL	0
VEGAN CALORIES	444
POLYUNSATS	★★☆
ANTIOXIDANTS	★★★
CALCIUM	★★☆
IRON	★★☆
B VITAMINS	★★☆

2 tbsp olive oil
½ red onion, chopped
1⅔ cups pumpkin, peeled, deseeded, and chopped
1 small sweet potato, peeled and chopped

3¾ cups vegetable stock
1 cup coconut milk
salt and black pepper to taste
1 tbsp cilantro leaves, chopped

Heat the oil in a pan and gently stir-fry the onion, pumpkin, and sweet potato for 3 minutes. Add the stock and the coconut milk, and season. Bring to a boil, cover, and simmer for 15 minutes. Check the seasoning and garnish with cilantro. Serve with corn bread.

188 CURRIED CARROT SOUP ★ ♥ ◆ ◆ ✕ ● ●

CALORIES	319
CHOLESTEROL	0
VEGAN CALORIES	319
POLYUNSATS	★★☆
ANTIOXIDANTS	★★★
CALCIUM	★★☆
IRON	★☆☆
B VITAMINS	★★☆

2 tbsp olive oil
2 cloves garlic, crushed
1 tsp curry powder
½ small green chili, deseeded and chopped
1 potato, chopped
1 lb carrots, chopped

1 tsp ginger, finely chopped
2½ cups vegetable stock
juice of 1 orange
juice of 1 lemon
salt and black pepper to taste
sugar or maple syrup to taste (optional)

Gently heat the oil in a large Dutch oven, add the garlic, curry powder, and chili and fry over a medium heat for 1 minute. Then add the potato and the carrots and stir-fry until they are well coated in the spices. Add the ginger and stir-fry for a further minute before adding the stock. Bring to a boil, cover, and simmer until the vegetables are soft. Remove from the heat, add the juice from the orange and the lemon, and season. Purée and check the seasoning. (You may need to add a little sugar or maple syrup, depending on the sweetness of the carrots and the size of the lemon.) Serve hot or cold.

189 MEXICAN AVOCADO SOUP ★ ♥ ✿ ●

CALORIES	464
CHOLESTEROL	28
VEGAN CALORIES	399
POLYUNSATS	★★★
ANTIOXIDANTS	★★★
CALCIUM	★★☆
IRON	★☆☆
B VITAMINS	★☆☆

2 tbsp corn oil
1 onion, finely chopped
1 tbsp wheat flour
4⅓ cups vegetable stock
1 large avocado, peeled, pitted, and mashed
1 pinch cayenne pepper

½ cup almond milk/light cream
salt to taste
½ yellow bell pepper, finely chopped
½ red bell pepper, finely chopped
1 tsp paprika

Gently fry the onion in a Dutch oven with the oil. Sprinkle with the flour and stir-fry until the onion is well coated. Continue to stir, and slowly add the stock. Bring to a boil, add the avocado and the cayenne pepper, and gently simmer for 5 minutes. Stir in the almond milk or cream, season, and serve garnished with red and yellow bell pepper and paprika.

190 QUICK TOMATO SOUP

CALORIES	46
CHOLESTEROL	0
VEGAN CALORIES	46
POLYUNSATS	★☆☆
ANTIOXIDANTS	★★★
CALCIUM	★☆☆
IRON	★☆☆
B VITAMINS	★☆☆

4 large tomatoes, stalks removed, quartered, and puréed
1 tsp tamari (soy sauce)
1 pinch ground coriander
1 tsp maple syrup
a pinch of Chinese five-spice
1 tbsp oregano, chopped
salt and black pepper to taste

Place all of the ingredients in a pan. Gently heat through, stirring often, and simmer for 5 minutes. Season and serve with croûtons.

191 SOUPE AU PISTOU

CALORIES	443
CHOLESTEROL	5
VEGAN CALORIES	431
POLYUNSATS	★★☆
ANTIOXIDANTS	★★★
CALCIUM	★★☆
IRON	★★★
B VITAMINS	★★☆

soup:
olive oil for frying
1 small leek, sliced
1 onion, halved and sliced
1 clove garlic, chopped
3 tomatoes, skinned and chopped
4⅓ cups vegetable stock
1 cup green beans, chopped
1 small stick celery, sliced
1 potato, diced
½ cup navy beans, cooked or canned
2 tbsp small macaroni pasta
salt and black pepper to taste

pistou:
a handful of basil leaves, chopped
3 cloves garlic
a little olive oil
Parmesan/brewer's yeast flakes to taste
a little salt

Heat a little oil in a Dutch oven and gently fry the leek, onion and garlic until soft. Add the tomatoes and cook for 5 minutes. Pour in the stock and bring to a boil. Add the remaining soup ingredients (except for the macaroni) and simmer until the vegetables are cooked. Add the macaroni, bring to a boil, and cook until the macaroni is soft, then season. Meanwhile, prepare the pistou by placing the basil and the garlic in a mortar with the oil, Parmesan or brewer's yeast flakes, and salt. Mash to a thick paste and add to the soup just before serving.

192 CHINESE CORN SOUP

CALORIES	162
CHOLESTEROL	98
VEGAN CALORIES	124
POLYUNSATS	★★☆
ANTIOXIDANTS	★★☆
CALCIUM	★☆☆
IRON	★★☆
B VITAMINS	★★☆

1 tsp ginger, finely chopped
2 tsp tamari (soy sauce)
2 tsp dry sherry
4⅓ cups vegetable stock
1 cup corn kernels
1 cinnamon stick
1 tsp cornstarch dissolved in a little
cold water
1 tsp almond butter
1 egg, beaten (optional)
salt and black pepper to taste
1 small bunch chives, finely chopped

Marinade the ginger in the tamari and sherry in a bowl. Bring the stock to a boil in a Dutch oven, add the corn, cinnamon, marinated ginger, and a little salt. Simmer for 10 minutes. Slowly add the dissolved cornstarch and the almond butter while stirring continuously. Then add the egg (if using). Season, heat through, and serve garnished with chives.

193 ◄ TOMATO SOUP WITH CILANTRO

⭐❤️💧❌🌿

CALORIES	213
CHOLESTEROL	0
VEGAN CALORIES	213
POLYUNSATS	★★☆
ANTIOXIDANTS	★★★
CALCIUM	★☆☆
IRON	★★☆
B VITAMINS	★★☆

2 tbsp olive oil
6 ripe tomatoes, quartered
   and stalks removed
1 red onion, chopped
1 clove garlic, chopped
1 cup vegetable stock

1 tsp raw cane sugar
1 handful cilantro leaves,
   chopped
salt and black pepper to taste
2 tbsp tamari (soy sauce)
1 tsp ginger, finely chopped

Gently sauté the tomatoes, onion, and garlic in a pan with the oil for approximately 10 minutes. Add the stock, sugar, and half of the cilantro leaves with a little salt and pepper. Bring to a boil, cover, and gently simmer for 10 minutes. Remove from the heat and purée, then add the tamari and ginger, and heat through. Check the seasoning and serve hot or cold, garnished with the remaining half of the cilantro leaves.

194 HOT PEAR SOUP

❤️💧❌🌿

CALORIES	241
CHOLESTEROL	0
VEGAN CALORIES	241
POLYUNSATS	★★★
ANTIOXIDANTS	★★☆
CALCIUM	★☆☆
IRON	★☆☆
B VITAMINS	★☆☆

2 tbsp grapeseed oil
3 ripe pears, peeled, cored, and
   chopped
1 tsp ginger, grated

1 tbsp lemon juice
1¼ cups water
salt and black pepper to taste

Gently stir-fry the pears and the ginger in a pan with the oil for 1 minute. Add the lemon juice and stir for a further 30 seconds. Then add the water, bring to a boil, cover, and simmer for 20 minutes. Purée and season. Serve hot or cold.

195 SPINACH AND GARBANZO SOUP

⭐❤️💧❌🌿☕

CALORIES	389
CHOLESTEROL	0
VEGAN CALORIES	389
POLYUNSATS	★★☆
ANTIOXIDANTS	★★★
CALCIUM	★★★
IRON	★★★
B VITAMINS	★★☆

2 tbsp olive oil, plus some for frying
1 bay leaf
1 pinch cayenne pepper
1 tsp ground cumin
1 tsp turmeric
1 packed cup garbanzos, cooked or
   canned
6 cups fresh spinach or Swiss chard,
   finely chopped

4⅓ cups vegetable stock
1 head garlic
1 whole onion, peeled
1 slice country bread (a few days
   old, if possible), crumbled
2 tbsp parsley, chopped
2 cloves garlic, crushed
salt to taste

Gently heat the oil in a pan and stir-fry the spices for 30 seconds. Add the garbanzos and stir-fry for 5 minutes, then add the spinach or Swiss chard and fry for a further minute. Add the stock, together with the head of garlic, the whole onion, and a little salt. Bring to a boil, cover, and simmer for 15 minutes. Meanwhile, heat a little oil in a skillet and gently fry the crumbled bread and the parsley for 2 minutes. Add the crushed garlic and mix with a little of the soup to make a thick paste. Add the paste to the soup and remove the head of garlic, whole onion, and bay leaf. Heat through, season, and serve.

196 WHITE CABBAGE, GRAPE, AND WALNUT SALAD

CALORIES	407
CHOLESTEROL	0
VEGAN CALORIES	407
POLYUNSATS	★★★
ANTIOXIDANTS	★★☆
CALCIUM	★★☆
IRON	★★☆
B VITAMINS	★★☆

1 packed cup white cabbage, finely
    shredded
⅓ cup raisins
1 red dessert apple, quartered,
    cored, and finely chopped
¼ cup cornichons

1 cup grapes, halved
1 tbsp tarragon vinegar
salt and black pepper to taste
2 tbsp walnut oil
¼ cup walnuts, shelled
1 tbsp parsley, finely chopped

Mix the cabbage, raisins, apple, cornichons, and grapes in a salad bowl.
Make the dressing by whisking the vinegar, salt, pepper, and oil in a bowl.
Then mix the dressing with the salad. Garnish with walnuts and parsley,
and serve with crusty bread.

197 CRUDITÉS WITH TAPENADE

CALORIES	652
CHOLESTEROL	0
VEGAN CALORIES	652
POLYUNSATS	★★★
ANTIOXIDANTS	★★★
CALCIUM	★★★
IRON	★★☆
B VITAMINS	★★☆

⅛ red cabbage, shredded
½ Florence fennel bulb, sliced
1½ cups cep mushrooms, sliced and
    stir-fried in a little oil
2 potatoes, parboiled and sliced
2 carrots, cut into fine sticks
2 tomatoes, cut into boats

1 handful Brazil nuts
¾ cup capers
½ cup black olives, pitted
2 cloves garlic, chopped
juice of 1 lemon
approximately ½ cup
    olive oil

Make the tapenade by puréeing the capers, olives, garlic, and lemon
juice with enough oil to make a reasonably smooth paste. Divide the red
cabbage between two large plates and place the remaining ingredients in
groups on top of the cabbage. Finish with a spoonful of tapenade in the
middle of the crudités. Serve with toasted bread.

198 AVOCADO AND MELON SALAD WITH CREAMY DRESSING

CALORIES	514
CHOLESTEROL	140
VEGAN CALORIES	748
POLYUNSATS	★★★
ANTIOXIDANTS	★★★
CALCIUM	★★★
IRON	★★★
B VITAMINS	★★☆

2 handfuls oakleaf lettuce
1 avocado, halved, pitted, peeled,
    and sliced
½ small melon, deseeded, peeled,
    and sliced
8 sun-dried tomatoes, thinly sliced
½ cup shrimp/cashew nuts (plus
    tamari [soy sauce])

½ cup plain/soy yogurt
1 tbsp olive oil
1 tbsp balsamic vinegar
1 tbsp tomato catsup
½ tsp salt
plenty of black pepper
1 small bunch dill

Arrange the lettuce leaves on two large plates. Add the avocado, followed
by the melon, sun-dried tomatoes, and shrimp or cashews (if you are using
cashews, dry-roast them first in a skillet with a little tamari). To make the
dressing, place the yogurt in a bowl, add the oil, vinegar, catsup, salt, and
pepper, and mix well. Spoon the dressing onto the salad. Garnish with
finely chopped dill and serve with fresh crusty bread.

199 CARROT SALAD WITH ALMOND DRESSING

CALORIES	394
CHOLESTEROL	25
VEGAN CALORIES	429
POLYUNSATS	★★★
ANTIOXIDANTS	★★★
CALCIUM	★★☆
IRON	★★☆
B VITAMINS	★★★

3 carrots, grated
2 tbsp light almond butter
1 tsp red wine vinegar
1 tsp lemon juice
1 tsp Dijon mustard
salt and white pepper to taste

2 tbsp almonds, chopped
2 tbsp parsley, finely chopped
oil for stir-frying (optional)
¾ cup ham/tempeh, sliced
1 small lettuce, shredded

Place the grated carrots in a salad bowl. To make the dressing, whisk the the almond butter, vinegar, lemon juice, mustard, salt, and pepper in a small bowl. Slowly add water until you have a smooth, even consistency. Add the dressing to the carrots, gently mix and garnish with almonds and parsley. If you are using tempeh, stir-fry the slices in a skillet with a little oil until golden. Divide the shredded lettuce between two plates, add the slices of ham or fried tempeh, top with the dressed salad, and serve.

200 TROPICAL SALAD

CALORIES	689
CHOLESTEROL	0
VEGAN CALORIES	689
POLYUNSATS	★★★
ANTIOXIDANTS	★★★
CALCIUM	★★☆
IRON	★★☆
B VITAMINS	★★☆

1 small butterhead lettuce, shredded
2 scallions, thinly sliced
1 bunch watercress, chopped
1 papaya, halved, deseeded, peeled, and diced
1 mango, peeled and diced

1 avocado, halved, pitted, peeled, and sliced
10 Brazil nuts, chopped
juice of 1 lime
3 tbsp walnut oil
salt and black pepper to taste

Arrange the salad ingredients on two large plates, in the order given. Sprinkle with the lime juice and walnut oil, season, and serve with corn bread or tortillas.

201 BALTIC SALAD

CALORIES	434
CHOLESTEROL	39
VEGAN CALORIES	317
POLYUNSATS	★★★
ANTIOXIDANTS	★★★
CALCIUM	★★★
IRON	★★★
B VITAMINS	★★★

½ celery root
2 carrots
1 rutabaga
2 potatoes
1 small beet
1 tbsp red wine vinegar
3 tbsp grapeseed oil

salt and black pepper to taste
2 cornichons, sliced
1 tbsp parsley, chopped
3 herring fillets, cut into chunks/ 1 cup marinated tofu, cut into chunks
1 small onion, sliced

Cut the celery root, carrots, rutagaba, and potatoes into small cubes and boil in a large pan until tender. Meanwhile, boil the beet in a separate pan until tender. Immediately cool the cooked vegetables under running water, drain, and set aside. Make the dressing by whisking the vinegar, oil, salt, and pepper in a bowl, and set aside. Place the cooked vegetables in a salad bowl with the cornichons and the parsley. Gently toss with the dressing. Garnish with the herring fillets or tofu chunks and the onion slices. Serve with whole wheat rolls.

202 BULGUR AND BEET SALAD

CALORIES	539
CHOLESTEROL	0
VEGAN CALORIES	539
POLYUNSATS	★★☆
ANTIOXIDANTS	★★☆
CALCIUM	★★☆
IRON	★★★
B VITAMINS	★★☆

½ cup bulgur wheat
1¼ cup red kidney beans,
   cooked or canned and rinsed
½ cup peas, fresh or
   defrosted
½ lb raw beets, cut into
   small cubes
1 scallion, finely chopped

1 tbsp mint, finely chopped
1 tbsp parsley, finely chopped
2 tbsp lemon juice
1 clove garlic, crushed
½ tsp Tabasco sauce
salt and pepper to taste
2 tbsp olive oil, plus some for frying

Heat a little oil in a skillet, add the bulgur, and stir-fry for 2 minutes until it begins to brown. Then add twice the volume of water and a pinch of salt, lower the heat, and very gently simmer for 10 minutes. Add the kidney beans and the peas for the last 2–3 minutes of the cooking time. Remove from the heat and place in a salad bowl. Add the beets, scallion, mint, and parsley to the bowl. Make the dressing by whisking the lemon juice, garlic, Tabasco sauce, salt, and pepper, then add the oil. Pour the dressing over the bulgur salad and gently toss. Serve warm or cold.

203 LEBANESE LIMA BEAN SALAD

CALORIES	350
CHOLESTEROL	0
VEGAN CALORIES	350
POLYUNSATS	★★★
ANTIOXIDANTS	★★★
CALCIUM	★★☆
IRON	★★★
B VITAMINS	★★☆

1¼ cups dried lima beans, cooked,
   or canned and blanched
1 scallion, finely chopped
1 handful parsley, chopped
3 thick slices lemon, peeled and
   chopped

3 tbsp walnut oil
1 clove garlic, crushed
salt and black pepper to taste
2 handfuls lettuce, shredded
12 cherry tomatoes, halved

Drain and cool the lima beans and place them in a bowl. Add the scallion, parsley, and lemon. Make a marinade by mixing the oil, garlic, salt, and pepper in a separate bowl. Then add the marinade to the lima beans and gently mix. Divide the shredded lettuce between two large plates. Add the lima bean mixture, garnish with cherry tomatoes, and serve with bread.

204 PASTA SALAD

CALORIES	422
CHOLESTEROL	0
VEGAN CALORIES	422
POLYUNSATS	★★★
ANTIOXIDANTS	★★★
CALCIUM	★☆☆
IRON	★★☆
B VITAMINS	★★☆

9oz cooked pasta of choice
1 green bell pepper, quartered
   and finely sliced
3 cherry tomatoes, quartered
1 large handful arugula,
   sliced
⅓ cup black olives, pitted

1 tbsp balsamic vinegar
1 clove garlic, crushed
salt and black pepper to taste
2 tbsp walnut oil
½ cup almonds, chopped and
   toasted

Place the cooked pasta, green bell pepper, tomatoes, arugula, and olives in a bowl. Make the dressing by whisking the vinegar, garlic, salt, and pepper, then add the oil and whisk to a smooth consistency. Drizzle the dressing over the salad and gently toss. Garnish with almonds, and serve.

205 ▲ CORN SALAD

⭐💜💧❌🫐

CALORIES	199
CHOLESTEROL	0
VEGAN CALORIES	199
POLYUNSATS	★★☆
ANTIOXIDANTS	★★★
CALCIUM	★☆☆
IRON	★★☆
B VITAMINS	★★☆

2 ears of corn, peeled and sliced
   into chunks
1 large handful lettuce
¼ cucumber, cut into sticks
2 tomatoes, cut into boats

1 small beet, cut into sticks
2 carrots, cut into sticks
12 black olives, pitted
salt and black pepper to taste

Plunge the corn chunks into a pan of boiling water and cook for
3–5 minutes. Meanwhile, arrange the salad ingredients on two plates,
in the order given. Top with the cooked corn, season, and serve with
French dressing (see p.23) and vegetable margarine or butter.

206 KASHA, CORN, AND BEAN SALAD

CALORIES	452
CHOLESTEROL	6
VEGAN CALORIES	449
POLYUNSATS	★★★
ANTIOXIDANTS	★★☆
CALCIUM	★★☆
IRON	★★☆
B VITAMINS	★★☆

½ cup kasha (roasted
　buckwheat)
1 cup water
2 cardamom pods
1 bay leaf
¼ tsp ground cinnamon
1 tsp ground cumin
2 tsp sunflower oil
½ cup corn kernels
⅔ cup flageolet beans, cooked or
　canned

1 small butterhead lettuce,
　shredded
1 tomato, sliced
¼ cucumber, sliced
1 small green bell pepper, sliced
1 shallot, finely chopped
½ cup plain/soy yogurt
1 tbsp lemon juice
2 tsp Dijon mustard
2 tsp tomato catsup
salt and black pepper to taste

Boil the kasha in the water in a pan, together with the spices until nearly all the water is absorbed. Remove from the heat, add the sunflower oil, and a pinch of salt. Stir, cover, and set aside. Cook the corn and the beans in a pan of boiling water for 1 minute. Drain and set aside. To make the dressing, combine the yogurt, lemon juice, mustard, and tomato catsup in a bowl. Set aside. Arrange the lettuce, tomato, cucumber, green bell pepper, and shallot on a large serving plate. Spoon the kasha onto the center of the plate and top with the corn and beans. Pour the dressing in a ring over the salad. Season and serve.

207 SALADE VERMEILLE

CALORIES	686
CHOLESTEROL	83
VEGAN CALORIES	577
POLYUNSATS	★★★
ANTIOXIDANTS	★★★
CALCIUM	★★☆
IRON	★★★
B VITAMINS	★★☆

4 tbsp olive oil
2 quails, cut into 4 pieces/
　6oz seitan
1 clove garlic, chopped
4 tbsp vinaigre de Banyuls (or white
　wine vinegar or sherry vinegar)

2 handfuls fresh spinach, shredded
1 curly endive, shredded
salt and black pepper to taste
4 slices bread, fried in a little oil and
　rubbed with garlic
1 tbsp parsley, finely chopped

Fry the quails or seitan in a skillet with a little oil until golden or brown and set aside. Add the garlic and vinaigre de Banyuls to the skillet and simmer for 5 minutes. Meanwhile, divide the spinach and the curly endive between two large plates, sprinkle with oil, and season. Place two slices of fried bread on the side of each plate, and top with the fried quail or seitan. Add the simmered garlic and vinegar, garnish with parsley, and serve immediately.

208 CARROT SALAD WITH SUNFLOWER SEEDS AND PARSLEY

CALORIES	258
CHOLESTEROL	0
VEGAN CALORIES	258
POLYUNSATS	★★★
ANTIOXIDANTS	★★★
CALCIUM	★☆☆
IRON	★★☆
B VITAMINS	★☆☆

1½ cups carrots, grated
2 tbsp sunflower seeds
2 tbsp lemon juice

2 tbsp sunflower oil
salt and black pepper to taste
2 tbsp parsley, finely chopped

Mix the grated carrots and sunflower seeds in a bowl with the lemon juice and oil. Season and garnish with parsley. Serve with toast and pâté.

209 ▲ FETTUCCINE WITH WALNUT PESTO
★♥🌾

CALORIES	637
CHOLESTEROL	0
VEGAN CALORIES	637
POLYUNSATS	★★★
ANTIOXIDANTS	★★☆
CALCIUM	★★☆
IRON	★★★
B VITAMINS	★★☆

7oz fettuccine pasta
¾ cup walnut halves
1 clove garlic, crushed
1 tbsp flat-leaf parsley,
   chopped

1 thick slice bread, crumbled and
   soaked in milk/soy milk
1 tbsp olive oil
2 tbsp basil, chopped
salt and black pepper to taste

Cook the pasta in plenty of boiling water with a little salt and oil. Meanwhile, pound the walnuts in a mortar (reserving a few to garnish), together with the garlic, parsley, and a little salt, until you have a rough paste. Squeeze the milk from the crumbled bread, add the bread to the mortar, and mix well. Then add the oil and the basil (and a little of the milk, if necessary), and mix until you have a thick green sauce. Drain the cooked pasta and stir in the pesto sauce. Season, garnish with walnut halves, and serve with Parmesan or brewer's yeast flakes.

210 GNOCCHI WITH SHIITAKE, LEMON, AND THYME SAUCE

CALORIES	581
CHOLESTEROL	30
VEGAN CALORIES	566
POLYUNSATS	★★☆
ANTIOXIDANTS	★★☆
CALCIUM	★★☆
IRON	★★☆
B VITAMINS	★★☆

1 tbsp olive oil
1 shallot, finely chopped
2 cloves garlic, crushed
1 knob vegetable margarine (or butter)
2½ cups fresh shiitake mushrooms, thinly sliced
salt to taste
2 tsp thyme leaves
1 cup plain/soy yogurt
1 tbsp lemon juice
1 package potato gnocchi pasta
paprika to garnish
black pepper to taste

Heat the oil in a skillet over a low heat. Add the shallot and the garlic and very gently cook for 5 minutes. Then add the margarine and the shiitake and stir until the margarine is dissolved. Continue to cook over a low heat until the shiitake give off their liquid. Season, add the thyme, and stir. Add the yogurt and the lemon juice and stir until the sauce is heated through. Cook the gnocchi as indicated on the package. Serve topped with the sauce and garnished with paprika and black pepper.

211 HOUMOUS AND CEP MACARONI

CALORIES	616
CHOLESTEROL	0
VEGAN CALORIES	616
POLYUNSATS	★★☆
ANTIOXIDANTS	★★☆
CALCIUM	★★☆
IRON	★★★
B VITAMINS	★★☆

1 cup garbanzos, cooked or canned
1 clove garlic, crushed
2 tbsp lemon juice
4 tbsp cold water
½ tsp salt
1 tbsp tahini
7oz macaroni pasta
3½ cups fresh cep mushrooms, sliced
1 tbsp olive oil
1 tbsp parsley, finely chopped
1 tsp paprika

Purée the garbanzos with the garlic, lemon juice, water, and salt in a bowl. Add the tahini and purée again to a smooth paste. Adjust the seasoning, and set aside. Cook the macaroni in plenty of boiling water with salt and oil. Meanwhile, thinly slice the ceps and gently stir-fry them in a skillet with the oil, until they begin to brown. Drain the cooked macaroni and mix with the garbanzo paste (houmous). Divide onto two plates and top with the fried ceps. Garnish with parsley and paprika and serve immediately.

212 PASTA WITH PERSILLADE TOPPING

CALORIES	651
CHOLESTEROL	25
VEGAN CALORIES	686
POLYUNSATS	★★☆
ANTIOXIDANTS	★★★
CALCIUM	★★☆
IRON	★★★
B VITAMINS	★★★

5oz lumache (pasta snails)
2 tbsp olive oil
1 red onion, halved and sliced
⅔ cup ham/5oz smoked tempeh, cubed
1 red apple, quartered and cored
1 large tomato
1 handful parsley, finely chopped
2 cloves garlic, crushed
salt and black pepper to taste

Cook the pasta in plenty of boiling water with a little salt and oil. Gently stir-fry the onion in a Dutch oven with the oil for 1 minute. Then add the ham or smoked tempeh and fry for a further 2 minutes. Chop the apple and the tomato and add them to the pan. Heat through. Add the parsley and the garlic, and season. Place the cooked and drained pasta on two large heated plates, top with the sauce, and serve immediately.

213 SPAGHETTI WITH SAUCE TOMATE CONCASSÉ

CALORIES	498
CHOLESTEROL	0
VEGAN CALORIES	498
POLYUNSATS	★☆☆
ANTIOXIDANTS	★★★
CALCIUM	★☆☆
IRON	★★☆
B VITAMINS	★★☆

sauce tomate concassé:
2 tbsp olive oil
1 onion, finely chopped
1 clove garlic, finely chopped
½ tsp sugar
1 pinch dried thyme
1 bay leaf
4 ripe tomatoes, peeled and
    finely chopped

5oz) spaghetti pasta
salt and black pepper to taste

To make the sauce tomate concassé, heat the oil in a Dutch oven and gently fry the onion until soft (don't let it brown). Add the garlic, sugar, thyme, bay leaf, and chopped tomatoes. Bring to a boil, cover and gently simmer for 20 minutes. Meanwhile, cook the spaghetti in plenty of water with a little salt and oil. Drain and season the cooked spaghetti, and serve with the hot sauce tomate concassé.

214 PASTA ALLA PUTTANESCA

CALORIES	524
CHOLESTEROL	19
VEGAN CALORIES	615
POLYUNSATS	★★★
ANTIOXIDANTS	★★★
CALCIUM	★★☆
IRON	★★★
B VITAMINS	★★☆

5oz) spaghetti pasta
2–3 anchovy fillets/4–6 sun-dried
    tomatoes
1 tbsp olive oil
2 cloves garlic, crushed
2 large, ripe tomatoes, chopped

12 black olives, pitted and chopped
1 tbsp capers
1 handful flat-leaf parsley, chopped
1 pinch cayenne pepper
salt and black pepper to taste

Cook the spaghetti in plenty of boiling water with a little salt and oil. Meanwhile, chop the anchovies or sun-dried tomatoes. Heat the oil in a skillet and add the garlic, then the chopped anchovies or sun-dried tomatoes. Stir-fry for 1 minute, add the tomatoes, and cook for 5 minutes. Add the olives, capers, parsley, and cayenne pepper. Season and gently simmer for a few minutes. Drain the cooked spaghetti, place in a large serving dish, and top with the sauce. Serve immediately.

215 CEPS WITH NOODLES

CALORIES	779
CHOLESTEROL	165
VEGAN CALORIES	439
POLYUNSATS	★★★
ANTIOXIDANTS	★★☆
CALCIUM	★☆☆
IRON	★★★
B VITAMINS	★★★

7oz fresh noodles
olive oil for cooking
5 cups fresh, firm cep
    mushrooms, sliced
10oz) pork fillet/

5oz seitan, sliced
1 small clove garlic, crushed
salt and black pepper to taste
1 tbsp parsley, chopped

Cook the noodles in plenty of boiling water with a little salt and oil. Meanwhile, fry the ceps in oil in a non-stick skillet until they give off their liquid. Remove from the skillet and set aside. Fry the pork or seitan slices in the same skillet with a little more oil. Add the ceps and garlic, and season. Mix in the cooked noodles and parsley. Serve on warmed plates.

216 ▼ PAPILLONS WITH CHANTERELLE AND THYME SAUCE

★♥🌾

CALORIES	626
CHOLESTEROL	38
VEGAN CALORIES	560
POLYUNSATS	★★★
ANTIOXIDANTS	★★☆
CALCIUM	★★☆
IRON	★★☆
B VITAMINS	★★☆

7oz papillons (farfalle pasta)
2 tbsp olive oil
½ cup smoked ham/tofu,
    cubed
2 cups fresh chanterelle
    mushrooms, quartered

1 small red onion, finely chopped
1 clove garlic, crushed
2 tbsp crème frâiche/soy cream
1 tsp dried thyme
salt and black pepper to taste

Cook the pasta in plenty of boiling water with a little salt and oil.
Meanwhile, heat the oil in a Dutch oven and stir-fry the ham or tofu,
chanterelles, onion, and garlic over a medium heat for 5 minutes.
Add the cream and the thyme, season and simmer for
a further 5 minutes. Check the seasoning. Place the
cooked pasta in a heated serving dish, top with
the sauce, and serve immediately.

217 RIGATONI WITH CREAM CHEESE AND HERB PANGRATTATO

CALORIES	996
CHOLESTEROL	104
VEGAN CALORIES	679
POLYUNSATS	★★★
ANTIOXIDANTS	★★☆
CALCIUM	★★★
IRON	★★★
B VITAMINS	★★★

1 cup mascarpone/soy cream
  cheese
3–4 tbsp olive oil
4 cloves garlic, crushed
2 tbsp Parmesan/1 tbsp brewer's
  yeast flakes
salt and black pepper to taste

7oz rigatoni pasta (or use macaroni
  pasta)
2 thick slices ciabatta bread,
  coarsely crumbled
1 tsp dried thyme
1 tsp dried oregano

Mix the cream cheese with 1 tablespoon of oil in a bowl. Add 2 cloves of
garlic and the Parmesan or brewer's yeast flakes, and season. Set aside.
Cook the pasta in plenty of boiling water with a little salt and oil. To make
the pangrattato, heat 2–3 tablespoons of oil in a small pan, add the
remaining 2 cloves of garlic and the crumbled bread, and stir-fry until
golden. Add the herbs at the last minute and remove from the heat.
Drain the cooked pasta and mix with the cream cheese sauce. Garnish
with the herb pangrattato, and serve immediately.

218 BUCATINI WITH SEAFOOD

CALORIES	523
CHOLESTEROL	29
VEGAN CALORIES	561
POLYUNSATS	★★☆
ANTIOXIDANTS	★★★
CALCIUM	★★☆
IRON	★★★
B VITAMINS	★★★

1 tbsp olive oil
1 clove garlic, chopped
1 pinch cayenne pepper
1 tbsp oregano, chopped
3 tbsp dry sherry/muscat wine
1 tsp paprika
2 large ripe tomatoes, chopped
1 cup mussel/soy-seaweed
  cooking/soaking liquid

2¼ lb mussels, cooked in shells,
  then shucked and chopped/
  2oz soy chunks, soaked with
  3 tbsp dried seaweed
1 tbsp flat-leaf parsley, chopped
salt and black pepper to taste
7oz bucatini pasta (or use pasta
  of choice)

Gently heat the oil in a pan, add the garlic, cayenne pepper and oregano
and stir-fry for 30 seconds. Then add the sherry or wine and the paprika
and cook for a further 30 seconds. Add the tomatoes, together with the
cooking or soaking liquid, and the soaked soy chunks and seaweed (if
using). Cook for 10 minutes, stirring regularly. Add the parsley, and the
mussels (if using). Season and heat through. Cook the pasta in plenty
of boiling water with a little salt and oil. Drain and add to the sauce.
Serve immediately.

219 SPAGHETTI WITH BROCCOLI IN YOGURT AND BASIL SAUCE

CALORIES	504
CHOLESTEROL	22
VEGAN CALORIES	494
POLYUNSATS	★★☆
ANTIOXIDANTS	★★☆
CALCIUM	★★★
IRON	★★★
B VITAMINS	★★☆

7oz spaghetti pasta
1 head broccoli, cut into florets
1 tbsp Dijon mustard
½ cup plain/soy yogurt

1 knob vegetable margarine or butter
½ small red onion, finely chopped
1 clove garlic, crushed
a handful of basil, finely chopped

Cook the spaghetti in plenty of boiling water with a little salt and olive oil. Add the broccoli to the pan for the last 4–5 minutes of the cooking time. Mix the mustard, yogurt, and margarine or butter in a bowl. Add the onion, garlic, and basil, season well, and set aside. Drain the spaghetti and broccoli in a colander. Put the sauce mixture into the pan and gently heat. Add the drained spaghetti and broccoli, and mix. Serve with a green side salad.

220 CORN PASTA AND SPINACH WITH OLIVE PASTE

CALORIES	632
CHOLESTEROL	36
VEGAN CALORIES	559
POLYUNSATS	★★★
ANTIOXIDANTS	★★★
CALCIUM	★★★
IRON	★★★
B VITAMINS	★★☆

6 cups fresh spinach, chopped
½ cup milk/soy milk
1 pinch nutmeg
salt and black pepper to taste
7oz corn pasta

⅔ cup black Niçoise olives
2 cloves garlic, chopped
2 tbsp basil, chopped
2 tbsp parsley, chopped
½ cup ricotta/soy cheese

Gently cook the spinach in a pan with a little water until soft. Add the milk and nutmeg, and heat through. Season and set aside. Cook the pasta in plenty of boiling water with a little salt and oil. Pit and finely chop the olives and mix with the garlic and herbs. Drain the cooked pasta and mix with the spinach. Then place in a serving bowl and top with the olive paste. Crumble the cheese and sprinkle over the pasta. Serve immediately.

221 PASTA FORESTIÈRE

CALORIES	823
CHOLESTEROL	125
VEGAN CALORIES	597
POLYUNSATS	★★☆
ANTIOXIDANTS	★★☆
CALCIUM	★☆☆
IRON	★★☆
B VITAMINS	★★☆

7oz fresh pasta of choice
oil for frying
10oz venison medallions/
    5oz seitan pieces
1 shallot, chopped
½ cup red wine

10 juniper berries
½ cup stock
1oz dried cep mushrooms, soaked
    in a bowl of warm water
1 tbsp crème fraîche/soy cream

Cook the pasta in plenty of boiling water with a little salt and oil. Heat some oil in a skillet and fry the venison or seitan until lightly browned. Set aside (keep warm). Add a little more oil to the pan and fry the shallot until soft, then add the wine and the juniper berries. Cook until the liquid is reduced by half its volume. Add the stock. Drain and rinse the ceps and add to the sauce. Cook until the liquid is reduced by half again. Add the cream, heat through, season, and cook until the sauce thickens. Serve the pasta and the venison or seitan on warmed plates, topped with the sauce.

222 ▲ PERUVIAN POLENTA CAKES

CALORIES	389
CHOLESTEROL	0
VEGAN CALORIES	389
POLYUNSATS	★★★
ANTIOXIDANTS	★★★
CALCIUM	★☆☆
IRON	★★☆
B VITAMINS	★★☆

10oz cooked polenta
1 fresh red chili, finely chopped
2 tbsp cilantro, finely chopped
½ tsp salt
approximately 1 cup
    boiling water
corn oil for frying

1 large tomato, diced
1 cucumber, grated
1 red bell pepper, quartered and
    sliced
2 tbsp lemon juice
1 tsp raw cane sugar
salt to taste

Place the polenta in a bowl. Add the chili, cilantro, and salt and mix
well. Gradually pour in the boiling water and stir to a thick consistency.
Let stand for 5 minutes, then mold the mixture with wet hands to make
twelve 2in x ½in round cakes. Fry the cakes in a skillet over a medium heat
with a little oil until golden, turning them frequently to prevent sticking.
Make the relish by mixing the tomato, cucumber, red bell pepper, lemon
juice, sugar, and salt. Serve the cakes hot with the relish.

223 EGYPTIAN CASSEROLE

CALORIES	348
CHOLESTEROL	0
VEGAN CALORIES	348
POLYUNSATS	★★☆
ANTIOXIDANTS	★★☆
CALCIUM	★☆☆
IRON	★★☆
B VITAMINS	★★☆

2 tbsp olive oil
1 leek, sliced
1 potato, diced
1 beet, diced
1 tsp ground cumin

½ cup red lentils
1 cup vegetable stock
2 tbsp lemon juice
salt and black pepper to taste
2 tbsp parsley, chopped

Heat the oil in a Dutch oven and gently stir-fry the leek, potato, and beet with the cumin for 5 minutes. Add the lentils and stir for a further 30 seconds, then add the stock. Bring to a boil, cover, and gently simmer until the lentils are soft, approximately 15 minutes. Stir from time to time (adding a little water, if necessary). Add the lemon juice, season, garnish with parsley, and serve with couscous, bulgur wheat or rice.

224 JAPANESE GOHAN

CALORIES	149
CHOLESTEROL	0
VEGAN CALORIES	149
POLYUNSATS	★★☆
ANTIOXIDANTS	★★☆
CALCIUM	★★★
IRON	★★☆
B VITAMINS	★★☆

1 cup tofu, cubed
1 tbsp tamari (soy sauce)
1 tbsp mirin or dry sherry
2 tsp sesame oil
1 pinch raw cane sugar
1¾oz cups shiitake mushrooms, sliced

2¼ cups vegetable stock
2¼ cups fresh spinach, cut into strips
½ tsp ginger, finely grated
1 scallion, finely sliced
salt to taste
4 thin slices lemon

Place the tofu cubes in a Dutch oven, add the tamari, mirin or sherry, sesame oil, and sugar and, mix well. Add the shiitake, mix again, and bring to a simmer. Cover and cook for 1 minute. Add the stock and spinach and very gently simmer for 3–4 minutes. Add the ginger and scallion, and heat through. Season, garnish with lemon slices, and serve with rice.

225 BRAZILIAN FEIJOADA

CALORIES	537
CHOLESTEROL	33
VEGAN CALORIES	447
POLYUNSATS	★★☆
ANTIOXIDANTS	★★★
CALCIUM	★★☆
IRON	★★★
B VITAMINS	★★★

2 cloves garlic, crushed
1 bay leaf
1 tsp paprika
1 tsp dried thyme
1 tsp ground cumin
1 leek, sliced
1 sweet potato, cubed
approximately 1 cup vegetable stock
oil for frying

½ cup bacon/smoked tofu
2⅓ cups black beans, cooked or canned
1 red bell pepper, deseeded and sliced
3 tomatoes, crushed
1 small bunch parsley and chives, finely chopped
salt and black pepper to taste
1 orange, thinly sliced

Place the garlic, spices, leek, and sweet potato in a medium Dutch oven. Cover with the stock, bring to a boil and simmer over a medium heat for 10 minutes. Meanwhile, heat a little oil in a skillet and stir-fry the bacon or smoked tofu and the beans for 2 minutes. Then add the red bell pepper, tomatoes, parsley, and chives, and stir-fry over a medium heat for a further 5 minutes. Add the bean mixture to the vegetables and heat through. Season, garnish with orange slices, and serve with rice.

226 LOUISIANA GUMBO

CALORIES	355
CHOLESTEROL	25
VEGAN CALORIES	287
POLYUNSATS	★★★
ANTIOXIDANTS	★★★
CALCIUM	★★☆
IRON	★★☆
B VITAMINS	★★☆

1 tbsp corn oil
1 small red onion, halved and sliced
1 bay leaf
1 pinch cayenne pepper
1 tsp paprika
½ green bell pepper, sliced
½ red bell pepper, sliced
1 stick celery, sliced

⅔ cup hokaido pumpkin, peeled, deseeded and chopped
1 tbsp wheat flour
3 tomatoes, chopped
1 cup vegetable stock
½ cup smoked sausage (meat/soy), sliced
salt and plenty of black pepper

Heat the oil in a heavy-based Dutch oven and gently sweat the onion with the spices. Add the bell pepper slices, followed by the celery and the pumpkin. Gently stir-fry for 3–5 minutes. Sprinkle with flour and stir for 1 minute to coat the vegetables. Add the tomatoes, stir, then add the stock. Bring to a boil, cover, and simmer for 10 minutes. Add the sausage and heat through. Season and serve with rice.

227 FLORENTINE SPINACH BAKE

CALORIES	763
CHOLESTEROL	74
VEGAN CALORIES	595
POLYUNSATS	★★★
ANTIOXIDANTS	★★★
CALCIUM	★★★
IRON	★★☆
B VITAMINS	★★☆

2 cups cooked rice
2 tbsp olive oil
1 small leek, sliced
6 cups fresh spinach, chopped
½ cup crème fraîche/soy cream

1 pinch nutmeg
salt and black pepper to taste
½ green bell pepper, sliced
2 ripe tomatoes, cut into boats
½ cup Emmental/soy cheese, grated

Preheat the oven to 220°C/425°F/gas mark 7. Press the cooked rice into the bottom of a large, flat, greased baking dish. Heat the oil in a Dutch oven and gently stir-fry the leek for 4–5 minutes. Add the spinach and cook until it is wilted. Then add the cream and heat through (don't let it boil). Add the nutmeg, and season. Spoon the spinach mixture over the rice and top with green bell pepper and tomato. Sprinkle with the grated cheese and bake in a hot oven until golden. Serve immediately.

228 AFRICAN CURRY

CALORIES	983
CHOLESTEROL	220
VEGAN CALORIES	743
POLYUNSATS	★★☆
ANTIOXIDANTS	★★☆
CALCIUM	★★☆
IRON	★★★
B VITAMINS	★★★

2 tbsp olive oil
2 cups pork fillet/14 oz tempeh, cut into chunks
1 tbsp curry powder
1 onion, halved and sliced
½ red bell pepper, sliced

1 clove garlic, crushed
1 cup coconut milk
1 apple, peeled, cored, and diced
salt and cayenne pepper to taste

Heat the oil in a Dutch oven. Add the pork or tempeh chunks, and half the curry powder. Stir-fry over a medium–high heat until the pork or tempeh chunks begin to brown. Remove from the pan and set aside. Stir-fry the onion, red bell pepper, and garlic in the same pan with the remaining curry powder (and a little more oil, if necessary). Add the coconut milk, apple, and cooked pork or tempeh. Bring to a boil and simmer for 5 minutes. Season and serve with rice.

229 ◄ KERALA CURRY WITH MANGO AND COCONUT
★♥▢

CALORIES	644
CHOLESTEROL	123
VEGAN CALORIES	608
POLYUNSATS	★★☆
ANTIOXIDANTS	★★★
CALCIUM	★★☆
IRON	★★★
B VITAMINS	★★★

2 tbsp olive oil
1 small onion, halved and sliced
1 clove garlic, crushed
1 tsp ginger, chopped
1½ cups chicken breast/6oz
tempeh, diced
1–2 tsp curry powder to taste
1 ripe mango, halved, pitted, peeled
and diced
1 cup coconut milk
1–2 tsp lemon juice (to taste)
salt and plenty of black pepper
water (optional)
1 handful cilantro leaves,
chopped

Heat the oil in a heavy-based pan or wok and gently stir-fry the onion and garlic until they begin to soften. Add the ginger and the chicken or tempeh and fry until the chicken or tempeh begins to brown. Add the curry powder and mix well before adding the mango and the coconut milk. Season and very gently simmer for 5–7 minutes. (You may need to add a little water to prevent the curry from drying.) Garnish with cilantro leaves, and serve with rice and/or chapati bread.

230 BOLIVIAN PALTA RELLEÑOS
★✖▢▢

CALORIES	369
CHOLESTEROL	140
VEGAN CALORIES	490
POLYUNSATS	★★★
ANTIOXIDANTS	★★★
CALCIUM	★★☆
IRON	★★☆
B VITAMINS	★★☆

2 avocados, halved and pitted
½ banana, peeled and diced
2 tbsp lemon juice
¼ small onion, finely chopped
½ green chili pepper, finely
chopped
1 tomato, finely chopped
½ tsp paprika
salt and cayenne pepper
to taste
½ cup shrimp, peeled and
cooked/½ cup Brazil nuts,
chopped

Scoop out the avocado flesh and place it in a bowl. Add the banana, lemon juice, onion, chili, tomato, and paprika. Gently mix and season. Spoon the mixture back into the avocado shells, garnish with shrimp or Brazil nuts, and serve immediately.

231 LEBANESE GREEN BEANS WITH POMEGRANATE
♥◗✖

CALORIES	226
CHOLESTEROL	0
VEGAN CALORIES	226
POLYUNSATS	★☆☆
ANTIOXIDANTS	★★☆
CALCIUM	★☆☆
IRON	★★☆
B VITAMINS	★☆☆

2¼ cups green beans, topped
and tailed
2 pomegranates, peeled and white
skin removed
2 tbsp olive oil
1 clove garlic, crushed
1 tbsp flat-leaf parsley,
chopped
salt to taste

Place the beans in a pan with as little boiling, salted water as possible, and cook over a low heat until tender. Drain and place in a serving bowl. Top with the pomegranate. Mix the oil and garlic with the chopped parsley in a small bowl, then pour the mixture over the beans and pomegranate. Gently mix, and serve with rice or flat Arabic bread.

232 CARIBBEAN CASSEROLE ★♥

CALORIES	530
CHOLESTEROL	37
VEGAN CALORIES	513
POLYUNSATS	★★☆
ANTIOXIDANTS	★★★
CALCIUM	★★★
IRON	★★★
B VITAMINS	★★☆

2 tbsp olive oil
1 sweet potato, peeled
   and diced
½ lb Savoy cabbage, chopped
1 cup hokaido pumpkin, peeled,
   deseeded and diced
2 cups fresh spinach, chopped
1 strip kombu seaweed, soaked in
   ½ cup water for 10 minutes
and chopped
1 tsp turmeric dissolved in 1 cup
   coconut milk
1 tsp dried thyme
1 tbsp parsley, chopped
salt and black pepper to taste
1¼ cups cod fillet/tofu, cut
   into chunks

Gently heat the oil in a heavy-based Dutch oven and stir-fry the sweet potato, Savoy cabbage, and pumpkin for 3 minutes until the cabbage begins to soften. Add the spinach, together with the seaweed and its soaking water, followed by the tumeric and coconut milk. Sprinkle over the thyme and parsley, and season. Bring to a boil, cover with a tight-fitting lid and simmer for 10 minutes. Add the cod or tofu chunks, and sprinkle with a little more salt. Cover and simmer for a further 5 minutes, then remove the lid, turn up the heat a little, and let the liquid reduce for 1 minute. Serve with rice.

233 KUWAITI OKRA ★♥◐▣◉◻

CALORIES	208
CHOLESTEROL	0
VEGAN CALORIES	208
POLYUNSATS	★☆☆
ANTIOXIDANTS	★★☆
CALCIUM	★★☆
IRON	★★☆
B VITAMINS	★★☆

2 tbsp olive oil
2 cloves garlic, crushed
10oz fresh okra (lady's
   fingers), trimmed
2 tomatoes, chopped
¼ cup water
1 pinch ground coriander
salt and cayenne pepper
   to taste
1 squeeze lemon juice

234 CHUNKY NORTH-INDIAN CURRY ★♥▣◉

CALORIES	365
CHOLESTEROL	55
VEGAN CALORIES	292
POLYUNSATS	★★☆
ANTIOXIDANTS	★★☆
CALCIUM	★☆☆
IRON	★★☆
B VITAMINS	★★☆

½ tsp cayenne pepper
1 tsp turmeric
1 tsp ground cumin
1 tsp ground coriander
2 tbsp olive oil
½ cup lamb fillet chunks/
1oz soy chunks (dry weight),
   soaked and drained
1 large eggplant, diced
2 potatoes, diced
1 tsp ginger, finely chopped
3 tomatoes, puréed

Place a dry Dutch oven or a wok over a medium heat, add the spices and stir for 10 seconds. Then add the oil and the lamb or soy chunks and stir for 1 minute before adding the eggplant and the potatoes. (If you are using soy chunks, you may need to add more oil at this point.) Stir-fry for a further 2 minutes, then add the ginger and the puréed tomatoes. Heat through, cover, and simmer for 15 minutes. Serve with rice.

235 ▼ EGGLESS SEAFOOD OMELET

CALORIES	491
CHOLESTEROL	0
VEGAN CALORIES	491
POLYUNSATS	★★★
ANTIOXIDANTS	★★★
CALCIUM	★★☆
IRON	★★☆
B VITAMINS	★★☆

batter:
⅔ cup wheat flour
1 tbsp brewer's yeast flakes
1 tsp baking powder
1 pinch saffron threads
¼ tsp salt
1 cup soy/rice milk
1 tsp olive oil, plus some for frying

filling:
1 sweet potato, chopped into
   thin sticks
1¾ cups fresh shiitake
   mushrooms, sliced
1 tbsp hiziki seaweed, soaked in hot
   water
1 tbsp tahini
salt and black pepper to taste
toasted ground salted sesame
   seeds (gomasio)

Mix the flour, brewer's yeast flakes, baking powder, saffron, and salt in
a bowl. Add the milk and the oil, and whisk to make a smooth batter. Set
aside. To prepare the filling, stir-fry the sweet potato and the shiitake in
a skillet with a little hot oil. Add the seaweed with a little of its soaking
water and cook for 5 minutes, then add the tahini, season, and sprinkle
over the toasted sesame seeds. Set aside (keep warm). Add the batter
to a clean, oiled skillet and cook over a medium heat until the top is dry.
Turn and cook the other side. Remove from the heat, top with the filling,
fold and serve.

236 FALL MUSHROOM OMELET

CALORIES	313
CHOLESTEROL	391
VEGAN CALORIES	322
POLYUNSATS	★★☆
ANTIOXIDANTS	★★☆
CALCIUM	★☆☆
IRON	★★☆
B VITAMINS	★★★

omelet:
4 eggs, beaten
salt and black pepper to taste
or 1 portion basic eggless omelet
     batter (see p.41)
olive oil for frying

topping:
1 small leek, sliced
3½ cups fresh cep mushrooms,
     sliced
1 tsp thyme

Mix your chosen batter ingredients and set aside. Gently stir-fry the leek in a skillet with a little oil until it begins to soften. Add the ceps and the thyme, and stir-fry for 3–5 minutes. Set aside. Pour the batter into an oiled skillet over a medium heat and cook until the top is dry. Turn and cook the other side. Remove from the heat, add the topping, and serve.

237 OMELET SANDWICH

CALORIES	366
CHOLESTEROL	418
VEGAN CALORIES	351
POLYUNSATS	★★★
ANTIOXIDANTS	★★★
CALCIUM	★★☆
IRON	★★☆
B VITAMINS	★★★

omelet:
4 eggs
a little milk/water
salt and black pepper to taste
or 1 portion basic eggless omelet
     batter (see p.41)
oil for frying

filling:
1 small red onion, finely chopped
1 small red bell pepper, finely
     chopped
½ cup bacon/smoked tempeh, diced
1 tbsp hazelnut butter
2 tbsp parsley, chopped
1 clove garlic, crushed

Mix your chosen batter ingredients in a bowl and add the red onion and red bell pepper to the batter. Fry the bacon or tempeh cubes and set aside (keep warm). Make two thin omelets out of the one mixture, and cook them in a clean, oiled skillet over a medium heat. Place the first omelet on a warmed serving plate, top with the bacon or tempeh cubes, and cover with the second omelet. Spread the hazelnut butter on top, then mix the parsley and garlic, and sprinkle over. Serve hot with tomato sauce.

238 OMELET WITH PINE KERNELS AND PARSLEY

CALORIES	401
CHOLESTEROL	391
VEGAN CALORIES	410
POLYUNSATS	★★★
ANTIOXIDANTS	★★☆
CALCIUM	★★☆
IRON	★★☆
B VITAMINS	★★☆

omelet:
4 eggs
a little milk/water
salt and black pepper to taste
or 1 portion basic eggless omelet
     batter (see p.41)
oil for frying

filling:
2 tbsp pine kernels
1 shallot, finely chopped
2 tbsp parsley

Mix your chosen batter ingredients in a bowl. Add the pine kernels, chopped shallot, and parsley to the batter and stir. Heat 1 tablespoon of oil in a skillet and pour in the omelet mixture. Reduce the heat and cook until the underside is firm and slightly brown. Turn and cook the other side. Serve hot with a tomato salad.

239 SPINACH PANCAKES WITH HOUMOUS AND MUSHROOMS

CALORIES	594
CHOLESTEROL	112
VEGAN CALORIES	524
POLYUNSATS	★★☆
ANTIOXIDANTS	★★☆
CALCIUM	★★☆
IRON	★★☆
B VITAMINS	★★★

pancakes:
1 portion basic pancake batter
(see p.42)
4½ cups fresh spinach, chopped,
cooked and drained
olive oil for frying

filling:
10oz fresh cep (or other wild)
mushrooms, chopped
2 cloves garlic, crushed
½ cup houmous
salt and black pepper to taste

Mix the batter. Add the spinach and mix well. Heat a little oil in a skillet and cook the pancakes over a medium–low heat. Add more oil to a separate pan and stir-fry the ceps with the garlic. Spread a spoonful of houmous over each pancake, add the seasoned ceps, fold and serve hot.

240 GARBANZO AND LEEK PANCAKES

CALORIES	664
CHOLESTEROL	112
VEGAN CALORIES	594
POLYUNSATS	★★★
ANTIOXIDANTS	★★★
CALCIUM	★★☆
IRON	★★★
B VITAMINS	★★★

pancakes:
1 generous cup wheat flour
1 egg/1 tbsp baking powder
1 pinch salt
1 cup milk/soy milk
1 cup water
1 tbsp grapeseed oil, plus some
for frying

filling:
1 leek, finely chopped
1½ cups garbanzos, cooked or
canned
1 bay leaf
1 tsp turmeric and 1 pinch cinnamon
1 green bell pepper, finely chopped
½ cup vegetable stock

Place the flour, baking powder or egg, and salt in a bowl and mix well. Add the milk, water, and oil, and whisk until smooth. Set aside. Stir-fry the leek in a Dutch oven with a little oil until soft. Add the garbanzos and spices and stir-fry for 2 minutes. Add the bell pepper and heat through, then add the stock. Bring to a boil and gently simmer while you fry six–eight pancakes in a skillet with a little oil. Fill the pancakes, roll and serve hot.

241 BUCKWHEAT PANCAKES

CALORIES	622
CHOLESTEROL	119
VEGAN CALORIES	529
POLYUNSATS	★★★
ANTIOXIDANTS	★★★
CALCIUM	★★☆
IRON	★★☆
B VITAMINS	★★☆

pancakes:
1 cup buckwheat flour
1 pinch salt
1 egg/2 tsp baking powder
1¼ cups milk/soy milk
grapeseed oil for frying

filling:
1 small onion, finely chopped
1 tsp cinnamon
2 tbsp pine kernels
2 carrots and 1 zucchini, grated
1 clove garlic, chopped
1 tbsp parsley, chopped
2 slices lemon, peeled and chopped

Mix the flour, salt, and baking powder or egg in a bowl. Add the milk little by little until you have a thick batter. Heat a little oil in a skillet and fry 6–8 pancakes over a medium–high heat. Gently heat a little oil in a Dutch oven and stir-fry the onion, cinnamon, and pine kernels for 3 minutes. Add the zucchini and carrot and stir-fry for a further 3 minutes. Add the garlic, parsley, and lemon. Season and serve with the pancakes.

242 CORN PANCAKES WITH KIDNEY BEAN FILLING

CALORIES	822
CHOLESTEROL	13
VEGAN CALORIES	798
POLYUNSATS	★★★
ANTIOXIDANTS	★★☆
CALCIUM	★★☆
IRON	★★☆
B VITAMINS	★★☆

pancakes:
1 cup cornstarch
1 cup wheat flour
1 tbsp baking powder
½ tsp salt
2 tbsp corn oil
1¼ cups water

filling:
1 shallot, finely chopped
1 tsp each of cumin and coriander
1½ cups red kidney beans, cooked or canned
1 small sweet potato, diced
½ cup water
salt and black pepper to taste
3 tbsp cheese/soy cheese, grated
corn oil for frying

Mix the two flours with the baking powder, salt, corn oil, and water in a bowl, and whisk until smooth. Set aside. Gently stir-fry the shallot in a Dutch oven with a little oil until soft. Add the spices, kidney beans, and sweet potato. Stir-fry over a medium heat for 5 minutes, then add the water, and season. Let simmer while you heat a little more oil in a skillet and fry six pancakes. Gently mash the sweet potato and some of the beans with a potato masher. Divide the filling among the pancakes. Sprinkle with grated cheese and serve hot.

243 TOMATO AND GARLIC PIZZA

CALORIES	556
CHOLESTEROL	29
VEGAN CALORIES	503
POLYUNSATS	★★☆
ANTIOXIDANTS	★★☆
CALCIUM	★★☆
IRON	★★☆
B VITAMINS	★★☆

1 pizza base
1 cup mozzarella/soy cheese
4 ripe tomatoes, chopped
4 cloves garlic, sliced and mixed
with 1 tbsp olive oil
10 black olives
salt and black pepper to taste
2 tbsp basil, chopped

Preheat the oven to 240°C/475°F/gas mark 9 and warm a baking sheet. Cut the cheese into cubes. Set aside. Spread the tomatoes over the pizza base and add a pinch of salt. Top with the garlic, cheese cubes, and olives. Season and bake in a hot oven for approximately 15 minutes. Garnish with basil and more black pepper. Serve hot.

244 ◄ PIZZA BROIL

CALORIES	462
CHOLESTEROL	29
VEGAN CALORIES	409
POLYUNSATS	★★☆
ANTIOXIDANTS	★★☆
CALCIUM	★★☆
IRON	★★☆
B VITAMINS	★★☆

French baguette (halved lengthwise) or 2 bagels (split), or 2 pitta bread
2 tbsp tomato sauce, passata, or sauce tomate concassé (see p.115)
1 cup mozzarella/soy cheese,
grated
1 tomato, sliced
1 small red onion, sliced
¼ red bell pepper, sliced
1 small fresh hot chili, sliced
2 cloves garlic, crushed
1 tbsp basil, chopped

Preheat the broiler and broil the underside of the bread. Turn and spread the tomato sauce over the uncooked side. Cover with the grated cheese and the remaining topping ingredients, and season. Broil for 4–5 minutes, or until the cheese has melted. Garnish with basil and serve

245 PIZZA A LA PIZZAIOLA

CALORIES	511
CHOLESTEROL	37
VEGAN CALORIES	447
POLYUNSATS	★★☆
ANTIOXIDANTS	★★★
CALCIUM	★★★
IRON	★★☆
B VITAMINS	★★☆

1 pizza base
3 tbsp tomato sauce, passata, or
  sauce tomate concassé
  (see p.115)
1 tsp dried thyme
1 tsp dried marjoram
1 bay leaf, crushed
1 clove garlic, crushed

¼ green bell pepper, finely sliced
¼ red bell pepper, finely sliced
¼ yellow bell pepper, finely sliced
¼ cup smoked ham/smoked tofu,
  thinly sliced
salt and black pepper to taste
1 cup mozzarella/soy cheese,
  grated

Preheat the oven to 240°C/475°F/gas mark 9 and warm a baking sheet. Spread the tomato sauce over the pizza base. Sprinkle with the thyme, marjoram, bay leaf, and garlic. Arrange the bell pepper slices and the smoked ham or smoked tofu on top. Season, sprinkle with the cheese and bake in a hot oven for approximately 15 minutes. Serve hot with a side salad.

246 FALL SPECIAL

CALORIES	618
CHOLESTEROL	62
VEGAN CALORIES	518
POLYUNSATS	★★☆
ANTIOXIDANTS	★★☆
CALCIUM	★★★
IRON	★★★
B VITAMINS	★★★

1 pizza base
2–3 tbsp tomato sauce, passata, or
  sauce tomate concassé
  (see p.115)
2½ cups fresh spinach, sautéed
2½ cups wild mushrooms
  (as available), chopped
2 cloves garlic, crushed

1 shallot, chopped
4 slices pancetta or bacon/smoked
  tempeh, fried
salt and black pepper to taste
1 cup mozzarella/soy cheese,
  grated
1 tbsp grated Parmesan/brewer's
  yeast flakes

Preheat the oven to 220°C/425°F/gas mark 7 and warm a baking sheet. Spread the tomato sauce over the pizza base. Cover with the sautéed spinach, wild mushrooms, garlic, shallot, and pancetta or bacon or smoked tempeh. Season, sprinkle with the grated cheese or brewer's yeast flakes, and bake in a hot oven for approximately 20 minutes. Serve hot with a side salad.

247 PIZZA AL FUNGHI

CALORIES	518
CHOLESTEROL	46
VEGAN CALORIES	488
POLYUNSATS	★★☆
ANTIOXIDANTS	★★☆
CALCIUM	★★☆
IRON	★★☆
B VITAMINS	★★★

1 pizza base
2–3 tbsp tomato sauce, passata, or
  sauce tomate concassé
  (see p.115)
½ small hot chili, finely chopped
4 mushrooms, sliced

½ cup ham/3oz tempeh, diced
1 scallion, sliced
a little oregano
salt and black pepper to taste
1 cup mozzarella/soy cheese,
  grated

Preheat the oven to 240°C/475°F/gas mark 9 and warm a baking sheet. Spread the tomato sauce over the pizza base and top with the hot chili, mushroom slices, ham or tempeh cubes, and scallion slices, then add a sprinkling of oregano. Season, sprinkle with the grated cheese, and bake in a hot oven for approximately 15 minutes. Serve hot with a side salad.

248 RICH CEP CASSEROLE
★✕✇

CALORIES	315
CHOLESTEROL	42
VEGAN CALORIES	298
POLYUNSATS	★★☆
ANTIOXIDANTS	★★☆
CALCIUM	★★☆
IRON	★★☆
B VITAMINS	★★☆

2 tbsp olive oil
1 small red onion, halved and sliced
½ cup venison steak, sliced into
   chunks/2oz soy chunks
   (dry weight), rehydrated
4½ cups fresh cep mushrooms,
   sliced into chunks
1 slice celery root, chopped

⅓ cup red wine
1¼ cups vegetable stock
1 tbsp tomato paste
5 black olives, pitted and chopped
1 tbsp red wine vinegar
1 tbsp tamari (soy sauce)
1 tsp dried thyme
salt and black pepper to taste

Heat the oil in a heavy-based Dutch oven and cook the onion over a medium heat for 1 minute. Add the venison chunks or soy chunks, turn up the heat and fry until they begin to brown, then add the ceps and fry for a further 2–3 minutes over a medium heat. Add the celery root, red wine and stock, and heat through before adding the tomato paste, olives, vinegar, tamari, and thyme. Stir, bring to a boil and gently simmer for 15 minutes. Season and serve with rice.

249 SPICY RAGOÛT
★✦✇

CALORIES	483
CHOLESTEROL	83
VEGAN CALORIES	357
POLYUNSATS	★★☆
ANTIOXIDANTS	★★★
CALCIUM	★★☆
IRON	★★☆
B VITAMINS	★★★

olive oil for frying
⅔ cup pork/5oz seitan, sliced
1 red onion, halved and sliced
2½ cups oyster mushrooms,
   sliced
1 sweet potato, cut into sticks
1 small zucchini, cut into sticks

1 small eggplant, cut into sticks
1 large tomato, finely chopped
½ tsp ground cinnamon
1 bay leaf
1 pinch turmeric
1 pinch cayenne pepper
½ cup vegetable stock

Heat some oil in a Dutch oven and fry the pork or seitan until brown. Add the onion and the mushrooms and stir for 3 minutes, then add the sweet potato, zucchini, and eggplant, and stir for a further 2 minutes. Add the tomato and the spices and, heat through. Heat the stock and add it to the pan. Season, bring to a boil, cover, and simmer for 10–15 minutes. Check the seasoning and serve with boiled or baked potatoes.

250 FALL BROIL
★✇◻

CALORIES	587
CHOLESTEROL	168
VEGAN CALORIES	629
POLYUNSATS	★★★
ANTIOXIDANTS	★★★
CALCIUM	★★☆
IRON	★★☆
B VITAMINS	★★★

2 ears of corn, sliced into chunks
1 yellow bell pepper, quartered
4 cep (or other) mushrooms,
   sliced
4 small tomatoes
1 sweet potato, cut into thick sticks
12 large shrimp/chestnuts

olive oil for brushing
salt and black pepper to taste
⅔ cup tomato catsup
2 tbsp lemon juice
⅓ cup red wine vinegar
1 tbsp raw cane sugar
1 tbsp mustard

Brush the ears of corn, yellow bell pepper, mushrooms, tomatoes, sweet potato, and shrimp (if using) with the oil and cook them on a hot grill with the shelled and peeled chestnuts (if using), then season. Meanwhile, make the barbecue sauce by mixing the tomato catsup, lemon juice, vinegar, sugar, and mustard. Serve the vegetables hot with the sauce.

251 ▼ BULGUR PILAF

CALORIES	440
CHOLESTEROL	17
VEGAN CALORIES	441
POLYUNSATS	★★★
ANTIOXIDANTS	★★★
CALCIUM	★★☆
IRON	★★☆
B VITAMINS	★★☆

2 tbsp grapeseed oil
½ cup smoked ham/⅔ cup garbanzos, cooked or canned
1 tbsp tamari (soy sauce) (optional)
½ cup bulgur wheat
1 cup hot water

½ cup green peas
salt and black pepper to taste
½ small red onion, finely chopped
½ lemon, peeled and chopped
10–12 small grape tomatoes, quartered
2–3 tbsp mint, finely chopped

Gently sweat the ham or garbanzos in a skillet with 1 tablespoon of oil until they begin to brown. Add the tamari (if using), then the bulgur wheat and stir-fry for 2–3 minutes. Pour in the water and simmer at the lowest possible heat for 10–12 minutes, adding the peas after 5 minutes. Stir from time to time (adding a little more water, if necessary). Remove from the heat and season. Add the onion, lemon, tomatoes and mint, and sprinkle with the remaining tablespoon of oil. Serve immediately.

252 TARTLETS PROVENÇALE

CALORIES	772
CHOLESTEROL	525
VEGAN CALORIES	663
POLYUNSATS	★★★
ANTIOXIDANTS	★★★
CALCIUM	★★☆
IRON	★★★
B VITAMINS	★★★

4oz ready-made tart dough,
  rolled out
10oz chicken liver, cut into strips/
  6oz tempeh, cut into chunks
1 sweet potato, cut into thin sticks
2 tbsp all-purpose flour
salt and black pepper to taste

olive oil for frying
1 small clove garlic, chopped
2 tbsp tomato paste
10 black olives, halved and pitted
½ cup vegetable stock
1 tbsp parsley, chopped

Use the tart dough to line two individual 4in round tart pans. Spread
a handful of dried beans or lentils over each one and bake at 220°C/
425°F/gas mark 7 until firm, 10–15 minutes. Let cool and remove the
beans. Meanwhile, flour the liver or tempeh, and the sweet potato,
season, and fry in a skillet with a little oil for 5 minutes. Add the garlic
and stir for 30 seconds before adding the tomato paste and the olives.
Then add the stock, heat the sauce, and let it thicken. Fill the tartlets with
the sauce and heat in the oven for 2 minutes. Garnish with parsley, and
serve with a seasonal salad (such as lamb's lettuce or arugula) and
vinaigrette dressing.

253 FALL CASSEROLE

CALORIES	559
CHOLESTEROL	88
VEGAN CALORIES	524
POLYUNSATS	★★☆
ANTIOXIDANTS	★★★
CALCIUM	★★☆
IRON	★★☆
B VITAMINS	★★☆

1¼ cups chicken breast, sliced/
  2oz soy chunks (dry weight),
  soaked and drained
1 tbsp maple syrup
1 tbsp tomato paste
1 tsp paprika
1 tsp ground cumin
seeds from 2 cardamom pods
1 tbsp tamari (soy sauce)
1 tbsp red wine vinegar

1 dash Tabasco sauce
2 tbsp olive oil
2 shallots, quartered
4 cloves garlic, quartered
½ lemon, cut into wedges
2 large sweet potatoes, sliced
salt and black pepper to taste
1 handful parsley, chopped
1 tsp maple syrup or raw cane sugar
  (optional)

In a bowl, marinate the chicken or soy chunks in the maple syrup, tomato
paste, paprika, cumin, cardamom seeds, tamari, vinegar, Tabasco sauce,
and 1 tablespoon of oil. Set aside. Gently heat the remaining tablespoon
of oil in a Dutch oven and stir-fry the shallots for 3 minutes. Add the
marinated chicken or soy chunks with their marinade and cook over
a medium heat for 5 minutes. Then add the garlic, lemon, and sweet
potatoes and heat through. Cover and simmer for 15 minutes or until
the chicken is tender. (Add a little water if necessary.) Season and garnish
with the parsley and maple syrup or sugar (if using). Serve with rice.

254 NORMANDIE SUPRÊME

CALORIES	581
CHOLESTEROL	292
VEGAN CALORIES	368
POLYUNSATS	★★★
ANTIOXIDANTS	★★☆
CALCIUM	★☆☆
IRON	★★☆
B VITAMINS	★★☆

vegetable oil for frying
2 pheasant breasts/6oz
    seitan, cut into strips
2 apples
1 pinch sugar
salt and black pepper to taste

¼ cup apple cider
½ cup stock
¼ cup crème fraîche/soy
    cream
4 tsp Calvados (apple brandy)

Fry the pheasant breasts or seitan strips in a skillet with a little oil. Remove from the pan and set aside (keep hot). Core and quarter the apples, then sauté them in the same skillet with a little more oil and the sugar and seasoning until they begin to brown. Remove from the skillet. Set aside. Add the cider and the stock to the skillet and let reduce by half the volume. Add the cream and the Calvados. Let reduce again, until the sauce thickens. Check the seasoning. Place the pheasant breast or seitan strips on a heated serving plate with the apples next to them, pour over the sauce, and serve with steamed potatoes and sautéed mushrooms.

255 SUSIE'S LENTILS

CALORIES	322
CHOLESTEROL	0
VEGAN CALORIES	322
POLYUNSATS	★★☆
ANTIOXIDANTS	★★★
CALCIUM	★☆☆
IRON	★★☆
B VITAMINS	★★☆

½ cup Puy lentils
olive oil for stir-frying
1 onion, finely chopped
2 carrots, finely chopped
2 cloves garlic, finely chopped

1 small zucchini, finely chopped
2 tomatoes, finely chopped
1 tbsp tamari (soy sauce)
1 bay leaf
1 tsp dried thyme

Bring the lentils to a boil in a pan with twice their volume of water and gently simmer while you prepare the other ingredients. Heat a little oil in a separate pan and stir-fry the onion, carrots, garlic, zucchini, and tomatoes (adding them one at a time). Then add the tamari, bay leaf, and thyme, together with the partially-cooked lentils and enough water to cover. Heat through and simmer until the lentils are soft, 10–15 minutes. Season, and serve with bread and slices of ham or fried tempeh.

256 FALL CHESTNUT CASSEROLE

CALORIES	327
CHOLESTEROL	0
VEGAN CALORIES	327
POLYUNSATS	★★☆
ANTIOXIDANTS	★★☆
CALCIUM	★★☆
IRON	★★☆
B VITAMINS	★★☆

oil for sautéing
1 shallot, sliced
1 clove garlic, sliced
9oz button mushrooms
1½ cups chestnuts, fresh,
    peeled or canned
1 tbsp wheat flour

¾in cube ginger, sliced
1 tsp curry powder
1¼ cup vegetable stock
1 sprinkle Tabasco sauce
1 tbsp horseradish root, freshly
    grated
2 tbsp parsley, finely chopped

Sweat the shallot, garlic, and mushrooms in a Dutch oven with a little oil for 3–4 minutes, stirring occasionally. Stir in the chestnuts and sauté for 3 minutes. Add the flour, ginger, and curry powder and cook for a few minutes. Then add the stock, Tabasco, and horseradish. Season and bring to a boil. Cover and gently simmer until the chestnuts are tender. Garnish with parsley and serve with green beans, carrots, and (mashed) potato.

257 WILD MUSHROOM PIE

CALORIES	475
CHOLESTEROL	203
VEGAN CALORIES	450
POLYUNSATS	★★★
ANTIOXIDANTS	★★★
CALCIUM	★★☆
IRON	★★☆
B VITAMINS	★★☆

7oz puff pastry, rolled out
2 tbsp olive oil
3 small shallots, halved and sliced
9oz wild mushrooms

1 tsp dried thyme
½ cup milk/soy milk
2 eggs/1 cup tofu, crumbled
1 pinch nutmeg

Use the pastry to line a 9in tart pan. Scatter with baking beans and bake blind in a preheated oven at 220°C/425°F/gas mark 7 for 10–15 minutes. Let cool and remove the beans. Gently sweat the shallots in a heavy-based skillet with the oil for 5 minutes. Add the mushrooms and the thyme and stir-fry for 10 minutes. Blend the milk, eggs or tofu, and nutmeg to a smooth consistency, and season. Place the mushrooms on the pastry, pour the blended mixture over them, return to the oven, and bake for 15–20 minutes until firm. Serve.

258 SPICY GARBANZOS WITH EGGPLANT

CALORIES	466
CHOLESTEROL	0
VEGAN CALORIES	466
POLYUNSATS	★☆☆
ANTIOXIDANTS	★★★
CALCIUM	★★☆
IRON	★★☆
B VITAMINS	★★☆

2 tbsp olive oil
1 leek, sliced
2¼ cup garbanzos, cooked
  or canned
1 eggplant, diced

1 clove garlic, crushed
½ tsp ground cumin
½ tsp ground coriander
6 tomatoes, chopped
salt and black pepper to taste

Heat the oil in a Dutch oven and gently sweat the leek for 5 minutes. Turn up the heat a little and add the garbanzos, eggplant, garlic, cumin, and coriander. Stir-fry for 5 minutes. Add the tomatoes and bring to a boil. Cover and simmer for 15 minutes (adding a little water, if necessary). Season and serve with rice.

259 TURKISH BOREG

CALORIES	658
CHOLESTEROL	55
VEGAN CALORIES	598
POLYUNSATS	★★★
ANTIOXIDANTS	★★★
CALCIUM	★★☆
IRON	★★★
B VITAMINS	★★★

2 tbsp olive oil
1 shallot, chopped
¼ cup ground pork/tempeh,
  grated
4 mushrooms, chopped
1 carrot, grated
9 oz couscous, covered with
  boiling water and soaked

  for 10 minutes
2 tbsp parsley, chopped
1 tsp dried thyme
zest of ½ lemon
salt and black pepper to taste
9oz ready-made shortcrust
  pastry, rolled out thinly

Preheat the oven to 220°C/425°F/gas mark 7. Soften the onion in a pan or a wok with the oil. Add the ground pork or grated tempeh and the mushrooms, and stir-fry for 5 minutes, then add the carrot, soaked couscous, parsley, thyme, and lemon zest, and season. Pile the filling onto the center of the rolled-out pastry and fold in the edges to form a parcel. Turn upside down onto a greased baking sheet. Glaze with cold water and bake for 15–20 minutes. Serve with steamed vegetables and plain or soy yogurt mixed with mint, cayenne pepper, and celery salt.

260 ▼ PURÉED PUMPKIN HOTPOT WITH BROILED FALL VEGETABLES

⭐❤️💧🌾🥜

CALORIES	580
CHOLESTEROL	70
VEGAN CALORIES	592
POLYUNSATS	★★★
ANTIOXIDANTS	★★★
CALCIUM	★★☆
IRON	★★☆
B VITAMINS	★★★

1 cup chicken breast/seitan,
   cut into chunks
1 parsnip, cut into chunks
1 small beet, quartered
4 potatoes, quartered
1 tbsp paprika
olive oil for stir-frying
1¼ cups pumpkin

1 red onion, halved and sliced
1 clove garlic, crushed
1 tbsp marjoram
1 cup vegetable stock,
   heated
1–2 tbsp white almond butter
salt and black pepper to taste

Preheat the oven to 220°C/425°F/gas mark 7. Scatter the chicken or seitan, parsnip, beet, and potatoes on an oiled baking sheet and sprinkle with paprika and a little salt and pepper. Broil in a hot oven until they begin to turn brown and soft. Check and turn from time to time. Meanwhile, peel, deseed, and chop the pumpkin, then gently stir-fry the pieces with the onion and garlic in a Dutch oven with a little oil for 5 minutes. Add the marjoram and the stock, and bring to a boil. Cover and gently simmer for 10 minutes. Purée the pumpkin mixture and add the almond butter. Season and serve with the broiled seitan or chicken and the broiled vegetables.

261 ▼ BAKED FRUIT KEBABS

♥☒◗

CALORIES	287
CHOLESTEROL	0
VEGAN CALORIES	287
POLYUNSATS	★☆☆
ANTIOXIDANTS	★★☆
CALCIUM	★☆☆
IRON	★☆☆
B VITAMINS	★☆☆

1 orange, peeled and cut into
    chunks
1 pear, cored and cut into chunks
1 apple, cored and cut into chunks
1 banana, peeled and cut into
    chunks

8 chestnuts, peeled
⅔ cup grape juice
2 tsp Grand Marnier
2 tsp maple syrup
oil for brushing

Preheat the oven to 240°C/475°F/gas mark 9. Thread the fruit chunks
and the chestnuts onto long skewers. Make a marinade of the grape
juice, Grand Marnier, and maple syrup, and brush over the fruit. Place
the skewers on oiled baking parchment. Wrap each skewer in the
parchment and bake in a hot oven for 15 minutes. Serve with the
remaining marinade as a dip.

262 MELLOW MELON

CALORIES	306
CHOLESTEROL	0
VEGAN CALORIES	306
POLYUNSATS	★☆☆
ANTIOXIDANTS	★★☆
CALCIUM	★★☆
IRON	★☆☆
B VITAMINS	★☆☆

½ Cantaloupe melon, peeled, deseeded and diced
1 bunch green grapes, halved
1 orange, peeled, halved and sliced

2 ripe green figs, quartered
1 banana, peeled and sliced
1 large fresh date, pitted
1 tsp maple syrup

Mix the melon, grapes, orange, and figs in a bowl. Purée the banana with the date, maple syrup, and enough water to make a thick, smooth sauce. Pour the sauce over the fruit and serve.

263 BLUEBERRY SALAD

CALORIES	220
CHOLESTEROL	0
VEGAN CALORIES	220
POLYUNSATS	★☆☆
ANTIOXIDANTS	★★★
CALCIUM	★★☆
IRON	★★☆
B VITAMINS	★☆☆

¾ cup blueberries
2⅓ cups red grapes, halved
1 banana, peeled and sliced

1 persimmon, halved and sliced
1 papaya, peeled and deseeded
4 fresh dark figs, chopped

Mix the blueberries, grapes, banana, and persimmon in a glass bowl. Chop the papaya and purée it with the figs and a little water to make a thick sauce. Pour the sauce over the berries and fruit, and serve.

264 PERSIMMON WITH JUICY PEARS

CALORIES	269
CHOLESTEROL	0
VEGAN CALORIES	269
POLYUNSATS	★☆☆
ANTIOXIDANTS	★★★
CALCIUM	★☆☆
IRON	★☆☆
B VITAMINS	★☆☆

1 persimmon, sliced
1 large ripe pear, halved, cored, and sliced
1 small bunch red grapes, halved

4 fresh dates, pitted and chopped
½ cup apple juice
1 pinch ground cinnamon
juice of 1 mandarin

Place the persimmon, pear, and grapes in a glass bowl. Purée the dates, apple juice, cinnamon, and mandarin juice. Pour the mixture over the fresh fruit and let marinate until serving.

265 PINEAPPLE BOATS

CALORIES	255
CHOLESTEROL	0
VEGAN CALORIES	255
POLYUNSATS	★☆☆
ANTIOXIDANTS	★★★
CALCIUM	★★☆
IRON	★☆☆
B VITAMINS	★☆☆

1 small pineapple, halved lengthwise
1 small bunch red grapes, halved
1 kiwi, peeled and diced
1 banana, peeled and sliced

zest and juice of ½ lime
1 tbsp maple syrup
juice of 1 orange
1 tbsp Grand Marnier (optional)
1 tsp ginger, finely chopped

Scoop out the pineapple flesh to make two boats and set the boats aside. Cut the pineapple flesh into chunks and place them in a bowl with the remaining ingredients. Gently toss, then spoon into the pineapple boats, and serve with plain or soy yogurt or custard (see p.140).

266 FALL COLORS

CALORIES	196
CHOLESTEROL	0
VEGAN CALORIES	196
POLYUNSATS	★☆☆
ANTIOXIDANTS	★★★
CALCIUM	★☆☆
IRON	★☆☆
B VITAMINS	★☆☆

1 red apple, cored and sliced
1 small bunch red grapes, halved
1 mango, peeled and sliced
1 pomelo, peeled and sliced
½ cup orange juice
1 tbsp lemon juice
2 tsp honey
cilantro leaves, chopped

Mix the fruit in a glass bowl. Heat the orange juice in a small Dutch oven, add the lemon juice and the honey, and simmer until the honey is dissolved. Remove from the heat, let cool a little, and pour over the fruit. Gently toss, garnish with cilantro, and serve.

267 PLUM TART

CALORIES	312
CHOLESTEROL	0
VEGAN CALORIES	312
POLYUNSATS	★★☆
ANTIOXIDANTS	★★☆
CALCIUM	★☆☆
IRON	★☆☆
B VITAMINS	★☆☆

6oz ready-made puff pastry,
   rolled out
1¼ cups ripe plums, quartered
   and pitted
1 tbsp liquid honey
1 pinch cinnamon

Preheat the oven to 220°C/425°F/gas mark 7. Place the rolled out pastry in an 8in round baking sheet. Line with the plums and brush with the honey. Sprinkle with the cinnamon and bake in a hot oven for 15 minutes. Serve with crème fraîche or soy cream.

268 APPLE SALAD, WALDORF-STYLE

CALORIES	478
CHOLESTEROL	0
VEGAN CALORIES	478
POLYUNSATS	★★★
ANTIOXIDANTS	★★★
CALCIUM	★☆☆
IRON	★★☆
B VITAMINS	★★☆

2 large lettuce leaves
2 red apples, cored and sliced
2 sticks celery, sliced
⅔ cup grapes, halved
⅔ cup raisins
½ cup apple juice
½ avocado, halved, pitted, peeled
   and chopped
2 tbsp pecan nuts

Place the lettuce leaves on two plates. Arrange the apples, celery, grapes, and raisins on top of the leaves. Purée the apple juice with the avocado and pour over the salads. Garnish with pecan nuts and serve.

269 FRESH AND FRUITY SALAD

CALORIES	137
CHOLESTEROL	0
VEGAN CALORIES	137
POLYUNSATS	★☆☆
ANTIOXIDANTS	★★★
CALCIUM	★★☆
IRON	★☆☆
B VITAMINS	★★★

1 handful Iceberg lettuce leaves,
   shredded
1 orange, peeled and sliced
1 carrot, grated
¼ cup blackberries
1 apple, cored and sliced
½ cup grape juice
½ lime, sliced

Place the lettuce on two plates. Top with the orange, carrot, blackberries, and apple. Sprinkle with grape juice, garnish with slices of lime, and serve.

270 SILKY FRUIT SALAD
★♥◊✕

CALORIES	356
CHOLESTEROL	0
VEGAN CALORIES	356
POLYUNSATS	★★★
ANTIOXIDANTS	★★☆
CALCIUM	★☆☆
IRON	★★☆
B VITAMINS	★★☆

2 tbsp dried apricots, sliced
½ cup grape juice
1 banana, peeled and sliced
1 persimmon, halved and sliced

1 large ripe pear, cored and sliced
2 plums, pitted and sliced
1 pomegranate, peeled and chopped
2 tbsp pine kernels, chopped

Soak the dried apricots in the grape juice while you prepare the other fruit. Then place all the fresh fruit in a glass bowl, add the soaked apricots together with the grape juice, and gently toss. Garnish with chopped pine kernels and serve.

271 ORCHARD HARVEST WITH CUSTARD
★♥

CALORIES	370
CHOLESTEROL	18
VEGAN CALORIES	320
POLYUNSATS	★☆☆
ANTIOXIDANTS	★★☆
CALCIUM	★☆☆
IRON	★☆☆
B VITAMINS	★★☆

2 ripe pears, cored and sliced
1 red apple, cored and sliced
1 persimmon, sliced
2 fresh figs, quartered
2 plums, pitted and quartered

custard:
1 tbsp cornstarch
1 tbsp raw cane sugar
1 tsp vanilla extract
1 pinch salt
scant 1¼ cups milk/soy milk

Arrange the fruit on two plates. To make the custard, put the cornstarch into a bowl with the sugar, vanilla extract, salt and enough milk to make a smooth paste. Heat the remaining milk in a pan (don't let it boil), then slowly add it to the cornstarch mixture, stirring continuously. Pour the custard back into the pan, stir and bring to a boil. Remove from the heat and serve with the fruit.

272 APPLE CRUMBLE
★♥

CALORIES	534
CHOLESTEROL	0
VEGAN CALORIES	534
POLYUNSATS	★★★
ANTIOXIDANTS	★★☆
CALCIUM	★☆☆
IRON	★★☆
B VITAMINS	★★☆

1½ tbsp raisins
1 tbsp rum (optional)
2 (Reinette) apples, thinly sliced
1 tbsp grapeseed oil

⅔ cup rolled oats
¼ cup chopped walnuts
2 tbsp maple syrup

Preheat the oven to 230°C/450°F/gas mark 8. Soak the raisins in a bowl with the rum (if using) and enough cold water to cover. Place the sliced apples in an oiled baking dish. Cover with the soaked raisins and their liquid. Heat the oil in a small skillet and stir in the oats and the walnuts. Add the maple syrup and gently heat through for 1 minute, stirring continuously. Evenly spoon the crumble mixture over the apples and bake in a hot oven for approximately 15 minutes until the topping is golden brown. Serve with ice cream or soy ice cream.

273 ▼ LAYERED FRUIT SALAD

⭐💟🔥

CALORIES	402
CHOLESTEROL	6
VEGAN CALORIES	399
POLYUNSATS	★★☆
ANTIOXIDANTS	★★★
CALCIUM	★★☆
IRON	★★☆
B VITAMINS	★★☆

1 mango, peeled and sliced
1 banana, peeled and sliced
   lengthwise
4 plums, pitted and sliced
⅔ cup raspberries

1 papaya, peeled, deseeded
   and diced
2 tbsp cashew nuts
1 tbsp maple syrup
½ cup plain/soy yogurt

Arrange the mango, banana, plums, and raspberries in layers in a dish.
Purée the papaya with the cashew nuts, maple syrup, and yogurt.
Pour the sauce over the fruit layers and serve.

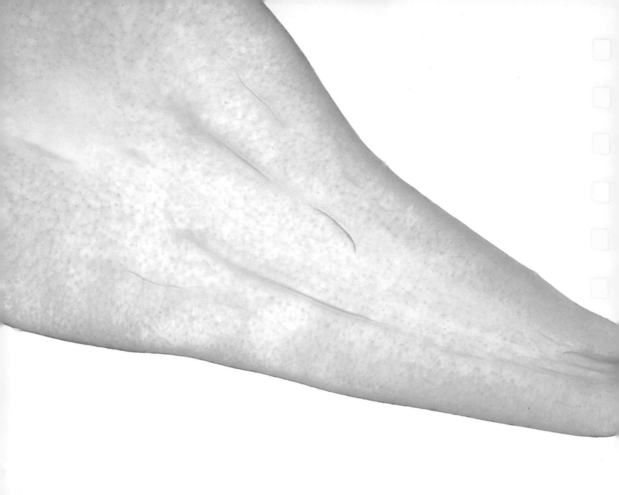

WINTER
RECIPES

Winter is the lean season. The energy is resting deep in the ground and, in Chinese philosophy, it is thought of as the season of most yin, when the energy is inward-looking. Nature sleeps and prepares, and it is time to let go of the old and to favour peace. Outside, all is barren and still, but inside there is warmth, an opportunity to study and learn, time for leisure, culture, and rest.

Winter is also the festive season, where we gather to enjoy each other's company in coziness indoors. It is the inner light that shines while we wait for the sun to return and, from a nutritional viewpoint, winter is the time to use the reserves that have been built up in the fall. We need more calorie-rich meals to keep us warm, and the most favored ingredients are pulses, rice and grain, cabbage, leeks, and root vegetables. Fish and fatty foods help keep us warm and dried fruits provide energy. The element of this season is water, which corresponds to the kidneys and the bladder, and special attention should be paid to the basic life energies. Keep warm and well nourished, stay quiet and peaceful, and enjoy this season of still life.

274 WALNUT AND CELERY SOUP

CALORIES	579
CHOLESTEROL	18
VEGAN CALORIES	529
POLYUNSATS	★★★
ANTIOXIDANTS	★★☆
CALCIUM	★★☆
IRON	★★☆
B VITAMINS	★★☆

30 walnut halves, shelled
2 tbsp olive oil
1 shallot, sliced
2 cloves garlic, chopped
2 sticks celery, chopped
1 cup water

1 pinch ground mace
2 tbsp tamari (soy sauce)
1 tbsp lemon juice
1¼ cups milk/soy milk
salt and black pepper to taste

Place the walnut halves in a pan of boiling water for 2 minutes. Drain and set aside. Heat the oil in a pan and gently fry the shallots until soft. Add the garlic and celery and fry for a further minute. Pour in the water and bring to a boil. Simmer for 5 minutes. Remove from the heat. Add the cooked walnuts, mace, tamari, lemon juice, and milk. Gently heat through, stirring continuously. Season and serve with crusty bread rolls.

275 CALDO VERDE

CALORIES	302
CHOLESTEROL	25
VEGAN CALORIES	235
POLYUNSATS	★★☆
ANTIOXIDANTS	★★★
CALCIUM	★☆☆
IRON	★★☆
B VITAMINS	★★☆

3¾ cups water or vegetable
   stock
½ cup curly kale leaves,
   chopped
2 potatoes, diced
1 shallot, chopped

4 cloves garlic, chopped
salt and black pepper to taste
½ cup spicy sausage (pork/soy),
   sliced
1 tbsp olive oil, plus some for frying

Bring the water or stock to a boil in a pan with the curly kale, potatoes, shallot, garlic, and a little salt. Heat through and simmer for 20 minutes. Meanwhile, fry the sausage slices in a skillet with a little oil. Set aside. Purée the soup, check the seasoning, and add the oil. Garnish with pepper and spicy sausage and serve hot with corn bread.

276 UKRAINIAN BORSCH

CALORIES	294
CHOLESTEROL	0
VEGAN CALORIES	294
POLYUNSATS	★☆☆
ANTIOXIDANTS	★★★
CALCIUM	★★☆
IRON	★★☆
B VITAMINS	★★☆

2 tbsp olive oil
1 onion, chopped
½ cup raw beet, diced
¼ white cabbage,
   shredded
1 carrot, diced
1 potato, diced
2 cups mushrooms, chopped

1 stick celery, finely chopped
1 tbsp wheat flour
2 ripe tomatoes, puréed
4⅓ cup vegetable stock
1 handful parsley, finely
   chopped
salt and black pepper to taste

Gently stir-fry the onion, beet, cabbage, carrot, and potato in a pan with the oil for 5 minutes. Add the mushrooms and the celery and stir-fry for a further 3 minutes. Sprinkle the flour into the pan and mix with the vegetables for 1 minute. Continue to stir while adding the puréed tomatoes, followed by the stock. Bring to a boil, add the parsley, and simmer for 20 minutes. Season and serve with garlic croutons.

277 CHINESE SOUP WITH SHIITAKE AND NOODLES

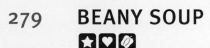

CALORIES	344
CHOLESTEROL	0
VEGAN CALORIES	344
POLYUNSATS	★★☆
ANTIOXIDANTS	★★★
CALCIUM	★★★
IRON	★★☆
B VITAMINS	★★☆

2 tbsp olive oil
1 scallion, chopped
1 cup tofu
1½ cups shiitake mushrooms, sliced
5 pieces bamboo shoots, cut into squares
1 small carrot, sliced into sticks

4⅓ cups vegetable stock
2 tbsp tamari (soy sauce)
2 tbsp dry sherry
1 pinch Chinese five-spice powder
1 small bunch watercress, chopped
1 tsp sesame oil
a handful of noodles

Gently heat the oil in a Dutch oven and stir-fry the scallion for 30 seconds. Add the tofu, shiitake, bamboo shoots, and carrot and stir-fry for 2 minutes before adding the stock, tamari, sherry, five-spice powder, and watercress. Bring to a boil. Add the oil and noodles. Cover, remove from the heat, leave for 2 minutes until the noodles are cooked, and serve.

278 LEEK AND POTATO SOUP

CALORIES	223
CHOLESTEROL	0
VEGAN CALORIES	223
POLYUNSATS	★★☆
ANTIOXIDANTS	★★☆
CALCIUM	★☆☆
IRON	★★☆
B VITAMINS	★★☆

2 tbsp olive oil
2 leeks, sliced
2 potatoes, diced

4⅓ cups vegetable stock
salt and black pepper to taste

Gently heat the oil in a pan, add the leeks and the potatoes and sauté for 3 minutes, then add the stock. Heat through and simmer for 15 minutes. Season, and serve with croutons.

279 BEANY SOUP

CALORIES	429
CHOLESTEROL	0
VEGAN CALORIES	429
POLYUNSATS	★☆☆
ANTIOXIDANTS	★★★
CALCIUM	★★☆
IRON	★★☆
B VITAMINS	★★☆

½ cup green lentils
3 tbsp olive oil
1 small leek, sliced
1 thin slice celery root, diced
1 small carrot, sliced
1 tsp paprika
4⅓ cups vegetable stock
1 packed cup red kidney beans, cooked or canned

½ cup fava beans, fresh or frozen
½ cup green beans, chopped
1 bay leaf
1 tbsp tomato paste
1 tsp dried thyme
1 tsp dried sage
salt and black pepper to taste
parsley to garnish (optional)

Boil the lentils in a pan with plenty of water. Meanwhile, gently heat the oil in a large Dutch oven and stir-fry the leek for 1 minute. Add the celery root, carrot, and paprika and stir-fry for a further minute, then add the stock. Bring to a boil, add the remaining ingredients (except for the parsley), and heat through. Add the partially-cooked lentils with a little of their cooking water. Bring to a boil again and simmer for 10 minutes until the lentils are cooked. Remove the bay leaf, check the seasoning, and serve garnished with parsley (if using).

280 ▼ JAPANESE SPINACH SOUP

CALORIES	207
CHOLESTEROL	0
VEGAN CALORIES	207
POLYUNSATS	★★★
ANTIOXIDANTS	★★★
CALCIUM	★★★
IRON	★★☆
B VITAMINS	★★☆

1 tbsp grapeseed oil
1 shallot, sliced
1 small carrot, finely chopped
1 cup tofu, diced
4 mushrooms, sliced
1¾ cups spinach, chopped
   into strips
2 tsp tamari (soy sauce)
4in strip kombu seaweed

¼ tsp raw cane sugar
1 tsp mirin (Japanese rice wine),
   or dry sherry (optional)
4⅓ cups water
salt and black pepper to taste
½ tsp sesame oil
1 tsp lemon juice
lemon zest, cut into strips
   to garnish

Heat the grapeseed oil in a pan, add the shallot, carrot, and tofu cubes, and stir-fry for 1 minute. Add the mushrooms and stir for a further minute, then add the spinach and continue to stir over a medium heat until the spinach is wilted. Add the remaining ingredients (except for the sesame oil, lemon juice, and lemon zest). Bring to a boil and simmer for 10 minutes. Then add the sesame oil and lemon juice. Check the seasoning and serve garnished with strips of lemon zest.

281 CREAMY PARSNIP SOUP

CALORIES	396
CHOLESTEROL	6
VEGAN CALORIES	393
POLYUNSATS	★★☆
ANTIOXIDANTS	★★☆
CALCIUM	★★☆
IRON	★★☆
B VITAMINS	★★☆

2 tbsp olive oil
2 tsp mustard powder
2¾ cups parsnips,
   chopped
1 tart apple, peeled, cored
   and chopped

4⅓ cups vegetable stock
1 tbsp tamari (soy sauce)
1 tsp dried thyme
salt and black pepper to taste
½ cup plain/soy yogurt

Gently heat the oil in a large pan. Stir in the mustard powder and let dissolve. Add the parsnips and the apple and stir-fry for a few minutes, then add the stock and bring to a boil. Cover and simmer for 10 minutes. Add the tamari and the thyme, and season. Purée to a rich, creamy texture, check the seasoning, and serve with a spoonful of plain or soy yogurt in each bowl.

282 MONKFISH AND FENNEL SOUP

CALORIES	317
CHOLESTEROL	26
VEGAN CALORIES	281
POLYUNSATS	★★☆
ANTIOXIDANTS	★★★
CALCIUM	★★☆
IRON	★★☆
B VITAMINS	★★☆

2 tbsp olive oil
1 small red onion, sliced
1 Florence fennel bulb, halved
   and sliced
2 potatoes, diced
2¼ cups vegetable/fish stock
½ cup dry white wine
½ unpeeled lemon, quartered
   and sliced

1 tsp raw cane sugar
2 tbsp tomato paste
1½ cups monkfish, skinned,
   boned and diced/1 cup tofu,
   diced and fried with a little
   tamari (soy sauce)
2 tbsp dill, finely chopped
salt and black pepper to taste

Heat the oil in a saucepan and sweat the onion over a low heat for 2–3 minutes. Add the fennel and the potatoes, turn the heat to medium and sauté for 2 minutes. Then add the stock, wine, lemon, sugar, and tomato paste. Bring to a boil, add the monkfish or tofu, and gently simmer for 5–7 minutes. Garnish with dill and season. Serve with crusty bread rolls.

283 CAULIFLOWER SOUP

CALORIES	281
CHOLESTEROL	7
VEGAN CALORIES	261
POLYUNSATS	★★☆
ANTIOXIDANTS	★★★
CALCIUM	★★☆
IRON	★★☆
B VITAMINS	★★☆

3¾ cups vegetable stock
1 small cauliflower, cut into
   small florets
1 small onion, finely chopped
1 small carrot, finely chopped
2 potatoes, finely chopped

2 tbsp olive oil
1 pinch asafoetida
1 pinch saffron threads
salt and black pepper to taste
½ cup milk/soy milk
1 handful parsley, chopped

Bring the stock to the boil in a Dutch oven with the cauliflower florets and the chopped onion, carrot, and potatoes. Add the oil, asafoetida, saffron, and a little seasoning. Simmer for 10–15 minutes. Turn off the heat and add the milk. Purée if you prefer. Adjust the seasoning, garnish with the parsley, and serve with fresh country bread and goat's cheese or soy cheese.

284 ▶ WINTER VEGETABLE SOUP
★♥⌀

CALORIES	524
CHOLESTEROL	20
VEGAN CALORIES	444
POLYUNSATS	★★☆
ANTIOXIDANTS	★★★
CALCIUM	★★☆
IRON	★★★
B VITAMINS	★★★

⅓ cup Puy lentils, rinsed
3 tbsp olive oil
1 small leek, sliced
⅓ cup bacon/3oz smoked tempeh, diced
1 carrot, sliced
1 thin slice celery root, diced

12 shiitake mushrooms, sliced
¼ cabbage, finely sliced
4⅓ cups vegetable stock
1 bay leaf
1 tsp dried thyme
1 tbsp tomato paste
salt and black pepper to taste

Boil the lentils in a pan with twice their volume of water. Meanwhile, gently heat the oil in a pan, add the leek and the smoked bacon or tempeh, and stir-fry for 2 minutes. Add the carrot, celery root, shiitake, and cabbage and continue to stir-fry for a further 5 minutes. Stir in the stock, bay leaf, thyme, and tomato paste and bring to a boil. Drain the partially-cooked lentils and add them to the pan. Bring the soup to a boil again, and simmer for 10 minutes, or until the lentils are soft. Remove the bay leaf, season, and serve with warm, crusty bread rolls.

285 CURLY KALE SOUP
★♥◊✖✦⌀

CALORIES	315
CHOLESTEROL	0
VEGAN CALORIES	315
POLYUNSATS	★★☆
ANTIOXIDANTS	★★★
CALCIUM	★★☆
IRON	★★☆
B VITAMINS	★★☆

2 tbsp olive oil
1 tsp turmeric
1 small leek, sliced
1 small carrot, sliced
1 small parsley root, quartered and sliced

1 potato, quartered and sliced
1 bay leaf
1 tbsp wheat flour
4⅓ cups vegetable stock
2 cups curly kale, chopped
salt and black pepper to taste

Gently heat the oil in a saucepan. Add the turmeric and the leek, followed by the carrot, parsley root, potato, and bay leaf. Stir-fry for 2 minutes over a medium heat. Sprinkle the flour into the pan and stir until the vegetables are coated in flour. Continue to stir while you add the stock and bring to a boil. Simmer for 10 minutes. Add the curly kale and boil for a further 5 minutes. Season and serve with croûtons.

286 SMOKY LIMA BEAN SOUP
★♥

CALORIES	493
CHOLESTEROL	47
VEGAN CALORIES	475
POLYUNSATS	★☆☆
ANTIOXIDANTS	★★☆
CALCIUM	★★☆
IRON	★★☆
B VITAMINS	★★★

2 tbsp olive oil
1 leek, sliced
1 lb lima beans, cooked or canned
4⅓ cups vegetable stock

1¼ cups smoked haddock, skinned, boned and cubed/4oz smoked tempeh, cubed
salt and black pepper to taste
1 tbsp dill, finely chopped

Gently stir-fry the leek in a pan with the oil until soft. Add the lima beans. Then mash the beans a little and stir-fry for a further 3–5 minutes. Pour in the stock and bring to a boil. Cover and simmer for 5 minutes. Add the smoked haddock or smoked tempeh cubes and simmer for a further 10 minutes. Season, garnish with chopped dill, and serve with soft bread.

287 WINTER CRUDITÉS WITH AVOCADO DRESSING

CALORIES	570
CHOLESTEROL	0
VEGAN CALORIES	570
POLYUNSATS	★★★
ANTIOXIDANTS	★★★
CALCIUM	★★☆
IRON	★★☆
B VITAMINS	★★★

2 potatoes, parboiled and sliced
⅛ white cabbage, shredded
¼ celery root, cut into thin sticks
8 cremini mushrooms, sliced
1 black radish, sliced
2 avocados, halved, pitted, and
   flesh scooped out
juice of ½ lemon

salt to taste
½ small red chili, deseeded and
   finely chopped
½ small onion, finely chopped
2–4 curly kale leaves, finely
   chopped
a handful of walnuts, shelled

Arrange the potatoes, cabbage, celery root, mushrooms, and radish on two large plates. Purée the avocado flesh with lemon juice and salt. Add the chili and onion, mix and spoon onto the middle of each plate. Garnish with curly kale and walnuts, and serve with whole wheat rolls.

288 SPANISH POTATO SALAD

CALORIES	628
CHOLESTEROL	70
VEGAN CALORIES	502
POLYUNSATS	★★★
ANTIOXIDANTS	★★★
CALCIUM	★★★
IRON	★★★
B VITAMINS	★★☆

2 tbsp olive oil
1 tsp paprika
2 potatoes, sliced
½ Spanish onion, finely chopped
2 cloves garlic, chopped
salt and black pepper to taste
⅓ cup water

2 Belgian endive, sliced
   lengthwise
1 tbsp walnut oil
1 tbsp red wine vinegar
1 handful parsley, chopped
1¼ cups goat's/soy cheese,
   sliced

Heat the oil in a skillet, add the paprika and stir in the potatoes, onion, and garlic. Season and stir-fry for 5 minutes. Add the water and bring to a boil. Cover and gently simmer for 10 minutes until the potatoes are tender. Arrange the Belgian endive on two plates, top with the potato slices and drizzle with the walnut oil and the vinegar. Check the seasoning, sprinkle with parsley and cheese, and serve.

289 WARM PASTA SALAD

CALORIES	444
CHOLESTEROL	26
VEGAN CALORIES	392
POLYUNSATS	★★☆
ANTIOXIDANTS	★★★
CALCIUM	★★☆
IRON	★★★
B VITAMINS	★★★

6oz tricolor pasta
1 thick slice celery root, chopped
   into matchsticks
1 leek, chopped into matchsticks
1 carrot, chopped into matchsticks
2 tbsp olive oil
juice of ½ lemon

salt and black pepper to taste
1 pinch ground coriander
5oz smoked salmon/1¼ cups tofu,
   cut into strips
4 mushrooms, sliced and sprinkled
   with lemon juice
2 tsp parsley, finely chopped

Cook the pasta in boiling water with a little salt and oil. Drain and set aside. Blanch the celery root, leek, and carrot in a pan of boiling water for 1 minute. Drain and set aside. Make the dressing by whisking the oil, lemon juice, salt, pepper, and coriander in a bowl. Mix the cooked pasta, vegetables, smoked salmon or tofu, and mushrooms in a salad bowl. Add the dressing and gently toss. Garnish with parsley and serve.

290 CARROT, DATE, AND, PECAN SALAD WITH GINGER DRESSING AND PAN BREAD

CALORIES	824
CHOLESTEROL	0
VEGAN CALORIES	824
POLYUNSATS	★★★
ANTIOXIDANTS	★★★
CALCIUM	★★☆
IRON	★★☆
B VITAMINS	★★☆

2 cups carrots, grated
½ cup dates, pitted
   and chopped
¾ cup pecans, chopped
3 tbsp lemon juice
2 tsp ginger, finely chopped
1 tsp liquid honey

pan bread:
1½ cups wheat flour
1 tsp baking powder
1 pinch salt
vegetable oil for frying

Mix the carrots, dates, and pecans in a salad bowl. To make the dressing, pour the lemon juice into a small bowl and mix in the ginger and honey. Set aside. Place the wheat flour in a bowl, mix in the baking powder and salt, and add enough water to form a soft dough. Break the dough into small balls, then flatten into thick pancakes and fry in a skillet with a little oil over a medium–high heat. Mix the dressing with the salad and serve with the hot pan bread, and cream cheese or soy cheese mixed with basil. Alternately, you can serve the dressed salad with pitta bread.

291 RED CABBAGE SALAD

CALORIES	698
CHOLESTEROL	94
VEGAN CALORIES	385
POLYUNSATS	★★★
ANTIOXIDANTS	★★☆
CALCIUM	★☆☆
IRON	★★☆
B VITAMINS	★★☆

1 duck breast/5oz seitan, cut into
   chunks
oil for frying (optional)
½ small red cabbage, finely sliced
1 apple, cored and cubed

1 stick celery, sliced
1 tbsp cider vinegar
2 tbsp walnut oil
salt and black pepper to taste
8 walnut halves

Fry the duck breast in a skillet (without oil, beginning with the skin-side facing downward), and set aside. Alternately, fry the seitan pieces in a skillet with a little oil. Slice and set aside. To make the vinaigrette, mix the vinegar, oil, salt, and pepper in a small bowl. Place the red cabbage, apple, and celery in a large bowl, add the vinaigrette, and mix well. Place on a serving dish and top with the fried duck or seitan, and the walnut halves. Serve with French baguette.

292 FRUITY AVOCADO SALAD

CALORIES	642
CHOLESTEROL	0
VEGAN CALORIES	642
POLYUNSATS	★★★
ANTIOXIDANTS	★★★
CALCIUM	★★☆
IRON	★★☆
B VITAMINS	★★☆

1 handful arugula or curly kale,
   chopped
2 avocados, quartered, pitted,
   peeled and sliced
1 small pink grapefruit, quartered,
   peeled and diced

1 large ripe pear or apple,
   quartered and sliced
12 Brazil nuts, chopped
3 tbsp walnut oil
1 tbsp balsamic vinegar
salt and black pepper to taste

Place the arugula or curly kale, avocados, grapefruit, pear or apple, and Brazil nuts in a salad bowl. Add the walnut oil and the vinegar, and season. Gently toss, and serve with bread and cheese or soy cheese.

293 ▲ WILD RICE SALAD
★ ♥ 🌢 ▢

CALORIES	483
CHOLESTEROL	0
VEGAN CALORIES	483
POLYUNSATS	★★☆
ANTIOXIDANTS	★★☆
CALCIUM	★★☆
IRON	★★☆
B VITAMINS	★★☆

½ cup wild rice, cooked
2½ cups fresh raw baby leaf
   spinach, chopped
½ red onion, finely chopped
½ Florence fennel bulb,
   sliced
1 thick slice pineapple,
   chopped

1 tbsp lemon juice
1 tsp Dijon mustard
1 tsp maple syrup
salt and black pepper to taste
3 tbsp hazelnut oil
a handful of bean sprouts
¼ cup hazelnuts, chopped

Place the cooked rice in a salad bowl with the spinach, onion, fennel,
and pineapple, and mix well. To make the dressing, whisk the lemon juice,
mustard, maple syrup, salt, and pepper in a small bowl, slowly adding
the oil. Pour the dressing over the rice salad, garnish with bean sprouts
and hazelnuts, and serve.

294 ARUGULA AND TROUT SALAD

★♥✕▢

CALORIES	370
CHOLESTEROL	56
VEGAN CALORIES	392
POLYUNSATS	★★★
ANTIOXIDANTS	★★★
CALCIUM	★★★
IRON	★★☆
B VITAMINS	★★★

1 large bunch arugula (or curly
   kale), chopped
1 handful radicchio leaves
1 pear, cored and sliced
1 handful chopped walnuts
5oz smoked trout/tempeh

3 tbsp plain/soy yogurt
1 tbsp lemon juice
1 tsp grated horseradish
2 tsp tamari (soy sauce)
salt and black pepper to taste

Place the salad leaves in a large bowl. Add the pear and the walnuts. Cut
the tempeh or trout into chunks. Fry or broil the tempeh until golden (if
using) and add to the salad, or add the trout. Make the dressing by mixing
the yogurt with the lemon juice, horseradish, and tamari in a bowl. Pour
over the salad and gently toss. Season and serve with fresh bread.

295 DRESSED WINTER SALAD

★♥◊◖

CALORIES	521
CHOLESTEROL	6
VEGAN CALORIES	518
POLYUNSATS	★★★
ANTIOXIDANTS	★★★
CALCIUM	★★★
IRON	★★★
B VITAMINS	★★☆

1½ cups red kidney beans, cooked
   or canned
1¼ cups lima beans, cooked or
   canned
1¾ cups button mushrooms,
   sliced
¼ lb artichoke hearts, sliced
1 small shallot, finely chopped

2 Belgian endive, sliced
   lengthwise
¼ cup plain/soy yogurt
1 tsp Dijon mustard
1 tbsp lemon juice
1 tbsp tarragon, chopped
salt and black pepper to taste
½ cup Brazil nuts, chopped

Rinse the beans and blanch them in a pan of boiling water for 1 minute.
Drain, cool under running water, and set aside to dry. Mix the mushrooms,
artichoke hearts, and shallot in a bowl. To make the dressing, pour the
yogurt into a bowl, add the mustard, lemon juice, tarragon, salt, and
pepper. Mix well and spoon over the vegetables. Add the beans and
gently toss. Arrange the endive on a large serving plate, top with the
dressed beans and vegetables, garnish with Brazil nuts, and serve.

296 RED CABBAGE AND POTATO SALAD

★♥◊⊘

CALORIES	796
CHOLESTEROL	0
VEGAN CALORIES	796
POLYUNSATS	★★★
ANTIOXIDANTS	★★★
CALCIUM	★★☆
IRON	★★☆
B VITAMINS	★★★

¼ fresh red cabbage, finely
   shredded
4 tbsp red wine vinegar, boiling
1 tsp raw cane sugar
2 large potatoes, washed
2 tbsp grapeseed oil
1 small raw beet, grated
1 cup cauliflower florets

1 small shallot, finely chopped
½ red bell pepper, grated (optional)
1 stick celery, finely chopped
a handful of raisins
a handful of walnuts, shelled
2 tbsp walnut oil
celery salt and black pepper to taste

Place the red cabbage in a heatproof bowl. Pour the boiling vinegar over
and add the sugar. Mix well and set aside. Slice and season the potatoes
and sauté them in a skillet with the grapeseed oil until golden brown. Set
aside. Add the beetroot, cauliflower, shallot, red bell pepper (if using),
celery, raisins, and walnuts to the bowl of red cabbage. Drizzle with
walnut oil and season. Gently toss and serve with the sautéed potatoes.

297 ROYAL COUSCOUS

CALORIES	983
CHOLESTEROL	47
VEGAN CALORIES	983
POLYUNSATS	★★★
ANTIOXIDANTS	★★☆
CALCIUM	★★☆
IRON	★★★
B VITAMINS	★★☆

1 cup couscous
2oz coconut, freshly grated, or
    unsweetened shredded
½ tsp salt
1 cup boiling water
1 tbsp olive oil

¾ cup pine kernels
1 tbsp tamari (soy sauce)
1 Little Gem lettuce, shredded
10 dried apricots, chopped
10 sun-dried tomatoes, chopped
French dressing (see p.23)

Place the couscous in a medium bowl. Mix in the coconut and salt. Pour the boiling water over the couscous and let stand for a few minutes. When the water is absorbed, add the oil and mix well. Dry-roast the pine kernels in a skillet. When they start to brown, add the tamari, remove from the heat, and stir until the kernels are well coated. Divide the lettuce between two plates. Add the couscous, then the apricots, sun-dried tomatoes, and roasted pine kernels. Top with French dressing and serve.

298 SMOKY WINTER SALAD

CALORIES	277
CHOLESTEROL	18
VEGAN CALORIES	243
POLYUNSATS	★★★
ANTIOXIDANTS	★★☆
CALCIUM	★★☆
IRON	★★☆
B VITAMINS	★★☆

2 Belgian endive,
    sliced diagonally
1 radicchio, shredded
1 handful lamb's lettuce
1¾ cups mushrooms, sliced
¼ lb smoked fish

(salmon, trout or eel), sliced/
    1 cup smoked tofu, cut into cubes
juice of 1 lemon
3 tbsp grapeseed oil
salt and black pepper to taste

Make a vinaigrette by whisking the lemon juice, oil, salt, and pepper in a small bowl. Place the endive, radicchio, lamb's lettuce, and mushrooms in a salad bowl. Add the vinaigrette and gently toss. Top with the smoked fish or tofu and serve with thick slices of country bread.

299 BEET SALAD WITH BAKED POTATOES

CALORIES	414
CHOLESTEROL	52
VEGAN CALORIES	360
POLYUNSATS	★★★
ANTIOXIDANTS	★★★
CALCIUM	★★☆
IRON	★★☆
B VITAMINS	★★★

4 potatoes, halved and slices
    cut nearly all the way through
    each half
grapeseed oil for brushing
    and stir-frying
½ cup turkey breast/1 cup tofu,
    diced
a little tamari (soy sauce)

1 large raw beet, grated
1 stick celery, finely chopped
½ apple, cored and chopped
½ cup plain/soy yogurt
1 tbsp lemon juice
2 tsp Dijon mustard
salt and black pepper to taste

Place the potato halves on an oiled baking sheet, brush with oil, sprinkle with salt, and bake at 200°C/400°F/gas mark 6 for 30 minutes, or until golden. Meanwhile, gently stir-fry the turkey or tofu in a skillet with a little oil until golden, sprinkling with a little tamari as you remove from the heat. Mix the beet, celery, and apple in a salad bowl. Make a dressing of the yogurt, lemon juice, mustard, salt, and pepper in a bowl, and mix with the beet salad. Serve with the baked potatoes.

300 ▲ LEBANESE MACARONI
★ ♥ 🌾

CALORIES	718
CHOLESTEROL	6
VEGAN CALORIES	715
POLYUNSATS	★★★
ANTIOXIDANTS	★★☆
CALCIUM	★★☆
IRON	★★☆
B VITAMINS	★★☆

½ lb macaroni pasta
½ cup plain/soy yogurt
2 cloves garlic, crushed
1 tbsp mint leaves, chopped

salt and black pepper to taste
¾ cup pine kernels
1 tbsp olive oil
2 tsp tamari (soy sauce)

Boil the macaroni in plenty of water with a little salt and oil until just tender. Meanwhile, mix the yogurt, garlic, and mint in a bowl, and season. Roast the skillet in a frying pan with the oil until they begin to brown. Remove from the heat, quickly add the tamari, and stir well. Set aside. Drain the cooked macaroni, rinse it under cold running water for a few seconds, and drain again. Place in a serving bowl and gently mix in the yogurt mixture. Garnish with roasted pine kernels and serve.

301 SPINACH AND ARTICHOKE TAGLIATELLE

⭐❤️💧🌿☕

CALORIES	568
CHOLESTEROL	0
VEGAN CALORIES	568
POLYUNSATS	★★☆
ANTIOXIDANTS	★★★
CALCIUM	★★★
IRON	★★★
B VITAMINS	★★☆

7oz tagliatelle pasta
2 tbsp olive oil
1 small onion, chopped
1 clove garlic, chopped
6 cups fresh spinach, chopped
1½ cups flageolet beans, cooked
   or canned

9oz artichoke hearts, cooked or
   canned
1 tbsp tomato paste
1 tsp herbes de Provence
a little grated Parmesan/brewer's
   yeast flakes (optional)

Cook the pasta in plenty of boiling water with a little salt and oil. Heat the oil in a skillet or a wok and gently stir-fry the onion for 1 minute. Add the garlic and the spinach, and cook until the spinach is soft. Add the beans, artichoke hearts, and tomato paste. Heat through. Add the herbs and season. Serve on top of the cooked and drained pasta, sprinkled with Parmesan or brewer's yeast flakes (if using).

302 PASTA TRICOLOR IN WALNUT SAUCE

⭐❤️💧🌿

CALORIES	893
CHOLESTEROL	0
VEGAN CALORIES	893
POLYUNSATS	★★★
ANTIOXIDANTS	★★★
CALCIUM	★★☆
IRON	★★★
B VITAMINS	★★☆

7oz tricolor fusilli pasta
1 cup walnuts, shelled and crushed
   in a mortar
2 cloves garlic, crushed
2 tbsp olive oil
1 tbsp balsamic vinegar

a handful of parsley or basil
1 small beet, finely chopped
¼ celery root, finely chopped
1 carrot, finely chopped
¼ Florence fennel bulb, chopped
salt and black pepper to taste

Boil the pasta in plenty of water with a little salt and oil. Mix the walnuts, garlic, oil, vinegar, and herbs with 1 tablespoon of salt in a bowl to make a sauce. Set aside. Heat a little oil in the pan, add the vegetables and stir-fry for a couple of minutes over a medium heat. Add the cooked and drained pasta, and the sauce, and gently mix. Heat through, season, and serve.

303 CONCHIGLIE WITH CHUNKY SAUCE

⭐❤️🌿☕

CALORIES	664
CHOLESTEROL	38
VEGAN CALORIES	563
POLYUNSATS	★★☆
ANTIOXIDANTS	★★☆
CALCIUM	★★☆
IRON	★★★
B VITAMINS	★★☆

7oz conchiglie pasta
olive oil for stir-frying
1 small red onion, halved and sliced
⅔ cup spicy sausage (pork/soy),
   sliced
1½ cups shiitake mushrooms,
   sliced

1 clove garlic, chopped
1 cup vegetable stock
½ cup peas
2 tbsp tomato paste
1 tsp maple syrup
2 tsp dried oregano
salt and black pepper to taste

Boil the pasta in plenty of water with a little salt and oil. Gently stir-fry the onion in a skillet or a wok with a little oil until soft. Add the sausage, turn up the heat, and sauté for 1 minute. Then add the shiitake and continue to stir-fry until the sausage and mushrooms begin to brown. Add the garlic, stock, and peas, and heat through. Then add the tomato paste, maple syrup, and oregano. Season and let simmer until the pasta is cooked. Drain the pasta and serve immediately, topped with the sauce.

304 PASTA WITH VEGETABLES AND CREAMY MUSTARD SAUCE

CALORIES	631
CHOLESTEROL	0
VEGAN CALORIES	631
POLYUNSATS	★★☆
ANTIOXIDANTS	★★★
CALCIUM	★★☆
IRON	★★★
B VITAMINS	★★☆

7oz pasta shapes
1 small leek, finely sliced
½ small hokaido pumpkin, deseeded, peeled, and diced
1 small head broccoli, cut into small florets
1 handful parsley, finely chopped,

plus some to garnish
1 tbsp tarragon, finely chopped (or 1 tsp dried)
2 tbsp Dijon mustard
1 clove garlic, crushed
3 tbsp olive oil
salt and black pepper to taste

Boil the pasta in plenty of water with a little salt and oil. After 4 minutes, add the vegetables and continue to boil until the pasta is just cooked. Mix the herbs with the mustard, garlic, oil, salt, and pepper in a bowl. Drain the cooked pasta and vegetables in a colander. Gently heat the mustard sauce in the pasta pan. Return the pasta and vegetables to the pan and gently mix. Check the seasoning and serve garnished with parsley.

305 PENNE WITH SMOKY PESTO SAUCE

CALORIES	859
CHOLESTEROL	41
VEGAN CALORIES	807
POLYUNSATS	★★★
ANTIOXIDANTS	★★☆
CALCIUM	★★☆
IRON	★★★
B VITAMINS	★★★

2 tbsp pine kernels
3 tbsp basil, finely chopped
3 tbsp olive oil, plus some for frying
1–2 cloves garlic, crushed (optional)
7oz penne pasta

1½ cups green beans, chopped
½ cup smoked bacon/tempeh
½ cup plain/soy yogurt
1 tbsp grated Parmesan/brewer's yeast flakes

Crush the pine kernels in a mortar and mix in the basil, oil, garlic (if using) and a little salt to make the pesto. Boil the pasta in plenty of water with a little salt and oil. After 4 minutes, add the beans. Cut the bacon or tempeh into cubes and sauté them in a skillet with oil until they begin to brown. Remove from the heat, add the pesto and the yogurt, and mix well. Return the drained pasta and beans to the pan, add the pesto sauce, and gently mix. Sprinkle with Parmesan or brewer's yeast and serve.

306 PASTA WITH SAUCE PROVENÇALE

CALORIES	674
CHOLESTEROL	32
VEGAN CALORIES	658
POLYUNSATS	★★☆
ANTIOXIDANTS	★★★
CALCIUM	★★☆
IRON	★★★
B VITAMINS	★★★

olive oil for stir-frying
1 onion, chopped
1lb tomatoes, chopped
1 clove garlic, crushed
¼ cup vegetable stock
¼ cup dry white wine

1 tbsp herbes de Provence
5oz tuna in oil/1¼ cups smoked tofu, cubed
7oz macaroni pasta
a handful of black olives, pitted
goat's/soy cheese (optional)

Gently fry the onion in a pan with the oil until soft. Add the tomatoes and simmer for 10 minutes, then add the garlic, stock, wine, and herbs. Season and continue to simmer. Stir-fry the tuna or tofu in a separate pan with a little oil until golden. Set aside. Boil the pasta in plenty of water with a little salt and oil. Drain and place in a large serving dish. Pour the sauce over and top with the fried tuna or tofu and the olives. Sprinkle with a little grated cheese (if using) and serve.

307 LINGUINE MUSCOLI

★ ♥ ☘ ▣

CALORIES	518
CHOLESTEROL	23
VEGAN CALORIES	575
POLYUNSATS	★☆☆
ANTIOXIDANTS	★★☆
CALCIUM	★★☆
IRON	★★★
B VITAMINS	★★☆

1 tbsp olive oil
2 shallots, finely chopped
½ cup dry white wine
1½ lb mussels (with shells)/
    2oz soy chunks, soaked in water
    with mixed seaweed
1½ cups mushrooms, sliced

juice of ¼ lemon
5oz linguine pasta
1 tsp cornstarch dissolved in a little
    cold water
salt and black pepper to taste
1 tbsp parsley, finely chopped

Gently fry the shallots in a large Dutch oven with the oil until soft.
Add the wine and the mussels or soy chunks (with their soaking water)
and boil for 5 minutes, or until the mussels have opened (shake from
time to time to ensure they cook evenly). Drain and set aside, reserving
the cooking liquid. (If you are using mussels, shell them, strain their liquid
and add it to the reserved cooking liquid.) Bring the cooking liquid to a
boil, add the mushrooms and lemon juice and let the sauce reduce for
5 minutes. Meanwhile, cook the pasta in plenty of boiling water with a
little salt and oil. Drain. Thicken the sauce with the dissolved cornstarch.
Season and add the parsley and the mussels or soy chunks. Divide the
pasta between two plates, top with the sauce, and serve.

308 BUCKWHEAT PASTA WITH
SWEET AND SOUR SAUCE

♥ ◊ ☘ ◉

CALORIES	558
CHOLESTEROL	61
VEGAN CALORIES	569
POLYUNSATS	★☆☆
ANTIOXIDANTS	★★☆
CALCIUM	★☆☆
IRON	★★☆
B VITAMINS	★★☆

olive oil for stir-frying
2 shallots, sliced
1 tsp ground coriander
6oz chicken breast/seitan,
    cut into chunks
1 red apple, cored
    and sliced
3 small zucchini, sliced
2 cloves garlic, crushed

1 tbsp cider vinegar
1 tsp maple syrup
1 tsp Tabasco sauce
1 tbsp tamari (soy sauce)
1 cup vegetable stock
7oz buckwheat pasta
1 tsp cornstarch diluted in a
    little cold water
salt and black pepper to taste

Heat a little oil in a Dutch oven and stir-fry the shallots, coriander,
and chicken or seitan chunks over a medium heat until golden. Add
the apple, zucchini, and garlic, turn up the heat a little, and stir-fry for a
further minute. Lower the heat, add the vinegar, maple syrup, Tabasco
sauce, tamari, and stock. Bring to the boil and simmer for 5–10 minutes,
or until the chicken is tender. Meanwhile, boil the pasta in plenty of water
with a little salt and oil. Add the diluted cornstarch to the sauce and heat
through, stirring continuously, until the sauce thickens. Season and serve
with the cooked and drained pasta.

309 ▼ SPAGHETTI BOLOGNESE

⭐💚🌿☕

CALORIES	728
CHOLESTEROL	47
VEGAN CALORIES	758
POLYUNSATS	★★☆
ANTIOXIDANTS	★★★
CALCIUM	★★☆
IRON	★★★
B VITAMINS	★★★

3 tbsp olive oil
1 onion, chopped
⅔ cup ground pork/
    3oz burgamix (dry weight)
2 cloves garlic, crushed
1 carrot, diced
1 stick celery (with leaves), chopped
2 tsp dried thyme
1 sprig each of rosemary and sage

1 tbsp basil (or 1 tsp dried)
1 tbsp tamari (soy sauce)
5 tomatoes, puréed
1 tsp raw cane sugar
2 tbsp tomato paste
salt
7oz spaghetti
parsley and black pepper
    to garnish

Gently fry the onion in the oil until soft. Add the ground pork or burgamix, together with the garlic, and stir-fry until it browns. (If you are using burgamix, you may need to add more oil.) Add the carrot, celery, herbs, and tamari. Heat through, then add the puréed tomatoes, sugar, and tomato paste. Bring to a boil and simmer for 10 minutes, stirring occasionally. Meanwhile, boil the spaghetti in plenty of water with a little salt and oil. Drain. Season the sauce. Divide the cooked spaghetti between two large plates. Top with the Bolognese sauce, garnish with plenty of parsley and black pepper, and serve immediately.

310 TAGLIATELLE WITH A-PLUS SAUCE

CALORIES	817
CHOLESTEROL	219
VEGAN CALORIES	785
POLYUNSATS	★★☆
ANTIOXIDANTS	★★★
CALCIUM	★★☆
IRON	★★★
B VITAMINS	★★★

7oz tagliatelle pasta
olive oil for stir-frying
1 small leek, sliced
2 cloves garlic, chopped
½ cup chicken livers/4 oz
    seitan, sliced
2 carrots, diced

½lb spinach or Swiss chard,
    chopped
2 tsp paprika
1 small bunch parsley, chopped
1 sprig sage, chopped
½ cup port wine
salt and black pepper to taste

Boil the pasta in plenty of water with a little salt and oil. Drain. Gently stir-fry the leek and garlic in a skillet with a little oil. Add the chicken or seitan slices, turn up the heat, and stir-fry until they begin to brown. Add the carrots, spinach or Swiss chard, and herbs. Heat through, add the port wine, and season. Continue to stir while you let the ingredients blend. Place the cooked pasta in a serving dish, add the sauce, mix, and serve.

311 SPAGHETTI WITH CREOLE SAUCE

CALORIES	693
CHOLESTEROL	31
VEGAN CALORIES	679
POLYUNSATS	★★☆
ANTIOXIDANTS	★★★
CALCIUM	★★★
IRON	★★★
B VITAMINS	★★★

2 tbsp olive oil
1¾ cup mushrooms, sliced
⅔ cups cod fillet/1¼ cups tofu,
    cut into chunks
2 tbsp parsley, chopped
1 tsp each of thyme and turmeric
1 tsp black pepper

1 cup yellow pumpkin, diced
3½ cups spinach, chopped
3 tbsp dried mixed seaweed flakes,
    soaked in water for 10 minutes
½ cup coconut milk
7oz spaghetti pasta
salt to taste

Sauté the mushrooms and the cod or tofu in a wok or a skillet with the oil for 3 minutes. Add the herbs and spices, followed by the pumpkin and spinach, then add the seaweed (with its soaking water). Heat through, add the coconut milk, partially cover, and gently simmer for 10 minutes. Boil the pasta in plenty of water with a little salt and oil. Check the seasoning of the sauce and serve with the cooked and drained pasta.

312 PASTA WITH GOUJONS IN A SPINACH SAUCE

CALORIES	922
CHOLESTEROL	177
VEGAN CALORIES	694
POLYUNSATS	★★★
ANTIOXIDANTS	★★★
CALCIUM	★★☆
IRON	★★★
B VITAMINS	★★★

⅔ cup crème fraîche/soy cream
1 pinch freshly grated nutmeg
6 cups fresh spinach, cooked in
    boiling water, drained, rinsed,
    and water pressed out
salt and black pepper to taste

5oz penne pasta
olive oil for frying
½lb turkey breast/9oz seitan,
    sliced
1 tomato, broiled whole

Heat the cream in a Dutch oven with the nutmeg. When it boils, add the spinach. Mix well, season, and set aside. Cook the pasta in plenty of boiling water with a little salt and oil. Heat a little oil in a skillet and sauté the turkey or seitan slices over a medium heat for 5 minutes. Reheat the sauce. Place the pasta on a large plate with the turkey or seitan slices, pour the sauce over, garnish with the broiled tomato, and serve.

313 MOROCCAN TAJINE

CALORIES	515
CHOLESTEROL	0
VEGAN CALORIES	515
POLYUNSATS	★☆☆
ANTIOXIDANTS	★★★
CALCIUM	★★☆
IRON	★★☆
B VITAMINS	★★☆

2 tbsp olive oil
1 shallot, sliced
1 cinnamon stick (¾in long)
½ tsp ground cumin
½ tsp ground coriander
2 cloves garlic, crushed
1 cup hokaido pumpkin, peeled,
   deseeded, and cubed
1 small sweet potato, peeled
   and cubed

1 packed cup garbanzos, cooked
   or canned
1 tbsp tomato paste
½ cup red wine
1 cup vegetable stock
a handful of dried (unsulphured)
   apricots, or raisins
salt, saffron threads, and cayenne
   pepper to taste

Heat the oil in a heavy-based Dutch oven (or a tajine), add the
shallot and gently sweat for 2 minutes. Then add the spices and the
garlic, and fry for 30 seconds before adding the pumpkin, sweet potato
and garbanzos. Stir-fry for 3 minutes, then add the tomato paste, red wine,
stock, and apricots or raisins. Season, bring to a boil and simmer until the
vegetables are soft. Serve with steamed couscous.

314 ARABIAN HALF-MOON PASTRIES

CALORIES	425
CHOLESTEROL	0
VEGAN CALORIES	425
POLYUNSATS	★★★
ANTIOXIDANTS	★★★
CALCIUM	★★★
IRON	★★★
B VITAMINS	★★☆

7oz ready-made tart dough, rolled
   out thinly
1 lb spinach, curly kale, or Swiss
   chard, chopped

2 tbsp lemon juice
2 tbsp olive oil
½ tsp allspice and 1 pinch salt
1 tsp sumac (optional)

Preheat the oven to 200°C/400°F/gas mark 6. Cut the tart dough into
approximately 4in rounds with a cookie cutter. Place the spinach, curly
kale, or Swiss chard in a bowl and mix in the remaining ingredients.
Place a large spoonful of filling on each dough round and fold each one
into a half-moon shape. Firmly pinch together the edges of each pastry
and place them on a greased baking sheet. Bake in the middle of a hot
oven until they brown – approximately 15 minutes. Serve with a salad.

315 INDIAN KORMA

CALORIES	587
CHOLESTEROL	125
VEGAN CALORIES	465
POLYUNSATS	★★★
ANTIOXIDANTS	★★☆
CALCIUM	★★☆
IRON	★★☆
B VITAMINS	★★☆

2 tbsp olive oil
1 small onion, chopped
1 clove garlic, chopped
1½ cups chicken breast/
   tofu, diced
2 tbsp wheat flour
1 tbsp mild curry powder

1 tbsp raisins
1 cup chicken/vegetable stock
2 tsp lemon juice
1 tbsp plain/soy yogurt
1 tbsp almond butter
salt and black pepper to taste
1 tbsp flaked almonds, toasted

Heat the oil in a heavy-based pan and gently stir-fry the onion and garlic
until they begin to soften. Coat the chicken or tofu cubes with a mixture
of flour and curry powder, add to the pan, and fry until they begin to
brown. Add the raisins and stock, bring to a boil, and simmer for 10
minutes. Remove from the heat, add the lemon juice, yogurt, and almond
butter. Season, garnish with toasted almond flakes, and serve with rice.

316 ◄ CUBAN COD
★ ♥ ⊘

CALORIES	522
CHOLESTEROL	98
VEGAN CALORIES	405
POLYUNSATS	★★★
ANTIOXIDANTS	★★★
CALCIUM	★★☆
IRON	★★☆
B VITAMINS	★★☆

1 large potato, finely sliced
corn oil for drizzling and frying
1 onion, chopped
1 clove garlic, chopped
1 tsp tomato paste
1 cup fish/vegetable stock

pinch saffron threads
2 dried hot chilies
14oz fresh cod fillet, halved/
   1¾ cups marinated tofu,
sliced
salt and cayenne pepper

Preheat the oven to 220°C/425°F/gas mark 7. Place the potato slices in a baking dish and drizzle with oil. Bake in a hot oven for 10 minutes. Meanwhile, fry the onion and the garlic in a skillet with a little oil, add the tomato paste, stock, saffron, and chilies, and bring to a boil. Season to taste, and set aside. Place the cod fillet or tofu slices on top of the partially-cooked potato slices. Pour the sauce over and bake for a further 10 minutes until the fish is tender. Serve with wedges of lemon.

317 TURKISH PILAF
★ ♥ 🌿

CALORIES	549
CHOLESTEROL	52
VEGAN CALORIES	558
POLYUNSATS	★★☆
ANTIOXIDANTS	★★★
CALCIUM	★★☆
IRON	★★★
B VITAMINS	★★☆

¾ cup Puy lentils
5oz chicken breast/seitan
2 tbsp olive oil
½ tsp ground cinnamon
½ tsp ground coriander
1 tsp turmeric
1 leek, sliced

1 carrot, sliced
½ cup bulgur
1 tbsp raisins
⅔ cup vegetable stock
salt and black pepper to taste
a handful of cilantro leaves

Boil the lentils in a saucepan with three times their volume of water. Cut the chicken or seitan into cubes. Heat the oil in a heavy-based pan and add the spices, then the leek. Add the chicken or seitan cubes and stir-fry for 5 minutes until they begin to brown. Add the carrot, bulgur, and raisins. Stir-fry for a further minute before adding the stock. Bring to a boil. Add the partially-cooked lentils (with their cooking water), cover, and very gently simmer for 10–15 minutes until the water is absorbed. Season, garnish with cilantro leaves, and serve hot with plain or soy yogurt.

318 SRI LANKAN MALLUNG
★ ♥ ⊘ ◻

CALORIES	495
CHOLESTEROL	0
VEGAN CALORIES	495
POLYUNSATS	★★★
ANTIOXIDANTS	★★★
CALCIUM	★★☆
IRON	★★☆
B VITAMINS	★★☆

2 tbsp grapeseed oil
1 leek, sliced
1 clove garlic, crushed
1 tsp black mustard seeds
1 pinch cayenne pepper
½ tsp each of turmeric and cumin

2¼ cups broccoli florets
1¾ cups pumpkin, peeled,
   deseeded, and cubed
1 cup coconut milk
1 tbsp lime juice
2 tbsp shredded fresh coconut

Gently heat the oil in a large Dutch oven or a wok and sweat the leek for 2 minutes, then add the garlic and the spices. When the mustard seeds start to pop, add the broccoli and pumpkin, and stir-fry for 3–5 minutes. Add the coconut milk and bring to a boil. Gently simmer until the broccoli is tender. Spoon in the lime juice, and season with salt to taste. Remove from the heat, garnish with the shredded coconut, and serve with rice.

319 RUSSIAN PARCELS

CALORIES	569
CHOLESTEROL	35
VEGAN CALORIES	577
POLYUNSATS	★★★
ANTIOXIDANTS	★★★
CALCIUM	★★★
IRON	★★☆
B VITAMINS	★★☆

olive oil for frying and brushing
5oz smoked salmon/tempeh, coarsely chopped
6 cups fresh curly kale, chopped
1 small black radish, finely chopped

1 tbsp capers
10 black olives, pitted, and chopped
1 pinch cayenne pepper
salt to taste
8 phyllo pastry sheets

Preheat the oven to 220°C/425°F/gas mark 7. Heat a little oil in a large Dutch oven and fry the smoked salmon or tempeh for 2 minutes until golden. Add the curly kale and gently stir-fry until it begins to soften. Then add the black radish, capers, and olives, stir-fry for a further minute, and season. Lay a pastry sheet on another sheet. Use two sheets to make each parcel. Brush the top of the pastry with oil and place a generous portion of filling in the middle. Fold into parcels and firmly press together the edges. (Make as many parcels as you have filling or pastry for.) Brush each parcel with a little more oil and place on a greased baking sheet. Bake in the oven until golden, approximately 10 minutes, and serve.

320 SWEDISH PYTTIPANNA

CALORIES	635
CHOLESTEROL	25
VEGAN CALORIES	568
POLYUNSATS	★★☆
ANTIOXIDANTS	★★☆
CALCIUM	★★☆
IRON	★★☆
B VITAMINS	★★☆

oil for stir-frying
1 onion, halved and sliced
2 spicy sausages (pork/soy), sliced
8–10 mushrooms, sliced
1 lb potatoes, diced

2 sticks celery, sliced
1½ cups kidney beans, cooked or canned
¼ lb green beans
salt and black pepper to taste

Heat a little oil in a large skillet and stir-fry the onion over a medium heat for 2 minutes. Add the sausages and the mushrooms, followed by the potatoes, and gently stir-fry for several more minutes until the potatoes begin to brown. Add the celery and beans. Heat through, season, and serve hot, accompanied by tomato catsup and mustard.

321 CHINESE SWEET AND SOUR VEGETABLES

CALORIES	574
CHOLESTEROL	0
VEGAN CALORIES	574
POLYUNSATS	★★★
ANTIOXIDANTS	★★☆
CALCIUM	★★☆
IRON	★★☆
B VITAMINS	★★☆

2 tbsp grapeseed oil
1 tbsp honey
1 tsp ginger, chopped
1 pinch cayenne pepper
1 leek, diagonally sliced
1 celery root, cut into sticks

2 tbsp white wine vinegar
3 tbsp miso or vegetable stock
¼ small white cabbage, finely sliced
¼ lb rice noodles
30 almonds, chopped and toasted

Heat the oil in a wok or a heavy-based skillet over a medium heat and add the honey, ginger, and cayenne pepper. Add the leek and celery root, and stir-fry for 30 seconds. Turn down the heat, cover, and simmer for 5 minutes. Add the vinegar and the miso or stock. Continue to simmer for a further 5 minutes. Add the cabbage and noodles, and stirring, simmer until the noodles are cooked. (Add a little more stock or water if necessary.) Garnish with the toasted almonds, and serve immediately.

322 ▼ SCANDINAVIAN BEET BURGERS

★♥🌿

CALORIES	485
CHOLESTEROL	0
VEGAN CALORIES	485
POLYUNSATS	★★★
ANTIOXIDANTS	★★☆
CALCIUM	★★★
IRON	★★☆
B VITAMINS	★★☆

1 generous cup well-cooked rice
1 cup tofu, grated
1 medium beet, grated
1 cup fresh bread crumbs
1 tbsp red wine vinegar

1 tbsp olive oil, plus some for frying
1 tsp dried basil
salt and black pepper to taste
all-purpose flour for dipping

Mix the cooked rice, tofu, beet, bread crumbs, vinegar, oil, and basil in a bowl. Season and shape into six flat cakes. Dip the flat cakes in the flour and fry in a skillet with a little oil over a high heat for 2 minutes on each side. Turn down the heat and continue to fry for approximately 5 minutes on each side. Serve each burger in a bun with mustard, tomato catsup, red onion, lettuce, tomato, and dill pickles.

323 MUMBAI CAULIFLOWER CURRY
★♥⊘◐

CALORIES	579
CHOLESTEROL	0
VEGAN CALORIES	579
POLYUNSATS	★★☆
ANTIOXIDANTS	★★★
CALCIUM	★★☆
IRON	★★★
B VITAMINS	★★☆

vegetable oil for stir-frying
1 small red onion, chopped
1 small red bell pepper, quartered, deseeded, and chopped
1 small eggplant, chopped
1 small cauliflower, cut into florets
½ cup flageolet beans, cooked or canned

1 tsp curry powder
½ tsp ground coriander
1¾ cups coconut milk
1 clove garlic, crushed
½ lime, peeled and chopped
1 tsp maple syrup
1 pinch cayenne pepper
1 tbsp almonds, chopped and toasted

Stir-fry the vegetables and the beans in a heavy-based pan with a little oil, adding them in the order given. Add the curry powder and coriander and stir for 30 seconds, then add the coconut milk, garlic, lime, maple syrup, cayenne pepper, and a little salt. Bring to a boil and simmer until the cauliflower is tender. Garnish with toasted almonds and serve with rice.

324 TROPICAL FILLETS
★♥⊘◐

CALORIES	413
CHOLESTEROL	91
VEGAN CALORIES	390
POLYUNSATS	★★☆
ANTIOXIDANTS	★★☆
CALCIUM	★★☆
IRON	★★★
B VITAMINS	★★☆

½ lb sole fillets/tofu strips
salt for rubbing
juice of 1 lemon
½ cup cold water
2 tsp ginger, finely chopped
1 tsp black pepper
1 tsp ground cinnamon

1 tbsp olive oil
2 cloves garlic, crushed
1 small green chili, finely sliced
1 onion, sliced
1 pinch saffron threads
1 cup coconut milk
1 lime, cut into wedges

Rub the sole or tofu with salt. Mix the lemon juice, water, ginger, black pepper, and cinnamon in a bowl, and marinate the sole or tofu for 15 minutes. Meanwhile, heat the oil in a large skillet or a wok, and gently stir-fry the garlic, chili, and onion for 2 minutes. Stir in the saffron and coconut milk, and very gently simmer for 2 minutes. Add the sole or tofu (with the marinade), and gently simmer for a further 7–10 minutes or until the fish is tender. Garnish with wedges of lime and serve with wild rice.

325 CHINESE CAULIFLOWER AND OYSTER MUSHROOMS
♥✖

CALORIES	195
CHOLESTEROL	0
VEGAN CALORIES	195
POLYUNSATS	★★★
ANTIOXIDANTS	★★☆
CALCIUM	★☆☆
IRON	★☆☆
B VITAMINS	★★☆

2 tbsp vegetable oil
1 shallot, finely chopped
1½ cups oyster mushrooms, sliced
1 small cauliflower, cut into florets
2 tsp tamari (soy sauce)
1 clove garlic, finely chopped

½ tsp Chinese five-spice powder
1 cup vegetable stock
1 tsp cornstarch dissolved in a little cold water
salt and black pepper to taste

Heat the oil in a skillet or a wok and stir-fry the shallot for 30 seconds. Add the mushrooms and cauliflower, and stir-fry for 2–3 minutes, then add the tamari, garlic, five-spice powder, and stock. Bring to a boil and simmer until the cauliflower is tender. Add the dissolved cornstarch and heat through until the sauce thickens. Season and serve with rice or noodles.

326 ITALIAN OMELET

CALORIES	400
CHOLESTEROL	391
VEGAN CALORIES	409
POLYUNSATS	★★★
ANTIOXIDANTS	★★★
CALCIUM	★★☆
IRON	★★☆
B VITAMINS	★★☆

omelet:
4 eggs
a little milk/cold water
salt and black pepper to taste
or 1 portion basic eggless omelet
   batter (see p.41)

filling:
oil for frying
1¾ cups mushrooms, chopped
4 sun-dried tomatoes, chopped
2 artichoke hearts, chopped
salt and black pepper to taste
a little vegetable margarine or butter
1 tbsp parsley mixed with 1 crushed
   clove garlic

Sauté the mushrooms in a skillet with a little oil for 2 minutes. Add the tomatoes and the artichoke hearts, and heat through. Season and set aside. Beat the eggs in a bowl, add the milk or water, and season. Alternately, prepare the eggless omelet batter. Add the filling to the batter and pour into an oiled skillet. Reduce the heat and cook each side until firm. Fold and remove from the heat. Spread a little margarine or butter over the top, garnish with the mixed parsley and garlic, and serve.

327 SPICY GARBANZO PANCAKE

CALORIES	316
CHOLESTEROL	0
VEGAN CALORIES	316
POLYUNSATS	★★☆
ANTIOXIDANTS	★★★
CALCIUM	★★☆
IRON	★★☆
B VITAMINS	★★☆

batter:
⅔ cup garbanzo flour
1 tsp ginger, finely chopped
1 pinch salt
1 tsp baking powder
1 cup water
olive oil for frying

filling:
1 small red onion
2 potatoes, finely diced
4½ cups fresh curly kale (or
   spinach), chopped
¼ tsp ground cardamom seeds
¼ tsp hot chili paste

Mix the batter ingredients in a bowl and pour into an oiled skillet. Turn down the heat and gently fry each side until golden brown. Meanwhile, stir-fry the onion and potatoes in a separate pan with a little oil until they begin to soften. Add the curly kale, the cardamom seeds and a little water. Season and simmer until the potatoes are soft. Place the filling on one half of the omelet, spread the chili paste on the other half, fold, and serve.

328 BEIJING-STYLE OMELET

CALORIES	249
CHOLESTEROL	391
VEGAN CALORIES	258
POLYUNSATS	★★☆
ANTIOXIDANTS	★★☆
CALCIUM	★★☆
IRON	★★☆
B VITAMINS	★★☆

batter:
4 eggs
a little milk/water
salt and black pepper to taste
or 1 portion basic eggless omelet
   batter (see p.41)

filling:
1 pinch Chinese five-spice powder
2 scallions or 1 small leek
oil for frying
oyster mushrooms, sliced and fried,
   and bean sprouts to garnish

Beat the eggs in a bowl, add the milk or water, and season. Alternately, prepare the eggless omelet batter. Chop the scallions or leek and add to your chosen batter, together with the five-spice powder. Pour the batter into an oiled skillet. Reduce the heat and fry each side until firm. Serve garnished with oyster mushrooms and bean sprouts.

329 SPICY WINTER OMELET

★ ✕ 🌿 ⬭

CALORIES	351
CHOLESTEROL	417
VEGAN CALORIES	389
POLYUNSATS	★★☆
ANTIOXIDANTS	★★★
CALCIUM	★★☆
IRON	★★☆
B VITAMINS	★★★

omelet:
4 eggs, beaten and seasoned
1 tbsp milk
¼ tsp hot chili paste
1 tsp ginger, finely chopped
or 1 portion basic eggless omelet
   batter (see p.41)

filling:
olive oil for frying
1 shallot, finely sliced
⅔ cup ham/5oz smoked tempeh,
   diced
1 carrot, grated
2 tbsp parsley, finely chopped

Mix your chosen batter ingredients and set aside. Sweat the onion in a skillet with a little oil until soft. Add the ham or tempeh and the carrot and fry for 5 minutes, then add the parsley, and season. Heat a little oil in a separate pan. Pour in the batter and stir with a fork. When the omelet is cooked, add the filling, fold, and serve.

330 LEEK AND POTATO PANCAKES

★ 🌿 ⬭

CALORIES	605
CHOLESTEROL	112
VEGAN CALORIES	603
POLYUNSATS	★★★
ANTIOXIDANTS	★★★
CALCIUM	★★☆
IRON	★★☆
B VITAMINS	★★☆

pancakes:
1 portion basic pancake batter
   (see p.42)
grapeseed oil for frying

filling:
4 slim leeks, trimmed, kept whole
2 carrots and 2 potatoes, diced
½ tsp caraway seeds, crushed
1 handful parsley, chopped
salt and black pepper to taste

Cook the leeks in a pan of boiling, salted water until tender, then halve them lengthwise. Mix the pancake batter and set aside. Cook the carrots and potatoes in the leek pan with a little boiling, salted water until soft, then purée with the caraway seeds, parsley, and a little cooking water. Fry the pancakes in a skillet with a little oil. When they are cooked, place some of the purée and one leek on each one, fold, and serve.

331 ENCHILADAS WITH BRAZIL NUTS AND POMEGRANATE

★ ♥ ⬭

CALORIES	842
CHOLESTEROL	0
VEGAN CALORIES	842
POLYUNSATS	★★★
ANTIOXIDANTS	★★★
CALCIUM	★★☆
IRON	★★☆
B VITAMINS	★★☆

enchiladas:
6 corn tortillas

filling:
corn oil for frying
1 small leek, finely sliced
½ cup Brazil nuts, chopped
1 stick celery (with leaves), chopped

½ cup vegetable stock
1 tbsp tomato paste
1 tbsp raisins
1 clove garlic, crushed
1 dash Tabasco sauce
salt and black pepper to taste
1 pomegranate, quartered, peeled,
   and seeds separated

Gently stir-fry the leek in a Dutch oven with a little oil for 3 minutes. Add the Brazil nuts and celery, and stir-fry for a further 3 minutes, then add the stock, tomato paste, and raisins. Bring to a boil. Add the garlic and Tabasco sauce, and season. Let simmer while you heat the tortillas as indicated on the package. Add the pomegranate seeds to the filling, heat through, divide among the tortillas, and serve.

332 ▲ INDIAN PANCAKES

CALORIES	386
CHOLESTEROL	6
VEGAN CALORIES	383
POLYUNSATS	★☆☆
ANTIOXIDANTS	★★☆
CALCIUM	★★☆
IRON	★★☆
B VITAMINS	★★☆

pancakes:
⅔ cup wheat flour
1 tbsp unsweetened shredded
   coconut
½ cup plain/soy yogurt
1 pinch cayenne pepper
1 pinch salt
oil for frying

filling:
1 black radish, chopped into thin
   sticks
1 handful bean sprouts
½ lb green beans, topped, tailed and
   blanched
1 handful cilantro leaves
1 tsp tamari (soy sauce)

Mix the flour, coconut, yogurt, cayenne pepper and salt with enough water
to make a smooth batter in a bowl, then cook four thin pancakes in a
skillet with a little oil. Set aside (keep warm). Stir-fry the black radish,
bean sprouts, and green beans In a separate pan with a little oil. Add the
tamari just before removing from the heat and garnish with cilantro. Fill
and fold the pancakes, and serve with mango chutney.

333 BUCKWHEAT GALETTES
★♥

CALORIES	548
CHOLESTEROL	98
VEGAN CALORIES	455
POLYUNSATS	★★★
ANTIOXIDANTS	★★☆
CALCIUM	★★☆
IRON	★★☆
B VITAMINS	★★★

galettes:
1 cup buckwheat flour
1 pinch salt
1 egg/2 tsp baking powder
2 tbsp grapeseed oil, plus some for
    frying
1¼ cups milk/soy milk

filling:
1 shallot, finely chopped

1 bay leaf
1 pinch mace
1 clove garlic, crushed
4½ cups mushrooms, chopped
1 cup vegetable stock
1 tsp cornstarch dissolved in a little
    cold water
1 cup each of green beans (chopped
    into tiny pieces) and corn kernels,
    cooked

Mix the flour, salt, and egg or baking powder in a bowl. Add the oil and
the milk, little by little, until you have a smooth batter. Set aside. Gently
fry the shallot in a Dutch oven with a little oil for 3 minutes. Add the bay
leaf, mace, and garlic. Heat through and add the mushrooms. Stir-fry for
2 minutes, then add the stock. Let simmer while you fry the galettes in a
skillet with a little oil. Add the cornstarch to the mushroom sauce and
cook until it thickens. Fill the galettes with a spoonful each of the
mushroom sauce and the cooked bean and corn mixture, and serve.

334 PIZZA NAPOLETANA
★♥🌾⊘

CALORIES	501
CHOLESTEROL	45
VEGAN CALORIES	426
POLYUNSATS	★★☆
ANTIOXIDANTS	★★☆
CALCIUM	★★☆
IRON	★★☆
B VITAMINS	★★☆

1 pizza base
3 tbsp tomato sauce, passata, or
    sauce tomate concassé
    (see p.115)
1 cup mozzarella/soy cheese,
    thinly sliced

2oz anchovy fillets/⅓ cup black
    olives, pitted
1¾ cups mushrooms, sliced
1 tbsp capers
1 pinch oregano
salt and black pepper to taste

Preheat the oven to 240°C/475°F/gas mark 9 and warm a baking sheet.
Cover the pizza base with the tomato sauce, followed by the cheese.
Top with the anchovies or olives, mushrooms, and capers. Season
(remembering that anchovies and olives are both quite salty) and bake
in the oven for approximately 20 minutes. Serve hot with a side salad.

335 WINTER SPECIAL
★♥🌾⊘

CALORIES	503
CHOLESTEROL	29
VEGAN CALORIES	450
POLYUNSATS	★★☆
ANTIOXIDANTS	★★☆
CALCIUM	★★☆
IRON	★★☆
B VITAMINS	★★☆

1 pizza base
2–3 tbsp tomato sauce, passata, or
    sauce tomate concassé
    (see p.115)
1 clove garlic, finely chopped
1 onion, finely chopped

1 cup shiitake mushrooms
1½ cups broccoli florets,
    blanched
oregano, salt and black pepper
1 cup mozzarella/soy cheese,
    grated

Preheat the oven to 240°C/475°F/gas mark 9 and warm a baking sheet.
Spread the tomato sauce over the pizza base and sprinkle with garlic and
onion. Slice the shiitake and add them to the pizza, together with the
broccoli. Season to taste, sprinkle with cheese, and bake in the oven
for approximately 15 minutes. Serve hot with a side salad.

336 PIZZA POSILLIPO

CALORIES	510
CHOLESTEROL	197
VEGAN CALORIES	750
POLYUNSATS	★★☆
ANTIOXIDANTS	★★★
CALCIUM	★★★
IRON	★★★
B VITAMINS	★★★

1 pizza base
2 tbsp tomato sauce, passata, or
   sauce tomate concassé
   (see p.115)
½ cup shrimp and 8 prepared
   calamares/1 cup walnuts and
   1 sheet toasted nori seaweed

½ small red chili, finely chopped
2 cups fresh spinach, sautéed
juice of ½ lime
salt and black pepper to taste
1 cup mozzarella/soy cheese,
   grated

Preheat the oven to 240°C/475°F/gas mark 9 and warm a baking sheet. Cover the pizza base with the tomato sauce. Top with the shrimp and calamares or walnuts and nori. Add the chili and the spinach. Sprinkle with lime juice, season, and sprinkle with cheese. Bake in the oven for approximately 15 minutes. Serve hot with a side salad.

337 PIZZA MARIO

CALORIES	495
CHOLESTEROL	39
VEGAN CALORIES	462
POLYUNSATS	★★☆
ANTIOXIDANTS	★★☆
CALCIUM	★★☆
IRON	★★☆
B VITAMINS	★★★

1 pizza base
2–3 tbsp tomato sauce, passata, or
   sauce tomate concassé
   (see p.115)
8 cooked mussels/2oz
   seitan, cut into chunks
1 shallot, finely chopped

6 anchovy fillets/12 black olives,
   pitted and chopped, plus some
   to garnish
salt and black pepper to taste
2 tbsp Parmesan/brewer's yeast
   flakes
1 tbsp olive oil

Preheat the oven to 230°C/450°F/gas mark 8 and warm a baking sheet. Mix the tomato sauce with the mussels or seitan, shallot and anchovies or olives in a bowl, and season. Place the pizza base on the preheated, oiled sheet and spread the topping over it. Garnish with anchovies or olives, sprinkle with Parmesan or brewer's yeast flakes, and drizzle with oil. Bake in a hot oven for 12–15 minutes. Serve hot with a side salad.

338 PIZZA QUATTRO STAGIONI (FOUR SEASONS)

CALORIES	510
CHOLESTEROL	35
VEGAN CALORIES	450
POLYUNSATS	★★☆
ANTIOXIDANTS	★★☆
CALCIUM	★★☆
IRON	★★☆
B VITAMINS	★★☆

1 pizza base
2–3 tbsp tomato sauce, passata or
   sauce tomate concassé
   (see p.115)
2 artichoke hearts (in oil), sliced
1 tomato and ½ green bell pepper
100g (3½oz) mushrooms, sliced and

   sautéed
1 clove garlic, crushed
3 anchovy fillets/8 black olives,
   pitted
oregano, salt and black pepper
100g (3½oz) mozzarella/soya
   cheese, grated

Preheat the oven to 240°C/475°F/gas mark 9 and warm a baking sheet. Spread the tomato sauce over the pizza base and divide into quarters. Top the first quarter with artichoke, the second with sliced tomato and bell pepper, the third with mushrooms and garlic, and the fourth with anchovies or olives. Season to taste, sprinkle with cheese, and bake in the oven for approximately 20 minutes. Serve hot with a side salad.

PIZZA CALZONE

CALORIES	527
CHOLESTEROL	46
VEGAN CALORIES	497
POLYUNSATS	★★☆
ANTIOXIDANTS	★★☆
CALCIUM	★★☆
IRON	★★☆
B VITAMINS	★★★

1 unbaked pizza base
2–3 tbsp tomato sauce, passata, or
   sauce tomate concassé
   (see p.115)
½ cup cooked ham/4 oz tempeh,
   cubed

1¾ cups oyster mushrooms,
   sautéed
2 tbsp fresh pineapple chunks
oregano, salt and black pepper
1 cup mozzarella/soy cheese,
   grated

Preheat the oven to 220°C/425°F/gas mark 7 and warm a baking sheet.
Spread the tomato sauce over half of the pizza base. Top with the ham or
tempeh, mushrooms and pineapple chunks. Season to taste and sprinkle
with grated cheese. Fold the base over the filling, press the edges
together to seal, and cut a couple of slits over the top. Bake in the oven
for approximately 20 minutes, or until the crust is beginning to brown.
Serve hot with a side salad.

340 ▲ SPICED BEAN AND JUNIPER CASSEROLE

CALORIES	423
CHOLESTEROL	0
VEGAN CALORIES	423
POLYUNSATS	★☆☆
ANTIOXIDANTS	★★★
CALCIUM	★★☆
IRON	★★☆
B VITAMINS	★★☆

2 tbsp olive oil
1 red onion, chopped
1 clove garlic, crushed
1 potato, cut into chunks
1 carrot, sliced
1 stick celery, sliced
1 tsp ground cumin and coriander
salt and cayenne pepper
   to taste

2 cups dried lima beans, cooked,
   or canned and drained
3 tomatoes, chopped
1 sprig each of thyme and
   rosemary
1¼ cups vegetable stock, heated
4 juniper berries, lightly crushed
1 tbsp parsley, finely chopped

Heat the oil in a Dutch oven and gently sauté the onion, garlic, potato, carrot and celery for 5 minutes. Add the cumin and coriander, and season. Sauté for a couple more minutes, then add the beans, followed by the tomatoes, thyme, and rosemary. Sauté for a further 2 minutes, then add the stock and the juniper berries. Bring to a boil, cover and gently simmer until the vegetables are cooked. Garnish with parsley, and serve with rice or thick slices of whole wheat bread and cheese or soy cheese.

341 SCALLOPS IN MUSHROOM SAUCE

CALORIES	619
CHOLESTEROL	73
VEGAN CALORIES	611
POLYUNSATS	★★★
ANTIOXIDANTS	★★★
CALCIUM	★★☆
IRON	★★☆
B VITAMINS	★★★

2 turkey scallops, flattened and
  seasoned/2 ready-made
  vegetarian scallops
1 tsp paprika
olive oil for (stir-)frying
10oz mushrooms, chopped

1 tbsp wheat flour
6 tbsp water
1 tbsp lemon juice
approximately 2 tbsp cream/
  soy cream
salt to taste

Sprinkle the scallops with paprika and fry them in a skillet with a
little oil until golden and cooked through. Set aside (keep warm). Heat
a little more oil in a small Dutch oven, add the mushrooms, and stir-fry
until they give off their juices. Sprinkle with the flour and stir for a further
minute. Add the water and the lemon juice, and enough cream to make a
thick sauce. Gently simmer for 5 minutes, then season. Place the fried
scallops on two plates, cover with the mushroom sauce, and serve with
boiled potatoes and carrots.

342 SPICY PEAS AND POTATOES

CALORIES	408
CHOLESTEROL	0
VEGAN CALORIES	408
POLYUNSATS	★☆☆
ANTIOXIDANTS	★★☆
CALCIUM	★☆☆
IRON	★★☆
B VITAMINS	★★☆

2 tbsp olive oil
1 onion, chopped
1 large potato, chopped
1 cup garbanzos, cooked
  or canned
1 cup peas, fresh or frozen
1 tsp turmeric

1 pinch cayenne pepper
1 tsp ground cumin
1 cup water
1 tbsp tomato paste
1 pinch raw cane sugar and salt
½ tsp garam masala

Heat the oil in a Dutch oven or a wok, add the onion, followed by the
chopped potatoes and stir-fry for 2 minutes. Add the garbanzos, peas,
and spices. Stir-fry for a further 2 minutes, then pour in the water, and
bring to a boil. Add the tomato paste, sugar, and salt, and simmer for
10–15 minutes until the potatoes are tender. Check the seasoning,
garnish with garam masala, and serve with rice.

343 BROCCOLI AND BRAZIL NUT STIR-FRY

CALORIES	568
CHOLESTEROL	0
VEGAN CALORIES	568
POLYUNSATS	★★★
ANTIOXIDANTS	★★★
CALCIUM	★★★
IRON	★★☆
B VITAMINS	★★☆

2 tbsp olive oil
1 clove garlic, chopped
¾ cup Brazil nuts, chopped
1 lb broccoli
2 tbsp tamari (soy sauce)
½ cup vegetable stock

2 tbsp lemon juice
1 tbsp toasted sesame oil
2 tsp cornstarch dissolved in a
  little cold water
black pepper to taste

Heat the olive oil in a wok and add the garlic and Brazil nuts. Cut the
broccoli into florets and add to the wok. Stir-fry for 1 minute, then add the
tamari and the stock. Simmer for 5 minutes and add the lemon juice and
sesame oil. Add the cornstarch, stir, and simmer for a few more minutes
until the mixture thickens. Season and serve hot with rice noodles.

344 LEMON AND MUSHROOM RISOTTO

CALORIES	596
CHOLESTEROL	0
VEGAN CALORIES	596
POLYUNSATS	★★☆
ANTIOXIDANTS	★★☆
CALCIUM	★★☆
IRON	★★☆
B VITAMINS	★★☆

1 cup wholegrain rice
3 tbsp olive oil
1 onion, thinly sliced
2½ cups mushrooms, sliced
1¼ cups vegetable stock
salt to taste
1 tsp turmeric

4 cloves garlic, crushed
1 large handful parsley,
 chopped
flesh of ½ lemon, chopped
1 tbsp chervil, chopped
1 dash Tabasco sauce

Parboil the rice in a pan for 10 minutes. Meanwhile, gently stir-fry the onion and the mushrooms in a Dutch oven with 2 tablespoons of oil. Then add the parboiled and drained rice and stir-fry for a few more minutes before adding the stock and a little salt. Bring to a boil and simmer for 15 minutes. Add the rest of the ingredients except the oil. Heat through. Add the remaining tablespoon, of oil and serve immediately.

345 GARBANZOS AND POTATOES IN RICH TOMATO SAUCE

CALORIES	414
CHOLESTEROL	0
VEGAN CALORIES	414
POLYUNSATS	★★☆
ANTIOXIDANTS	★★☆
CALCIUM	★☆☆
IRON	★★☆
B VITAMINS	★★☆

3 tbsp olive oil
1 small onion, sliced
2 potatoes, sliced
1½ cups garbanzos, cooked or
 canned

⅓ cup water
1 tbsp tomato paste (purée)
2 cloves garlic, crushed
2 tsp maple syrup
salt and black pepper to taste

Gently stir-fry the onion in a heavy-based pan or a wok with the oil for 3 minutes. Add the potatoes and continue to stir-fry until they begin to brown. Add the garbanzos, stir-fry for 3 minutes and pour in the water. Bring to the boil and simmer until the potatoes are tender, approximately 5–10 minutes. Add the tomato paste, garlic and maple syrup. Season. Heat through, adjust the seasoning, and serve hot or cold with rice.

346 PICCATA IN GARLIC CREAM

CALORIES	815
CHOLESTEROL	222
VEGAN CALORIES	510
POLYUNSATS	★★★
ANTIOXIDANTS	★★★
CALCIUM	★★☆
IRON	★★☆
B VITAMINS	★★☆

olive oil for frying
2 shallots, chopped
2 cups carrots, sliced
4 cloves garlic
10oz pork scallops,
 flattened/2 ready-made

vegetarian scallops
½ cup white wine
½ cup vegetable stock
½ cup crème fraîche/soy cream
salt and black pepper to taste

Sweat the shallots in a Dutch oven with a little oil. Add the carrots, cover with cold water, season, bring to a boil and slowly cook until tender. Meanwhile, blanch the garlic in a saucepan of boiling water for 2 minutes. Fry the scallops in a skillet with a little oil until golden brown. Set aside (keep warm). Pour the wine and stock into the skillet, then add the blanched garlic and cream. Let reduce for 5 minutes. Purée and season. Divide the scallops between two plates with the carrots to the side. Top with the sauce. Serve with boiled potatoes and green beans.

WINTER TAPAS TARTS

CALORIES	521
CHOLESTEROL	77
VEGAN CALORIES	483
POLYUNSATS	★★★
ANTIOXIDANTS	★★★
CALCIUM	★★★
IRON	★★★
B VITAMINS	★★★

½ shallot, chopped
1 tbsp tomato paste
1 tbsp parsley, chopped
1 tsp paprika
1 pinch each of sugar and salt
1 dash Tabasco sauce
2 cloves garlic, chopped
oil for stir-frying
1 cup tuna, cut into chunks/
   2oz soy chunks, soaked in water
   with 2 tbsp seaweed for
   5–10 minutes

5oz ready-made puff pastry, halved
   and rolled out
1 cup cauliflower florets,
   blanched
8–10 cremini mushrooms, thinly
   sliced
salt and black pepper to taste
1 tbsp capers
¼ cup mozzarella/soy cheese,
   grated
2 tbsp Parmesan/brewer's yeast
   flakes

Preheat the oven to 220°C/425°F/gas mark 7. Blend the shallot, tomato paste, parsley, paprika, sugar, salt, Tabasco sauce, and garlic in a bowl with a little water. Stir-fry the tuna or soya chunks in a skillet with a little oil until golden. Line two 1½ x 4in tart pans with the pastry. Add the blended tomato mixture, followed by a layer of blanched cauliflower and mushroom slices. Season and sprinkle with capers and mozzarella or soy cheese. Sprinkle with Parmesan or brewer's yeast flakes, bake in the middle of a hot oven until the tarts begin to brown, and serve.

348 WINTER CHESTNUT CASSEROLE

CALORIES	467
CHOLESTEROL	0
VEGAN CALORIES	467
POLYUNSATS	★★☆
ANTIOXIDANTS	★★★
CALCIUM	★★☆
IRON	★★☆
B VITAMINS	★★☆

2 tbsp olive oil
½ cup shallots, kept whole
1⅓ cups peeled chestnuts,
   fresh, canned, or dried
   and soaked

1 cup vegetable stock
1¾ cups Brussels sprouts,
   trimmed
salt and black pepper to taste

Gently sauté the shallots in a Dutch oven with the oil until they begin to brown. Add the chestnuts and stir-fry for 5 minutes, then add the stock. Bring to a boil and gently simmer for 15 minutes. Add the Brussels sprouts and simmer until they are tender. Season and serve with rice.

349 LIVER OR SEITAN WITH GARLIC AND RED WINE VINEGAR

CALORIES	818
CHOLESTEROL	483
VEGAN CALORIES	601
POLYUNSATS	★★★
ANTIOXIDANTS	★★★
CALCIUM	★★☆
IRON	★★☆
B VITAMINS	★★★

10oz lamb's liver, sliced/
   6oz seitan, sliced
1 tbsp all-purpose flour
salt and black pepper to taste

vegetable oil for frying
2 cloves garlic, chopped
1 cup red wine vinegar
1 tbsp parsley, chopped

Flour the liver or seitan, season, and fry on both sides in a skillet with a little oil over a high heat. Set aside (keep hot). Fry the garlic in a separate pan with a little oil. Add the vinegar and let reduce to one-third of its volume. Season and add parsley. Cover the liver or seitan with the sauce, and serve on warmed plates with steamed potatoes, carrots, and broccoli.

350 SEAFOOD RISOTTO

CALORIES	594
CHOLESTEROL	72
VEGAN CALORIES	638
POLYUNSATS	★★★
ANTIOXIDANTS	★★★
CALCIUM	★★☆
IRON	★★☆
B VITAMINS	★★★

2 tbsp olive oil
1 small red onion, finely chopped
1 Florence fennel bulb, finely chopped
2 cloves garlic, crushed
½ tsp fennel seeds, crushed in a mortar
½ tsp cayenne pepper
1 pinch saffron threads
¾ cup risotto rice

1 cup dried hiziki seaweed, soaked in cold water
1 tbsp tomato paste
¼ cup dry white wine
3 cups fish/vegetable stock, heated
1 cup crabmeat/½ cup chopped walnuts
2 tbsp lemon juice
2 tbsp parsley, finely chopped

Heat the oil in a large, heavy-based Dutch oven and gently stir-fry the onion and the chopped fennel until soft. Add the garlic, fennel seeds, cayenne pepper, saffron, rice, and hiziki, and stir-fry for 3 minutes. Add the tomato paste and stir for 1 minute until the rice is coated. Pour in the wine and continue to stir until it is absorbed, then slowly add the stock. Bring to a boil, cover, and very gently simmer until the rice is cooked and all the liquid is absorbed. Stir in the crabmeat or walnuts and the lemon juice. Heat through. Adjust the seasoning, garnish with parsley, and serve.

351 TRANCHES LYONNAISES

CALORIES	711
CHOLESTEROL	483
VEGAN CALORIES	479
POLYUNSATS	★★☆
ANTIOXIDANTS	★★★
CALCIUM	★★☆
IRON	★★★
B VITAMINS	★★★

10oz lamb's liver, sliced/ 5oz seitan, sliced
2 tbsp all-purpose flour
2 onions, halved and sliced
½ cup white wine

½ cup meat/vegetable stock
salt and black pepper to taste
1 tbsp parsley, chopped

Flour the liver or seitan and fry in a skillet with a little oil until just brown on both sides. Set aside (keep hot). Add a little more oil to the pan and sweat the onions (don't let them brown). Add the white wine and the stock. Let reduce to one-third of the volume, then season. Return the fried liver or seitan to the pan, sprinkle with parsley, and serve with steamed potatoes and Brussels sprouts.

352 WINTER KEBABS

CALORIES	517
CHOLESTEROL	56
VEGAN CALORIES	455
POLYUNSATS	★★★
ANTIOXIDANTS	★★★
CALCIUM	★★☆
IRON	★★☆
B VITAMINS	★★☆

¾ cup turkey breast steaks/tofu, cut into chunks
1 sweet potato, cut into chunks
4 cloves garlic, kept whole
1 beet, cut into chunks
6 Brussels sprouts, blanched

6 button mushrooms, kept whole
2–3 tbsp olive oil
¼ cup finely chopped walnuts
1 tsp dried basil
salt to taste
1 tbsp tomato paste

Thread the turkey or tofu chunks and the vegetables alternately onto two metal skewers. Mix the oil with the chopped walnuts, basil, salt, and tomato paste in a bowl, and brush the kebabs with the mixture. Place on a greased baking sheet and broil for 5–6 minutes on each side, or until golden and cooked through. Serve on a bed of rice with a side salad.

353 TROPICAL FRUIT FLAMBÉ

CALORIES	508
CHOLESTEROL	0
VEGAN CALORIES	508
POLYUNSATS	★★★
ANTIOXIDANTS	★★★
CALCIUM	★★☆
IRON	★★☆
B VITAMINS	★☆☆

1 tbsp grapeseed oil
2 thick slices pineapple, peeled,
    cored, and halved
2 bananas, peeled and halved
    lengthwise
1 papaya, peeled, deseeded, and
    sliced
¼ fresh coconut, peeled, and thinly
    sliced
2 tbsp maple syrup
1 tbsp rum

Heat the oil in a skillet and fry the fruit pieces for 1 minute. Turn, sprinkle with the maple syrup, and fry for a further 1–2 minutes until the fruit is tender but still firm. Add the rum, heat through and carefully ignite the mixture with a taper. Gently shake the pan while allowing the rum to burn for a minute. When the rum has burned out, serve the sautéed fruit with ice cream, soy cream, plain or soy yogurt.

354 PINEAPPLE PIE

CALORIES	378
CHOLESTEROL	0
VEGAN CALORIES	378
POLYUNSATS	★★☆
ANTIOXIDANTS	★★☆
CALCIUM	★☆☆
IRON	★☆☆
B VITAMINS	★☆☆

½ pineapple, peeled, cored, and
    chopped, plus 2 thin slices
    (halved) to garnish
1 tsp maple syrup
1 tbsp agar-agar

3 tbsp water
1 prebaked 8in shortcrust
    tart case
2 tbsp fresh coconut, shredded

Purée the pineapple and maple syrup until smooth and set aside. Heat the agar-agar with the water in a small Dutch oven over a low heat, stirring continuously until the mixture bubbles and becomes gelatinous (3–4 minutes). Stir in the puréed pineapple and pour into the prebaked tart case. Let cool, then garnish with halved pineapple slices and coconut. Chill before serving.

355 BAKED CINNAMON APPLES

CALORIES	504
CHOLESTEROL	0
VEGAN CALORIES	504
POLYUNSATS	★★★
ANTIOXIDANTS	★★☆
CALCIUM	★★☆
IRON	★★☆
B VITAMINS	★★☆

2 apples, cored
2 bananas, peeled and mashed
4–6 dates, pitted and chopped
1 tbsp flaked almonds

ground cinnamon to taste
2 tbsp tahini
1 tbsp lemon juice
3 tbsp maple syrup

Preheat the oven to 180°C/350°F/gas mark 4. Cut a horizontal line in the skin of the apples around the middle and set aside. Mix one of the mashed bananas with the dates in a bowl. Stuff the cored apples with the banana and date mixture. Sprinkle the almonds and the cinnamon on top and bake in the oven for approximately 20 minutes. Meanwhile, mix the tahini with the remaining mashed banana, lemon juice, and maple syrup in a bowl with enough cold water to make a thick sauce. Place the baked apples on two dessert plates, garnish with the sauce, and serve.

356 CREAMY ORANGE SALAD

CALORIES	302
CHOLESTEROL	0
VEGAN CALORIES	302
POLYUNSATS	★★☆
ANTIOXIDANTS	★★★
CALCIUM	★★☆
IRON	★★☆
B VITAMINS	★★☆

2 oranges, peeled and diced
4 lichees, peeled, halved, and pitted
2 dates, pitted and sliced
2 mandarins, peeled and sliced

1 banana, peeled and chopped
1 tbsp cashew nuts
2 tsp maple syrup
approximately 2 tbsp almond milk

Divide the oranges, lichees, dates, and mandarins between two glass bowls. Purée the banana with the cashews, maple syrup, and enough almond milk to make a smooth cream, pour over the fruits, and serve.

357 ▼ HOT WAFFLES WITH FRESH FRUIT

CALORIES	464
CHOLESTEROL	0
VEGAN CALORIES	464
POLYUNSATS	★★☆
ANTIOXIDANTS	★★☆
CALCIUM	★★☆
IRON	★☆☆
B VITAMINS	★★☆

4 small waffles
2 mandarins, peeled and chopped
1 banana, peeled and sliced

1 pear, halved, cored, and sliced
1 tbsp chopped walnuts
2 tbsp maple syrup

Toast the waffles and place them on two dessert plates. Pile the fruit on top, sprinkle with walnuts and maple syrup, and serve immediately.

CITRUS FRUIT SALAD

CALORIES	94
CHOLESTEROL	0
VEGAN CALORIES	94
POLYUNSATS	★☆☆
ANTIOXIDANTS	★★★
CALCIUM	★☆☆
IRON	★☆☆
B VITAMINS	★☆☆

1 orange, peeled and sliced
1 pink grapefruit, peeled and sliced
1 clementine, peeled and sliced
maple syrup to taste

Place the fruit in a glass bowl. Drizzle with the maple syrup and serve.

WINTER FRUIT SALAD
WITH CREAMY DATE SAUCE

CALORIES	306
CHOLESTEROL	0
VEGAN CALORIES	306
POLYUNSATS	★☆☆
ANTIOXIDANTS	★★★
CALCIUM	★★☆
IRON	★★☆
B VITAMINS	★☆☆

1 papaya, peeled, deseeded, and
  sliced
2 kiwis, peeled and sliced
1 banana, peeled and sliced

6 dates, pitted and diced
1 tbsp lime juice
½ cup apple juice
1 tbsp rum (optional)

Arrange the papaya slices on two plates and top with the kiwi and banana slices. Purée the dates with the lime juice, apple juice and rum (if using) to make a sauce. Then heat the sauce in a small Dutch oven and pour over the fruit. Serve immediately.

FRUIT FLOWERS

CALORIES	237
CHOLESTEROL	0
VEGAN CALORIES	237
POLYUNSATS	★☆☆
ANTIOXIDANTS	★★★
CALCIUM	★★☆
IRON	★★☆
B VITAMINS	★★☆

2 oranges, peeled and horizontally
  sliced
1 banana, peeled and diagonally
  sliced
2 kiwis, peeled and horizontally

sliced
1 papaya, peeled, deseeded, and
  sliced lengthwise
2 tsp maple syrup (optional)

Arrange the fruit in layers on two flat plates, beginning from the middle and making flower-petal and leaf shapes with the fruit slices. Drizzle with the maple syrup (if using), and serve.

AFRICAN FRUIT SALAD

CALORIES	343
CHOLESTEROL	0
VEGAN CALORIES	343
POLYUNSATS	★★☆
ANTIOXIDANTS	★★★
CALCIUM	★☆☆
IRON	★☆☆
B VITAMINS	★★☆

1 avocado, halved, pitted, peeled,
  and sliced
1 guava, peeled, deseeded, and
  chopped
1 mango, peeled, deseeded, and
  chopped

1 pear, quartered, cored, and sliced
1 tangerine, peeled and chopped
1 tbsp lime juice
⅓ cup apple juice
1 tsp honey
1 tbsp grated coconut

Mix the fruit in a glass bowl and sprinkle with lime juice. Heat the apple juice in a pan and dissolve the honey. Allow the sauce to cool a little, pour over the fruit and gently mix. Garnish with coconut and serve.

PEAR TART

♡ 🌿

CALORIES	452
CHOLESTEROL	0
VEGAN CALORIES	452
POLYUNSATS	★★★
ANTIOXIDANTS	★★☆
CALCIUM	★★☆
IRON	★☆☆
B VITAMINS	★☆☆

7oz ready-made tart dough, rolled out
2 tbsp flaked almonds

2 large sweet, ripe pears, peeled, halved and cored
approximately 2oz almond paste

Preheat the oven to 200°C/400°F/gas mark 6. Use the tart dough to line an 8in square pie pan, leaving a generous rim hanging over the edge of the dish. Sprinkle with almonds. Place a knob of almond paste in the hollow of each pear half, then arrange all four pear halves in the tart case, stalk ends meeting in the middle. Fold the tart dough into the center to cover the base of the pears, and bake for 30 minutes until golden. Serve with plain or soy yogurt, crème fraîche or soy cream.

363 # FRUIT AND NUT SALAD

★ ♡ 💧 ▲ ✕

CALORIES	393
CHOLESTEROL	0
VEGAN CALORIES	393
POLYUNSATS	★★★
ANTIOXIDANTS	★★★
CALCIUM	★☆☆
IRON	★★☆
B VITAMINS	★★☆

1 banana, peeled and sliced
1 apple, cored and chopped
1 pear, cored and chopped
1 handful raisins

5 almonds, chopped
4 Brazil nuts, chopped
2 tbsp chopped walnuts
2 tbsp sunflower seeds

Mix the fresh fruit in a glass bowl. Add the raisins, nuts, and seeds and gently toss. Serve with yogurt or soy yogurt and maple syrup.

364 # APPLE SALAD WITH
CASHEW CREAM

★ ♡ 💧 ✕ 🍋

CALORIES	345
CHOLESTEROL	0
VEGAN CALORIES	345
POLYUNSATS	★★☆
ANTIOXIDANTS	★★☆
CALCIUM	★☆☆
IRON	★☆☆
B VITAMINS	★☆☆

2 dessert apples, cored and grated
2 mandarins, peeled and chopped
4 dates, pitted and chopped

⅓ cup cashew nuts
2–3 tbsp apple juice

Mix the apples, mandarins, and dates in a bowl. Purée the cashews with the apple juice to make a thick cream. Divide the apple salad between two dessert glasses, top with the cashew cream, and serve immediately.

365 # WINTER SUNSHINE SALAD

★ ♡ 💧 ✕ 🍋

CALORIES	260
CHOLESTEROL	0
VEGAN CALORIES	260
POLYUNSATS	★☆☆
ANTIOXIDANTS	★★★
CALCIUM	★☆☆
IRON	★☆☆
B VITAMINS	★☆☆

½ pineapple, peeled, cored, and cut into chunks
2 mandarins, peeled and divided into segments
1 persimmon, sliced

½ papaya, peeled, deseeded, and sliced
¼ cup orange juice
seeds from 1 pomegranate
1 dash maple syrup to taste

Divide the pineapple, mandarins, persimmon and papaya between two small glass bowls. Sprinkle with orange juice, pomegranate seeds, and maple syrup, and serve.

FOOD
FACTS

This chapter helps you to check how many calories you need each day and provides tables showing how much of each vitamin, mineral, and trace element you need for maximum health, followed by the top ten primary food sources of each micronutrient. Recommended daily amounts vary from country to country, and also evolve as our understanding of micronutrients grows; so, in reality, it is not possible to say precisely how much of a given nutrient an individual needs because we are all different and have different absorption rates and metabolisms. These figures, therefore, should be taken as guidelines for average needs of the population as a whole and not as hard and fast measurements.

Obtaining micronutrients from food is usually more efficient than taking nutritional supplements, because food provides nutrients in a steady stream as it is digested, thus making absorption more efficient. The top ten tables show you which foods to eat more of if you feel you need to increase your intake of a particular micronutrient and are intended as a guide to help you change your diet and improve health and well-being naturally.

VITAMIN A (retinol and beta-carotene)

Estimated Average Requirements
*6 micrograms of beta-carotene is equivalent to 1 microgram of retinol

AGE	MICROGRAMS RETINOL EQUIVALENT* PER DAY
0–1 year	250
1–6 years	300
7–14 years	375
From 15 years onward	500

Pregnant women should add 100 micrograms/day
Breastfeeding mothers should add 350 micrograms/day

Top Ten Foods
micrograms per 100 grams of food
*6 micrograms of beta-carotene is equivalent to 1 microgram of retinol

BETA-CAROTENE* FROM PLANT SOURCES

1. Paprika	36250
2. Carrots	12472
3. Sweet potato	8910
4. Spring greens	8295
5. Parsley	4040
6. Red bell pepper	3780
7. Spinach	3535
8. Curly kale	3145
9. Watercress	2520
10. Cantaloupe melon	1765

RETINOL FROM ANIMAL SOURCES

1. Liver	17300
2. Liver pâté	7300
3. Butter	958
4. Double cream	779
5. Margarine (average)	665
6. Crème fraîche	388
7. Cheese (average)	300
8. Light cream	291
9. Eggs	190
10. Greek-style yogurt	115

VITAMIN B1 (thiamin)

Estimated Average Requirements
amount needed per 1000 calories eaten

AGE	MILLIGRAMS PER DAY
0–12 months	0.23
From 1 year onward	0.30

Top Ten Foods
milligrams per 100 grams of food

1. Yeast extract	4.10
2. Wheat germ	2.01
3. Sunflower seeds	1.60
4. Breakfast cereals (average)	1.20
5. Peanuts	1.14
6. Pork	0.98
7. Sesame seeds	0.94
8. Oatmeal and wheat bran	0.90
9. Peas	0.74
10. Brown rice	0.59

VITAMIN B2 (riboflavin)

Estimated Average Requirements

AGF	MILLIGRAMS PER DAY
0–3 years	0.5
4–10 years	0.8
From 11 years onward	1.0

Pregnant women should add 0.3 milligrams/day
Breastfeeding mothers should add 0.5 milligrams/day

Top Ten Foods
milligrams per 100 grams of food

1 Yeast extract	11.90
2. Liver (average)	3.00
3. Breakfast cereals (average)	1.20
4. Crab	0.86
5. Almonds	0.75
6. Wheat germ	0.72
7. Venison, duck, and goose	0.60
8. Tempeh	0.48
9. Eggs and cheese (average)	0.45
10. Oyster mushrooms	0.40

VITAMIN B3 (niacin)

Estimated Average Requirements
amount needed per 1000 calories eaten

AGE	MILLIGRAMS PER DAY
From birth onward	5.5

Breastfeeding mothers should add 2.3 milligrams/day

Top Ten Foods
milligrams per 100 grams of food

1. Yeast extract	71.0
2. Wheat bran	32.6
3. Liver	19.4
4. Peanuts	19.3
5. Paprika	18.4
6. Breakfast cereals (average)	15.0
7. Game	12.0
8. Sesame seeds	10.4
9. Wheat germ	9.8
10. Tempeh	4.7

VITAMIN B5 (pantothenic acid)

Estimated Average Requirements

AGE	MILLIGRAMS PER DAY
0–1 years	1.7
From 1 year onward	3.0

Top Ten Foods
milligrams per 100 grams of food

1. Fava beans	3.8
2. Liver	3.8
3. Breakfast cereals (average)	3.8
4. Peanuts	2.7
5. Cod roe	2.6
6. Wheat bran and wheat germ	2.2
7. Sesame seeds	2.1
8. Mushrooms	2.0
9. Eggs	1.8
10. Trout	1.6

VITAMIN B6 (pyridoxine)

Estimated Average Requirements

AGE	MILLIGRAMS PER DAY
0–3 years	0.7
4–6 years	0.9
7–10 years	1.1
From 11 years onward	1.5

Pregnant women should add 0.2 milligrams/day
Breastfeeding mothers should add 0.3 milligrams/day

Top Ten Foods
milligrams per 100 grams of food

1. Wheat germ	3.30
2. Tempeh	1.86
3. Muesli	1.60
4. Yeast extract	1.60
5. Wheat bran	1.38
6. Sesame seeds	0.76
7. Salmon	0.75
8. Walnuts	0.67
9. Venison	0.65
10. Turkey	0.61

VITAMIN B12 (cobalamin)

Estimated Average Requirements

AGE	MICROGRAMS PER DAY
0–12 months	0.1–0.5
1–6 years	0.7–0.9
From 7 years onward	1.0

Breastfeeding mothers should add 0.5 micrograms/day

Top Ten Foods
micrograms per 100 grams of food

1. Liver	58.0
2. Mussels	35.0
3. Dried seaweed, nori	27.5
4. Yeast extract	13.3
5. Kippers, sardines, anchovies, and cod roe	11.0
6. Shrimp	8.0
7. Salmon, trout and mackerel	5.0
8. Duck, rabbit, beef, lamb, turkey, and goose	2.5
9. Eggs	2.5
10. Cheese	2.0

FOLATE (folic acid)

Estimated Average Requirements

AGE	MICROGRAMS PER DAY
0–3 years	50
4–6 years	75
From 7 years onward	150

Pregnant women should add 100 micrograms/day
Breastfeeding mothers should add 60 micrograms/day

Top Ten Foods
micrograms per 100 grams of food

1. Yeast extract	2620
2. Chicken liver	1350
3. Black-eyed beans	630
4. Soy flour and soy beans	345
5. Wheat bran	260
6. Lambs liver	250
7. Purple broccoli	195
8. Garbanzos, mung and, red kidney beans	180
9. Asparagus, parsley, Swiss chard, and Savoy cabbage	170
10. Beets	150

BIOTIN

Estimated Average Requirements

AGE	MICROGRAMS PER DAY
All ages	15–100

Top Ten Foods
micrograms per 100 grams of food

1. Chicken liver	216
2. Peanuts	110
3. Hazelnuts, almonds, and soy beans	65
4. Tempeh	53
5. Plaice	47
6. Wheat bran	45
7. Wheat germ	25
8. Eggs	20
9. Oatmeal	17
10. Mushrooms	15

VITAMIN C (ascorbic acid)

Estimated Average Requirements

AGE	MILLIGRAMS PER DAY
0–10 years	20
From 11 years onward	30

Pregnant and breastfeeding women should add
20 milligrams/day

Top Ten Foods
milligrams per 100 grams of food

1. Guava	230
2. Blackcurrants	200
3. Parsley	190
4. Spring greens	180
5. Green and red bell peppers, and chili peppers	120
6. Brussels sprouts	115
7. Curly kale	110
8. Broccoli	87
9. Watercress	62
10. Papaya	60

VITAMIN D (cholecalciferol)

Estimated Average Requirements
with daily exposure of the skin to sunshine
or skyshine no dietary vitamin D is needed

AGE	MICROGRAMS PER DAY
0–6 years	10
From 7 years onward	2.5

Pregnant and breastfeeding women should add
7.5 micrograms/day

Top Ten Foods
micrograms per 100 grams of food

1. Herring	19.0
2. Cod roe	17.0
3. Trout	9.6
4. Kipper and mackerel	8.1
5. Salmon	7.1
6. Sardines and tuna	4.0
7. Eggs	1.8
8. Pancakes (made with whole milk)	1.3
9. Liver	1.1
10. Butter and pork	0.9

VITAMIN E (tocopherols)

Estimated Average Requirements

AGE	MILLIGRAMS PER DAY
All ages	4

Top Ten Foods
milligrams per 100 grams of food

1. Wheat germ oil	136.7
2. Sunflower and safflower oil	45.0
3. Sunflower seeds	37.8
4. Almonds and hazelnuts	24.5
5. Sun-dried tomatoes	24.0
6. Wheat germ	22.0
7. Corn oil	17.2
8. Brazil nuts	7.18
9. Fresh mint	5.00
10. Avocado and walnuts	3.50

VITAMIN K

Estimated Average Requirements

AGE	MICROGRAMS PER DAY
0–1 year	10
From 1 year onward	1/kilo body weight

Top Ten Foods
micrograms per 100 grams of food

1. Curly kale	623
2. Parsley	548
3. Spinach and spring greens	394
4. Watercress	315
5. Cabbage	242
6. Broccoli	185
7. Brussels sprouts	153
8. Lettuce	129
9. Safflower oil	113
10. Asparagus	52

CALCIUM

Estimated Average Requirements

AGE	MILLIGRAMS PER DAY
0–3 years	400
4–10 years	450
11–18 years	800
From 18 years onward	700

Breastfeeding mothers should add 500 milligrams/day

Top Ten Foods
milligrams per 100 grams of food

1. Parmesan cheese	1025
2. Sesame seeds	670
3. Tofu	510
4. Cheese (average)	450
5. Anchovies and sardines	420
6. Dried figs, almonds, and yogurt	250
7. Purple sprouting broccoli	200
8. Spring greens, spinach, and curly kale	170
9. Okra, garbanzos, and Brazil nuts	160
10. Cow's milk	130

MAGNESIUM

Estimated Average Requirements

AGE	MILLIGRAMS PER DAY
0–1 years	40–60
1–3 years	65
4–6 years	90
7–10 years	150
11–14 years	230
From 14 years onward	250

Breastfeeding mothers should add 550 milligrams/day

Top Ten Foods
milligrams per 100 grams of food

1. Brazil nuts	410
2. Sesame and sunflower seeds	380
3. Almonds, cashews, pine kernels, and wheat germ	270
4. Walnuts	160
5. Beans and brown rice	110
6. Swiss chard, spinach, and okra	75
7. Anchovies, sardines, and shrimp	50
8. Whole wheat and rye bread	46
9. Cheddar cheese	39
10. Meat and fish (average)	25

IRON

Estimated Average Requirements

	MILLIGRAMS PER DAY	
AGE	BOYS/MEN	GIRLS/WOMEN
7–12 months	6.0	6.0
1–6 years	5.0	5.0
7–10 years	6.7	6.7
11–18 years	8.7	11.4
19–50 years	6.7	11.4
From 50 years onward	6.7	6.7

Top Ten Foods
milligrams per 100 grams of food

2. Wheat bran	12.9
2. Liver	11.3
3. Sesame and pumpkin seeds	10.4
4. Fresh mint	9.5
5. Kidney	9.0
6. Beans, garbanzos, lentils, and wheat germ	8.3
7. Parsley and black-eye beans	7.7
8. Dried peaches, soy flour, and mussels	6.8
9. Venison, shrimp, cashew nuts, and pine kernels	5.1
10. Anchovies and dried figs	4.1

POTASSIUM

Estimated Average Requirements

AGE	MILLIGRAMS PER DAY
0–3 years	800
4–6 years	1100
7–10 years	2000
From 11 years onward	3100

Top Ten Foods
milligrams per 100 grams of food

1. Yeast extract	2100
2. Dried apricots	1880
3. Wheat bran and wheat germ	1050
4. Beans, peas, and lentils	1000
5. Dried fruit	900
6. Nuts (average)	750
7. Sweet potato, avocado, greens, and cabbage	450
8. Banana	400
9. Potato, Belgian endive, and zucchini	360
10. Meat and fish (average)	350

ZINC

Estimated Average Requirements

AGE	MILLIGRAMS PER DAY	
	BOYS/MEN	GIRLS/WOMEN
0–3 years	3.8	3.8
4–6 years	5.0	5.0
7–10 years	5.4	5.4
11–14 years	7.0	7.0
From 15 years onward	7.3	5.5

Breastfeeding mothers should add 5 milligrams/day

Top Ten Foods
milligrams per 100 grams of food

1. Wheatgerm and bran	17.0
2. Liver	15.9
3. Nuts and seeds	5.3
4. Soy beans and lentils	4.0
5. Venison	3.9
6. Kidney, meat, and cheese	3.5
7. Cod roe, lamb, and turkey	3.3
8. Whole wheat flour and pasta, beans, and garbanzos	3.0
9. Anchovies and bacon	2.5
10. Sardines, shrimp, and mussels	2.3

SELENIUM

Estimated Average Requirements

AGE	MICROGRAMS PER DAY	
	BOYS/MEN	GIRLS/WOMEN
7–12 months	12	12
1–3 years	20	20
4–10 years	25	25
From 11 years onward	40	30

Pregnant women should add 5 micrograms/day

Breastfeeding mothers should add 10 micrograms/day

Top Ten Foods
micrograms per 100 grams of food

1. Brazil nuts	254
2. Kidney	209
3. Lentils	105
4. Tuna	78
5. Squid, lemon sole, and lobster	62
6. Liver	50
7. Sunflower seeds	49
8. Mussels	43
9. Sardines, plaice, kipper, and mackerel	39
10. Cashew nuts	34

IODINE

Estimated Average Requirements

AGE	MICROGRAMS PER DAY
0–1 years	50
1–6 years	90
7–10 years	120
From 11 years onward	150

Pregnant and breastfeeding women should add 50 micrograms/day

Top Ten Foods
micrograms per 100 grams of food

1. Dried seaweed, kombu	448670
2. Dried seaweed, arame	84140
3. Dried seaweed, hijiki	42670
4. Dried seaweed, wakame	16830
5. Dried seaweed, dulse	5970
6. Dried seaweed, nori	1470
7. Cockles and mussels	140
8. Cod and lobster	100
9. Kipper, yogurt, and eggs	63
10. Salmon, butter, milk, and cheese	31

INDEX